AMS Studies in the Eighteenth Century, No. 27

Woman and Poet in the Eighteenth Century

Mary Whateley Darwall, portrait silhouette

Woman and Poet in the Eighteenth Century

❀❀❀

The Life of Mary Whateley Darwall
(1738 – 1825)

❀❀❀

by
Ann Messenger

AMS PRESS, INC.
New York

Library of Congress Cataloging-in-Publication Data

Messenger, Ann, 1933-
  Woman and poet in the eighteenth century : the life of Mary
Whateley Darwall (1738-1825) / by Ann Messenger.
    (AMS Studies in the Eighteenth Century, ISSN
  0196-6561; no. 27)
    Includes bibliographical references and index.
    ISBN 0-404-63527-X
    1. Darwall, Mary Whateley, 1738-1825 —Biography.
    2. Women and literature—England—History—18th century.
    3. Women poets, English—18th century—Biography.
        I. Title.   II. Series.
PR3395.D87Z78   1999
821'.6—dc20   94-821
                                                                     CIP

All AMS Books are printed on acid-free paper that meets the guidelines for performance and durability of the Committee on Production Guidelines for Book Longevity of the Council on Library Resources.

Copyright © 1999 by AMS Press, Inc.
All rights reserved

AMS Press, Inc.
56 East 13th Street
New York, NY 10003-4686 U.S.A.

Manufactured in the United States of America

for my mother

in memoriam

CONTENTS

List of Illustrations	ix
Acknowledgments	xi
Introduction: A Minor Talent, a Private Life	1

Part I: VIRGIN (1738-1766)

1. Beoley (1738-1759)	9
2. Walsall (1759/60-1763)	24
3. Guides, Philosophers, and Friends: Shenstone, Langhorne, *et al.*	39
4. *Original Poems on Several Occasions* (1764)	60
5. Transition (1764-November 4, 1766)	75

Part II: WIFE (1766-1789)

6. "Now Darwall" (1766-1775)	87
7. Sylvia's Diary for 1776	109
8. "Fond Hearts . . . Ebbing Life" (1777-1789)	132

Part III: WIDOW (1789-1793)

9. "The Cares of the World" (1789-1793)	159

10. *Poems on Several Occasions* (1794)		180
11. Last Years (1795-1825)		196
Appendix:	Poems	213
	Family Trees	222
References		225
Notes		227

List of Illustrations

1. Mary Whateley Darwall, portrait silhouette — Frontispiece
2. St. Leonard's church, Beoley — 12
3. Whateley/Darwall marriage signatures — 82
4. Walsall vicarage stone inscription — 97
5. The Darwalls' Charity Hymn — 102
6. Hockley Abbey — 137
7. Honor Darwall — 206
8. Jane Hewitt — 206
9. Walsall, 1782 map — Endpapers

Acknowledgments

One of the many things I have learned during this my first venture into biography is that such work cannot be done alone. I used to regard the massive lists of acknowledgments in biographies with skepticism and puzzlement. But no longer.

It is a cliché to say that a book could not have been written without the help of one or more specific people. But it is nonetheless true that without two particular people this book would not exist. The first is Betty Rizzo. Some years ago, though we had never met, I wrote to ask her how one went about finding information on obscure women writers of the eighteenth century. And she told me. Her continuing help and encouragement have been of the greatest importance. The other is Juliet McLaren. She was doing some routine work for me as a research assistant when the subject of biography came up, and she admitted to being "an amateur genealogist." I doubt that professionals have greater skills in unravelling the mysteries of international indexes and parish registers; Juliet's researches have produced or confirmed most of the facts on the Whateley and Darwall families that form the essential underpinning of this book. As we worked together, I profited from her insights and suggestions in many other ways as well. I thank both Betty and Juliet for, genuinely, making this book possible.

It has been a great pleasure to work with the four main sources of information for Mrs. Darwall's and the Reverend John Darwall's lives: Thea Randall of the Staffordshire County Record Office; the late Jane Hampartumian of the Lichfield Joint Record Office; the staff of the Walsall Local History Centre, especially Marilyn Lewis and David Guy; and the staff of the Local Studies and Archives divisions of the Birmingham Reference Library, especially John Warner Davies (Archives). My warmest thanks to them all.

Another pleasure has been the friendship and help of the Darwall family: Richard Darwall, who put me in touch with others; Stephen Leicester Darwall, my first direct contact with "our Mary"; Mrs. Penelope Darwall, whose papers included the kind of material every biographer dreams of finding; and the Darwall-Smiths (Randle, Robin, and Alan) who have shared their family archives with me and assisted in other ways as well. Their enthusiasm for the project has spurred me on.

Some specific debts to the family and to other people and institutions are recorded in the footnotes. I also thank the following for a wide range of information and service:

The libraries of Cambridge University; Duke University; Harvard University; Simon Fraser University; Yale University; the universities of British Columbia, Chicago, Illinois at Urbana-Champaign, Manchester, Oregon, Oxford (Bodleian), and Virginia; the British Library (especially Scot McKendrick, Manuscripts); the Family History Library, Salt Lake City, Utah; the Huntington Library; Lincolnshire County Council Reference Library; Lincoln's Inn Library; the National Library of Wales; the New York Public Library; Shropshire County Library; Wells Cathedral Library; Westminster Abbey Library; William Andrews Clark Memorial Library; and the William Salt Library;

County Record Offices of Cumbria, Essex, Hereford and Worcester (especially A. M. Wherry), Kent, Powys, Shropshire, Somerset, and Warwickshire;

The Diocesan Registrar of the Lichfield Joint Record Office;

The Hyde Collection; the Public Record Offices of London and Kew; the Royal Commission on Historical Manuscripts; the Society of Genealogists; the *Times Literary Supplement*;

Major P. N. Chisholm (Staffordshire Regiment), Malcolm Cooper, C. J. L. Elwell, Philip Highfill, Glyn Tegai Hughes, C. R. Johnson, Paul Korshin, Roger Lonsdale, John H. Manners, V. A. Masters, William E. Messenger, Philip Mortiboy, Rev. J. W. Pearson, J. W. Phillips, Barbara Schnorrenberg, Arthur Sherbo, Margaret M. Smith, Fiona Tait, Elliott Viney, and Percy M. Young.

Introduction

A Minor Talent, a Private Life

Why read—indeed, why write—a book about a nearly forgotten poet of the eighteenth century who had only a minor talent and no particular historical or other importance? One could reply, rather rudely, with another question—why not? But the first question should be faced, not simply dismissed. For it is quite true that Mary Whateley Darwall was a minor poet, as the categories of "major" and "minor" are traditionally understood. Even when the canon of eighteenth-century poetry is reconsidered and she finds her place in it, it will not be a large place. She produced two books of verse, thirty years apart, followed by a few contributions to her younger daughter's book of poems and a small number of fugitive pieces. Several of Mrs. Darwall's poems were reprinted in magazines and newspapers, and a few found their way into both eighteenth- and nineteenth-century anthologies. But, although her first book was praised in detailed reviews and she was recognized as one of "the BRITISH NINE" in 1774, she was not on Anna Seward's list of seven worthy female poets in 1789. Her second book had only two brief notices, and as a poet she soon faded away. Until the last third of the twentieth century, when eighteenth-century scholars began to search for and find lost women writers, she had virtually vanished. Her books have never been reprinted. And while some of her poems deserve to be known, many are unremarkable. So she is not the usual subject for a literary biography, which as a rule examines historically and aesthetically significant work in the light of the writer's life and vice versa.

A Minor Talent, a Private Life

But Mary Darwall is a good subject to study to see how one person coped with being both a woman and a poet in the eighteenth century, a dual role and a problem in coping not limited to that time. Then, however, to be a woman was overwhelmingly a role or series of roles, even a full-time occupation. A woman was profoundly defined by her gender. Her marital status—virgin, wife, widow—was also always a major part of her identity. As a woman, she had to depend on men for her social status and her way of life in general; the rank, occupation, and financial circumstances of her father, brothers, husband, and sons shaped her life. Her acceptability in the world was determined by how well she understood and played the complex, restricted roles she was born to. If she had literary talent and wanted to be recognized and accepted as a writer, she knew she would always be judged as a woman writer—which is to say her moral character was considered to be inseparable from her work, and her work was assumed to be of a different order from a man's. A woman of great talent could strike out on her own; indeed, though an eighteenth-century woman writer could never escape or transcend her gender, the lives of the greater ones followed various, sometimes unusual, courses. A less unusual woman, however, lived a more ordinary life.

Mary Darwall is an interesting woman and poet partly just because she was ordinary. A middle-class woman from the middle of England, married at just above the average age, mother of an average number of children, a member of the established church, devoted to king and country, concerned with money and health and family and friends—to know her is to know much of what was typical of a woman's life at that time. And part of my purpose in telling her story is to show something of how women lived in the eighteenth century. Her poetry too is typical of her time: she wrote much conventional verse in the pastoral mode; she responded to the growing fashion of the gothic and the primitive. Her work supports the axiom that a minor writer is more fully representative of a literary period than a major figure could ever be. Her poetry is also typical of her

A Minor Talent, a Private Life

gender: she began by limiting herself to pastoral, which was considered suitable for ladies; throughout her writing life, she reacted in the usual verse forms to particular occasions in her world, rather than acting in verse to make an impact on the world. Yet with all this ordinariness and typicality, she was very much an individual, with great strength of character and conviction, vivid perceptions and passions, keen intelligence, a lively sense of humor, and a literary talent that she made an integral part of her busy life. She was an extraordinary ordinary woman.

The relationship she forged between her life and her writing is part of my story—a statement that requires some comment. In the decades since the Author has been pronounced Dead, controversy has raged over what if any connection exists between the life and character of a writer and the literature he or she produced. Instead of surveying this whole battleground, I will simply describe where I stand on it: the life matters. No literary biographer could think otherwise. It matters for both men and women, who lived as we do in specific times and places with their specific social and intellectual climates. Indeed, the very idea that the author is dead is symptomatic of a twentieth-century mind-set. Furthermore, the life—and the times—matter in an especially urgent way for women writers. Excluded from the comparatively timeless and universal world of education and from public life, their lives profoundly defined by their gender, women of the eighteenth century were more closely tied than men to the everyday and the local. It is small wonder that the poets among them almost invariably called their books *Poems upon Several Occasions*, a title much less popular among men; and to understand such poems, one has to know about the life, in general and in particular. Besides, to erase the life from the work is to erase the woman—again. This is not to say that the poems can not, or should not, also be studied from other points of view. I would welcome such attention. But exhaustive, theoretical analysis is not my purpose here. Instead, because they are unfamiliar, I find it necessary to describe simply what

A Minor Talent, a Private Life

the poems have to say. And I examine the connections between the poems and the poet's life, because my credo is that the life and the work go hand in hand.

Mary Whateley Darwall was simultaneously a woman living and a poet writing—a unity, despite the duality implied in my title. She wrote as a woman and somehow found time to write during an increasingly demanding domestic life. Indeed, her art was part of her life, part of her identity, in a more intimate way than a male writer's formal profession could be. And to some extent it reveals the course of her life.

Perhaps the most difficult and delicate problem in writing eighteenth-century literary biography is determining how much one can rely on the autobiographical "truth" of the subject's work. In an age of convention and persona, it can be disastrously wrong to take a body of poems as the record of a life. And yet, as the eighteenth century moved on towards the age of the Romantics, sincerity, even confession, in poetry gained strength as reliance on persona dwindled. On the other hand, however much a woman might wish to be sincere and to unburden her heart in verse, she was far more at risk than a man if she took off her clothes in public. So she was faced with difficult choices: whether or not to express her self, and if so, how.

I keep all this in mind as I use much of Mary Darwall's poetry as evidence about her life. The obviously and simply occasional poems are autobiographical; they do not present problems. The others, especially the most conventional, do. But I have been encouraged to make some use even of these—judiciously, I hope—by the fact that my conjectures about her life which were based solely on the poems, even on the most conventional poems, were confirmed time and again as information from other sources trickled in. So I think my picture of Mary Darwall is essentially true, despite the inevitable omissions, errors, and fictions of any biography.

My story is, then, firmly based in recorded fact, though a woman of the eighteenth century leaves few tracks for the hunter

A Minor Talent, a Private Life

to follow. For Mrs. Darwall, besides her poems I have found only dates in parish registers, some references in letters and poems by friends, and a few unpublished papers in record offices and family archives. But most of her men have left clear trails: degrees and other documents for the university men, leases for the renters of farm property, apprenticeship and patent records for the businessmen. Those engaged in the public worlds of the church and the law, the army, medicine, and education, have been relatively easy to trace. And a few left wills. However indirectly, their records reflect Mrs. Darwall's life, because these are the men whom she cared about and who shaped her life. So, with much emphasis on family, the woman's story can be told. To complete the picture of Mary Darwall as a poet, I describe separately the poems I do not incorporate directly into the story of her life.

To make my story readable, I have condensed what could have been overwhelming quantities of documentation, and I have omitted footnote numbers. The reader will find notes at the end of the book, keyed to page numbers. And I have tried, though not very successfully, to minimize the inevitable *apparently*'s and *probably*'s that accuracy demands. I have not always explained my logic in making deductions and reaching conclusions, which would have been tedious for the reader, but the reasoning process was as sound as I could make it. Most of the time I have tried to remain decently invisible as Mary Darwall's story unfolds, but occasionally it was more truthful to let the subjective "I" appear—at times to confess ignorance or explain method, and at times just to show how real she had become to me. I hope she will become real for the reader too; I hope that however minor her talent and however private her life, she will make the world of an eighteenth-century woman and poet come alive once more.

Part I

VIRGIN

1738-1766

Chapter 1

Beoley (1738-1759)

> ... near Arrowe's glassy Stream
> Reclin'd, I woo the museful Dream. ...
>
> Mary Whateley

In the winter of 1737-38, the Whateleys of Beoley in Worcestershire were expecting yet another addition to their family. Mary Bach Whateley had already borne eight babies in the twenty years of her marriage. The ninth was probably somewhat unexpected: Mary was forty-one, and it had been almost four years since the youngest, Henry, was born. Only two of the eight babies had died in infancy, and the farmhouse was getting more than a little crowded. But this impending birth would be the last, and this baby would be different.

The crowding in the farmhouse would be gradually relieved as the older children grew up. William Whateley did not own the farm; it was leased for ninety-nine years or three lives, and he was the third renter to occupy it. Other plans were being made for the children. In 1738, his oldest son, also named William, would turn nineteen and had already gone or would soon go into farming in the nearby community of Wooten Wawen. Martha, the next child, who was seventeen, was to marry a chandler named John Baylies, nine years hence, and move away from Beoley, probably taking with her the third child, Ann, three years her junior and an inseparable companion; they were still together, widow and spinster, when they died many years later. When they were old enough, John, now ten years old, would

Beoley (1738-1759)

follow William to farm in Wooten Wawen; George, eight, would be apprenticed. And little Henry was only four.

The Whateley farm was just prosperous enough to support such a brood. When William Whateley inherited the lease from his father, the estate was valued at 360 pounds. Most probably, he grew wheat, peas, and beans, the major crops in Beoley parish, and some fruit—his lease required him to add six more pear or apple trees to the orchards each year. There would also, of course, have been poultry for the womenfolk to tend and a few animals—cows and pigs—to supply the family with meat and milk, butter and cheese. Perhaps there were sheep and a spinning wheel as well. Farms tended to be self-sufficient, and there was no place to shop in the parish; its main settlement was only a small village called Holt End at a fork in the road. Indeed, when in 1720 the vicar wanted a new book in which to record the births, deaths, and marriages of his parishioners, he had to send one of his churchwardens—William Whateley himself—eleven miles to Birmingham to buy it. Although Beoley did have its parish church and its small village, its ancient castle had vanished long ago. Its manor house, Beoley Hall, rebuilt after being destroyed in the civil strife of the seventeenth century, was rented out to farming families. The Catholic lords of the manor, the Sheldons, lived elsewhere most of the time. There wasn't much in Beoley to attract a tourist.

But Beoley did have land, beautiful and productive land divided into deer park and woods and fields, land that sloped towards the west from Holt End to the church and then fell steeply to a flat, broad valley. The River Arrow darted through the valley just beyond the western edge of the parish. As it flowed south, it passed—and turned—grain mills and paper mills. But the mills weren't obtrusive enough to spoil the beauty of the countryside where the scattered farms, along with the small village, supported between five hundred and six hundred souls. There was plenty of room for oaks and pines, hazels and osiers, ring-doves and blackbirds and lambs, flower gardens

Beoley (1738-1759)

stocked with roses and carnations, and other rural beauties that would soon be celebrated in verse.

That verse would be written by Mary, the youngest Whateley, who was expected, and arrived, in the winter of 1737-38. They took her to the church, St. Leonard's, to be baptized by the Rev. Mr. Loggin on February 9. It was a dark church of respectable antiquity with a squat, square bell tower at one end and an unusually narrow chancel at the other, five steps up from the ill-lit nave. The Whateleys had belonged to it for several generations, and the baby's grandfather, John, had literally left his mark on it—two bells were inscribed with his name and the dates 1708 and 1709. And somewhere in the cold gloom of the church, perhaps in the elegant Sheldon chapel where it is today, there lurked a handsome, dark oak chest he had made and carved boldly with his initials, the date 1683, and "C W" to show the world that he had been a churchwarden even at the tender age of twenty-four. In fact, it was grandfather John's efforts, and respectability, that made it possible for Whateley men to write themselves gentleman.

John's father, William, had been ranked as a "yeoman." The first of the family to appear in Beoley records, in 1674 he was occupying a humble house with only one hearth. But he was an energetic man: he not only pursued his trade as a clockmaker but also, in less than ten years, became a farmer successful enough to rent part of Beoley Hall and some of its expensive properties. When he died in 1688, he was still called "yeoman," however, and the rank passed on to his son John, the poet's grandfather. John too was enterprising and energetic, and not only in serving as a churchwarden; he renewed the family tenure at the Hall and added substantially to the acreage he farmed. By 1698 he was unclassified in yet another lease, and when he died in 1726, the parish register records him unequivocally as "gent." He had come a long way.

The family energy seems to have skipped the next generation. William, the poet's father, retrenched rather than expanding his

Beoley (1738-1759)

St. Leonard's Church, Beoley.
(Photograph: W.E. Messenger.)

Beoley (1738-1759)

holdings: he accepted modest cash settlements instead of property from the tangled estates of his mother and his wife's mother, he returned a piece of land to the lord of the manor, and he allowed the lease on spacious Beoley Hall to run out, contenting himself, despite the size of his family, with the farmhouse on the much cheaper piece of land he had inherited. His rent there was only £1.13.8 a year. He kept the title of "gentleman," but the family fortunes, in tandem with those of the Catholic lord of the manor, had declined. His youngest daughter inherited gentility but not affluence.

She was christened Mary after her mother and in memory of an earlier baby who had lived only a few weeks. It is fanciful to imagine her taking note of her surroundings during the ceremony —like all new babies, she would have simply slept or cried—but given a recurring theme in the poetry she would write when she grew up, it is pleasant to visualize her carried up to the medieval stone font and, as Mr. Loggin dipped his fingers in the water, held close to the font's decorations: four women's faces with long braids that reached out to each other to form a continuous link around the bowl. For Mary's poems often celebrate her links with women friends. She never mentions her siblings; she barely nods to her parents; she addresses fellow poets, sometimes quite emotionally, on the subject of her art. But it is women friends whom she yearns to see, mourns for, and defends; it is to women friends that she addresses some of her most thoughtful and her most deeply felt poems.

It is not surprising that she turned to friends rather than family. Early-eighteenth-century families were not particularly close-knit, if Lawrence Stone is right. In any event, Mary's sisters were much older than she, essentially of a different generation, while her brothers, also older, lived boys' lives in which a younger girl could take little part. By the time she was eight, all but one of the other children had left home, for George had by then been apprenticed to a "toymaker" in Birmingham; he would do well in the trade and was to take out patents for new ways of plating gold and silver onto wire to

Beoley (1738-1759)

make lace and fringe. Only Henry was still in Beoley. Mary seems to have gotten along well with Henry, but soon he too would go, to the manufacturing town of Walsall, near Birmingham, to read law in an attorney's office. In her teens, then, she was virtually an only child. But she found companionship, even intimacy, with a friend—Elizabeth Loggin, the vicar's daughter, just two years older than she was. Elizabeth had a flock of younger brothers and sisters, but most of them died in infancy. Among Mary's earliest memories were the nearly annual births and nearly as frequent deaths of the Loggin babies. But Elizabeth survived to become her best friend. There were other friends as well: "Miss Smith of B———," "Miss M———" (also called "Monimia"), and more, mentioned in Mary's poems but disguised with pastoral names. Clearly, women friends were important to her.

But Elizabeth Loggin was special. Just enough older to be looked up to, coming from the cultivated home of the vicar, Elizabeth too was interested in books and in trying to write poetry: when Mary left Beoley, they wrote letters to each other about their reading and sent each other verses. As girls at home, they must have walked together by the River Arrow and tended their gardens together and talked of books, as well as of all the other things girls talk about. Their mothers no doubt did their best to keep them at their needles, however. Even though the Whateleys could probably afford more help as the older children left home, a farm was no place for idle hands.

A little evidence, but substantial evidence, survives about Mary's girlhood in Beoley. Dr. John Wall of Worcester, having seen some of her poems in manuscript, published two letters about her in the *Gentleman's Magazine* and elsewhere. At first he thought she was "employed in the common drudgery of a mean farm-house," but he corrected himself when he learned better:

> ... her father is a substantial farmer. ... Her education is such as is usually given to the daughters of persons in

Beoley (1738-1759)

> that station, reading, writing, and needle-work, comprehending most of what is thought necessary. But her genius is not confined to such slender limits. She had a great love for literature, and applied herself with great assiduity to the reading the best authors. This necessarily engaged a very considerable portion of her time.

Her mother, whose signature suggests that she was barely literate, can almost be heard scolding in the background. Dr. Wall notes that Mary's reading included the *Gentleman's Magazine*, which would have encouraged her to persevere in reading and writing, the *Spectator*, and Shakespeare. Her poems show that she also had access to Pope and Johnson, Anacreon and Tibullus, Milton, Gray, Whitehead, Langhorne, and many more. It is unlikely that she would have found all these at home. Her father had inherited "a parcell of old watches and books and other things" worth ten pounds (along with one of his grandfather's clocks), but none of these Whateleys were university men and only Henry (who became an attorney) went into a learned profession. It is more likely that Mary found so many books, including such recent ones, in the library of Elizabeth's father, the vicar. As Elizabeth's friend, she would have been welcome there. And the senior Loggins were kindly, friendly people: local memories—and country memory is long—preserve the appealing picture of Mr. and Mrs. Loggin visiting around the parish with Mrs. Loggin riding pillion; at the close of their visits, it was her husband's custom to say, "Well, Mrs. Loggin, we must be joggin'." Perhaps he too was a sort of poet.

The most important of the contemporary poets in Mary Whateley's early life, and no doubt another source of books, was William Shenstone, the gentleman of leisure who gardened and wrote pastoral verse at the Leasowes, about ten miles from Beoley. I cannot be sure just when and how they met, and their professional relationship belongs farther along in my story, but their acquaintance could have begun when Mary was only ten, or even younger. Shenstone had been visiting Henrietta, Lady Luxborough, in August 1748, at her estate at Barrels. When he

Beoley (1738-1759)

got back to the Leasowes, he wrote her a letter describing his return journey. He and his party got home late on a dark night, after they had "encounter[ed] certain Gate-posts in passing thro' some Neighbour's Grounds"; the lateness of their return had been caused partly by a "*Delay* at Mr. Loggin's." Beoley lies on the road between Barrels and the Leasowes, so this Mr. Loggin could well have been Mary's vicar. He and Shenstone were fellow Oxonians, though of somewhat different generations, and Loggin is not a common name. Shenstone certainly knew the neighborhood: he had cousins in Tardebigge, the next village on the road from Beoley to the Leasowes. So it is possible that Mary Whateley knew her most influential mentor from childhood. She had definitely absorbed his ideas about poetry during her formative years, absorbed them so thoroughly that she was later to be dubbed "Daughter of SHENSTONE."

No further clues have survived to tell what Mary Whateley did in her girlhood and her teens, or what her personal life was like. The agricultural life of Beoley, which surrounded her, had its changeless cycles, as did the life of the church with its festivals and ceremonies. The life of the nation was less repetitious. George II, when he wasn't off to Hanover, sat on the throne of England, quarreling with his son, pretending to be sorry when he died, and then trying (with limited success) to control his grandson. He looked uneasily at the growing power of France in North America and the growing restlessness of his own colonies there. Mid-century was a difficult time for the aging monarch.

Little of all this disturbed the placid life of rural England, however. But adolescence, no matter where or when one lives, is never entirely placid. Does anything more than pastoral convention lie behind the lament of Delia for Strephon's faithlessness in Mary's poems? Or Sylvia's sighs for Damon? Did Mary develop an interest in Elizabeth Loggin's brothers before they went off to Oxford? She was a plain girl—did they ignore her? One cannot say. But one can say that by 1759, when she was twenty-one, Mary was taking herself seriously as a poet and had already acquired considerable skill in versifying.

Her skill is apparent in the only poem in her first book that bears a date, "Elegy on a much lamented Friend, Who died in Autumn, 1759." It follows the conventions of elegy knowledgeably: the first paragraph dismisses joy and sets the gloomy scene; mourning dominates the second, as nymphs, shepherds, and Nature herself "Weep in the Stream, and languish in the Gale"; the third tells of the past sorrows and present peace of the dead Fidelia. The last, which describes the levelling power of death and concludes with a glimpse of heaven, will serve to illustrate the young poet's learning and technical skill:

> There, wrapt in Shade impervious, *Newton* lies;
> There lifeless *Lely*'s Hand, and *Myra*'s Eyes;
> There *Thomson*'s Harp forgets the moral Song,
> Deaf *Handel*'s Ear, and silent *Milton*'s Tongue.
> There ev'n this Heart, which melts to strains of Woe,
> Shall cease to grieve, these streaming Eyes to flow:
> This weary Clay, to *Death*'s cold Arms consign'd,
> Shall give to kindred Skies th'immortal Mind.

Mary Whateley kept up with the news—Handel had just died in April of that year—and already, though with modest indirectness, the poet is associating herself with other artists.

Dimly visible through the veil of convention in the poem, Fidelia's life takes on some individuality. Despite her "superior Worth," Fortune was "adverse." Envy and Malice pursued her to "the Gates of Death"; she had suffered wrongs and anguish and grown pallid with care. But death is truly a leveller: "And there shall sleep, in equal Night inurn'd, / The *Friend* that lov'd her, and the *Fool* that scorn'd." Unrequited love seems to have contributed to, or even caused, Fidelia's lamentable death. Such a deduction raises the difficult question of the relationship between poetry and the biographical and autobiographical facts of life, especially difficult in the case of highly conventional poetry. There is no evidence beyond the poem itself that Mary

Beoley (1738-1759)

Whateley had such a friend who met such a fate. But because real feeling breathes through the conventions here, and because such details as envy, malice, and "the *Fool*" go beyond the merely conventional, I read the poem as true to its author's experience—she lost a friend—and as evidence that she was already skilled in transforming experience into art.

And she was serious about her art. As a woman, Mary Whateley could not expect literature to be a profession for her as it had been for Pope and was being for Johnson. Women were making a precarious living as novelists and playwrights, but theater was unknown in Beoley, and perhaps Mr. Loggin had no novels by women in his vicarage study to serve as models. Besides, Mary was a gentlewoman, someone who would not even contemplate writing for a living. And she knew and cared about poetry, not novels and plays, though she admired Shakespeare. But if a fully professional career was closed to her, she could aspire to the level of gentleperson amateur—the level of Shenstone himself—and make a place for herself in the world of letters.

The *Gentleman's Magazine* was an important—perhaps the only—window on the world of current letters available in Beoley. Here Mary found both professional and amateur poetry, neatly segregated from the mixed bag of other contents and headed "Poetical Essays." Here were the poet laureate's official birthday and New Year's odes; and here were translations and parodies, fables, prologues and epilogues, pastoral effusions, lessons in morality—the full range of current versifying. A number of women contributed unexceptionable verse; on rare occasions, they used apparently real names, but most of the time modestly concealed their identity under "Myrtilla," "Dorinda," "Ophelia," or simply "a Lady." Their presence was clearly encouraging to an isolated country girl who saw, despite the name of the magazine, that one could be a woman, a woman of respectable sentiments, and a published poet at the same time. And who knew how many of the poems left unsigned or signed only with initials had been written by women?

Beoley (1738-1759)

Another attractive side to the "Poetical Essays" was evidence of communication and community among the contributors. Some of the poems were invitations to other poets; some were epitaphs or birthday greetings or other sorts of addresses. Occasionally, contributors responded to each other directly and sent in translations of someone's French or Latin verses or solutions to someone's riddle or rebus. One could join in the community of writers by appearing in the *Gentleman's Magazine*, and Mary Whateley did.

Beginning in 1758, Mary had found in the magazine some poems by "Jemmy Copywell of Lincoln's Inn," some comic, some serious. Something, perhaps two things, about Copywell caught her eye: his poems apparently appealed both to her liking for the moral and pastoral strains that were to dominate her own first book, and to the lively sense of humor that she only occasionally indulged in her writing. In her first two poems to be published, which appeared in the *Gentleman's Magazine*, she chose to demonstrate both sides of her talent with a conventional pastoral "To my Garden" and a partly comic address "To Mr. Copywell."

"To my Garden," signed "Harriott Airy" and dated from Worcestershire, June 21, 1759, seems to be a response to a garden poem by T.P. in May, a poem in Marvell's line, which rather lengthily prefers the pleasures and beauties of the garden to the pleasures and beauties of society, especially female society. "Harriott" too praises the pleasures and beauties to be found in the garden, but her conclusion differs: unlike T.P., she now finds the garden unsatisfactory, because the enchantment of the name of "Sweet *Alexis*" makes "each rural beauty" die. The address to Mr. Copywell which follows is quite different from her conventional garden poem. Amazingly bold, it is a "presumptuous" request to "partake" with him of "The good or ill with which [his] cup is fraught." She will "attend [his] pleasure" and learn from his muse. She even promises to make him splendid puddings (alluding to his comic January poem in praise of pudding) and says that his "moral lays would harmonize [her] soul." Despite her claims in the poem to a lofty personal morality, this is almost a proposition, and it is written for the most part in Copywell's own vaguely Miltonic blank verse.

Who could resist such an appeal? In the next issue of the *Gentleman's Magazine*, Copywell published a brief poem "To Miss Harriet [sic] Airy," praising both her "moral muse" and her "tender breast." He wants to know her better: a brief note, of a kind highly unusual in this magazine, follows his poem: "Miss Harriet is desired to signify how a letter may be conveyed to her, by a line directed to J.C. at Robin's Coffee house, Shire Lane, near Temple Barr."

Did she write to him? No letters have survived, but I think she did. Of course, discreet young ladies did not enter into epistolary relationships lightly. Nor did they address verses, especially verses which might be considered proposals of marriage or at least of discipleship, to unknown men in the public press, though the very openness of the press might be less compromising than a private correspondence. But Mary Whateley had determination, poetic ambitions, and, as a woman isolated in the country, very few opportunities to make contact with the literary world. She could no more have refused Copywell's advances than he could refuse hers.

There is a piece of evidence for a relationship of some sort over the next few months. The *Gentleman's Magazine* for October 1759, which also contains another poem by "Harriot Airy" (yet a third spelling), includes Jemmy Copywell's "Ode to Friendship," twelve unrhymed quatrains each composed of two octosyllabic lines followed by two pentameters, in which he calls upon Friendship to "Perch on [his] wounded breast" and cheer him up. Friendship is seen as a nymph with Advice, Truth, Generosity, and Honesty in her train, but is urged not to bring with her "That fiend ... / Hypocrisy ... / whose busy thought / Premeditates unmanly fraud!" In the next issue, Copywell gets an answer:

Beoley (1738-1759)

Ode to Truth

Descend fair Truth, celestial maid descend,
And with thy lustre radiate the dark cloud,
    Which deep invelopes half
    The sapient sons of men.
At thy approach shall the infernal train,
Which now oppress the human breast, depart,
    And, in primaeval night,
    Their fiend-like forms conceal.
There dark Distrust, and Incredulity,
Parents of Care, shall fly, when thou resum'st
    Thy godlike reign, in man's
    Deserted, chearless, breast.
Thro' thy transparent veil, the only charm
I have to boast, let all the world survey
    My guiless heart, and trace
    Each action to its spring.
If consciousness of curst Hypocrisy,
Or fraud unmanly, which my soul disdains,
    Produce one guilty pang,
    Let anguish be my lot.
But let me bless the providential hand,
Which kindly form'd me female, and deny'd,
Superior genius and superior pride;
Mistaken pride, which all desert confines
To man, and in his breast each virtue shrines,
Tho' learning's ample field he rules alone,
Nor fears a female near his awful throne,
Unsatiated with empire so immense,
He'd fain divest our sex of common sense.

                                          Harriot Airy

B———y, Worcestershire, Nov. 14, 1759.

"Harriot" has reversed Copywell's meter and improved it by shortening the shorter lines for greater contrast; then she slides gracefully into heroic couplets for her conclusion. His "fiend

Beoley (1738-1759)

... Hypocrisy" becomes "curst Hypocrisy," and "unmanly fraud" is turned into "fraud unmanly," which, despite some confusion of gender, her soul disdains. This is not the only confusion, or rather obscurity, in the poem. Who are "half / The sapient sons of men" who lack Truth? The male sex, including Copywell, or all misguided people—apparently including Copywell? He seems to have distrusted her, failed to believe her, but she claims to be honest; taking their two poems together, one can see that he seems to have questioned the sincerity of her friendship, a serious charge because friendship was always of central importance to her. He also seems to have sneered at her as a female without education, that male prerogative, and even without common sense. However, his own poem rejoices that Education has "Ne'er tutor'd" youthful Honesty. It doesn't quite add up. Too many facts are missing. But two points are clear: "Harriot Airy" will not tolerate an overbearing man, and the relationship with Copywell is over. "Harriot," though she published elsewhere, disappears from the pages of the *Gentleman's Magazine* (where she reappeared later both anonymously and as Miss Whateley), but "Copywell" goes on, sometimes using his own name.

"Jemmy Copywell" was William Woty. His career was not distinguished: he had experienced bankruptcy and Grub Street before he found security as legal advisor to Washington, Earl Ferrers. During all this, he went on writing verse. Perhaps he and Mary Whateley mended their fences: a Mrs. Woty subscribed for two copies of Miss Whateley's first book in 1764, as did Woty's patron, Earl Ferrers, and both the Rev. Mr. Darwall and Mrs. Darwall (née Whateley) subscribed in turn to Woty's book in 1770. Possibly his "The Female Advocate" (1770), which indicates a high opinion of women, mended the fence, though he seems to value them primarily as mothers. But he does praise them for honesty as well.

Mary Whateley had made a beginning. At the age of twenty-one, she had four poems in the *Gentleman's Magazine*, but the link to the world of letters which she had tried to forge by

Beoley (1738-1759)

addressing Copywell had apparently broken. She still loved her Beoley home, however, despite its isolation, and when she left it, within a few weeks of her attack on the overbearing Copywell, she dreaded the exchange of rural quiet for urban noise.

Chapter 2

Walsall (1759/60-1763)

... a very large, sooty, ill-paved town.

Gentleman's Magazine

As the eventful year of 1759 was ending, Mary Whateley went to Walsall, Staffordshire, to live with and keep house for her brother Henry. No evidence survives about why she went. Possibly her parents disapproved of her idle scribbling in the relative leisure of the depleted household, or possibly they felt that she badly needed a change of situation after the distressing Copywell affair. Certainly Henry could have used her help. Having finished his training in an attorney's office, he had taken accommodations, a house or lodgings of some sort, in Walsall's busy High Street and was setting up in business for himself. Before long, announcements of his participation in real estate sales began to appear in *Aris's Birmingham Gazette*, and although real estate was to be a profitable, lifelong part of his career, as an attorney he had other business as well, including collecting debts. He was not to marry for another fifteen years, so he needed a woman to look after him—or at least his mother probably thought he did. And who could be more suitable than his unattached younger sister?

Why Mary went to Walsall must be in part conjectural, but how she felt about the move is clear. She didn't like it. Two poems attest to the fact: "Elegy on leaving ———" and "Liberty." The "Elegy" is undated but obviously chronicles her feelings about having to trade rural peace for the "Crowds and Noise" of the town. One could, of course, read the poem simply as pastoral convention, but when it is taken in conjunction with "Liberty," its personal dimension becomes inescapable. In it she takes a "reluctant" farewell of bowers and streams, wooded hills and vales, the whole scene in which she had enjoyed "grateful Solitude." This was the setting in which she had read, and written, poetry for the first time:

> Rapt with the Melody of *Cynthio*'s Strains,
>   There first my Bosom felt poetic Flame;
> Mute was the bleating Language of the Plains,
>   And with *his* Lays the wanton Fawns grew tame.
>
> But, ah! those pleasing Hours are ever flown;
>   Ye Scenes of Transport from my Thoughts retire!
> Those rural Joys no more the Day shall crown,
>   No more my Hand shall wake the warbling Lyre.

The poem is quite clear, except for one detail: "Cynthio," a curious mixture of a muse and an Orpheus figure, may not be a specific poet; he could simply represent in a general way the poetry that inspired her. But I suspect that he is Shenstone: Lady Luxborough had used the name for him, and it is not the most common of pastoral names. Whichever is the case, Mary Whateley seems genuinely to believe the traditional pastoral tenet that the rural scene is the necessary context for writing. On the more mundane level, she knows that she will have much less leisure, quiet, and solitude at her brother's house in town than she has had in the country. She concludes, however, on a note of resignation:

> But come, sweet *Hope*, from thy divine Retreat
>   Come to my Breast, and chase my Cares away;
> Bring calm *Content* to gild my gloomy Seat,
>   And chear my Bosom with her heav'nly Ray.

Walsall (1759/60-1763)

She will make the best of it. *"Hope"* may even suggest a feeling that the town might turn out to have some advantages.

She soon learned that Walsall in December could be a prison despite its advantages. But books were available for escape—Walsall had no library, but it did have a bookstore, which also kept a stock of patent medicines—and Mary soon discovered and read Johnson's *Rasselas*. When she received a verse letter from Elizabeth Loggin asking for a descriptive poem in return, she could find nothing worth describing in the cold town and turned to *Rasselas* instead: "Now as the depth of *December* . . . affords no agreeable objects to furnish a description-piece, I have supposed myself one of the inhabitants of this romantic region [Abyssinia]; as confinement, however splendid, cannot be agreeable to human nature, were all this real . . . I should sigh for *Beoley*, frosty weather, and freedom." "Liberty," the poem that follows (see Appendix), expresses her sense of entrapment vividly. Like Rasselas in the Happy Valley, she is bored and frustrated by the sameness of things. She longs for escape, but the rocky summits close her in inexorably. The allegory is susceptible of further interpretation as well, but the first level of application is clear: the poet was unhappy in her confinement.

The confinement could well have amounted to virtual house arrest, given the state of Walsall's streets in the winter. The town was laid out in the form of a T (see map on endpapers). The upright began at the bridge that crossed a wide, shallow stream, and climbed, first gradually, then steeply, to a spot near the top of the hill, where it met the crossbars of the T. The more gradual slope was a broad street named Digbeth; the steeper slope was the High Street. A long flight of steps finished the climb from the top of the T to the top of the hill where the parish church looked down on the town. The crossbars of the T, Peal Street and Rushall Street, which met at the foot of the steps, were narrow and in bad repair; they stretched across the face of the hill and out into the surrounding countryside. Across the bridge, the bottom of the T also led off into the country between a row of buildings that soon petered out. Building,

Walsall (1759/60-1763)

mostly red brick and all soot-stained, was dense along the main body of the T, however, and even along the stairs to the church: shops and smithies, offices and dwellings, town hall, workhouse, grammar school and free school, inns, the old market cross— and the town pump.

Central Walsall got its water from a pump at the top of the High Street. There were, of course, splashes and spills, and sometimes the pump leaked. In winter, therefore, the High Street often turned into a sheet of ice, a very steep sheet. Mary could look out of her brother's windows and see carts and horses struggling in vain to negotiate the hill, and sliding painfully back down to the bridge. Small wonder that the town worthies, the Corporation, were discussing the possibility of another street to run from bridge to hilltop by a gentler route— and well away from the town pump. But, like all such bodies, they moved slowly; nothing was done until 1766, even though the High Street was dangerous. However allegorical, Mary's poem on "Liberty" probably represented a very literal imprisonment, at least during the winter when it was written.

But winter eventually loosened its grip, the ice melted, and Walsall life went on more conveniently. Now one could send the laundry down to the wash house at the bridge. Now one could step safely out the door and into the Tuesday and Saturday markets that rambled up and down the High Street, as they still do today. Unlike Beoley, here there was much to buy. Local farmers brought foodstuffs from the countryside for miles around and set them out on carts and stalls. Local manufacturers too displayed their wares: the shoe-buckles for which the town was famous; less glamorous but more necessary, the bits and other metal fittings that went into harnesses and saddles; and other ironmongery, including nails. Many of the six to seven thousand inhabitants were employed in the smithies that rang and roared throughout the town, puffing smoke and soot into the air. Women and children, black to the eyes, were as adept as men at making nails. They were certainly kept busy at these and other trades. Most of the children were even too

Walsall (1759/60-1763)

busy to go to the available schools, and as a result, Walsall had an unusually high number of illiterates in its largely working-class population.

But Walsall did have some cultural amenities and a small class of business people and professionals—doctors, lawyers, clergy—to support them and offer Mary Whateley society and friendship. When the ice melted and walking was easier, people gathered at the bookstore not only for books but also for magazines and newspapers sent in from nearby Birmingham. The amenities did not include a theater building, but the inns regularly provided space for travelling companies to perform. On September 22, 1760, Miss Whateley, who became quite addicted to theater, could have attended *The Spaniard Outwitted*, preceded by a concert of music (as the law required), interspersed with songs and dances, and followed by the afterpiece, Garrick's *Miss in Her Teens*. Walsall also offered music and dancing at occasional balls and assemblies. And people climbed, panting, to the church on the hilltop for sermons and prayers—and for more music. Not all eighteenth-century churches paid much attention to music, but Walsall's St. Matthew's did: it had an organ and an organist, John Balaam, who, though blind, played for church services and gave concerts as well. There was other music in town too, amateur music, produced by the Musical Society. There was even a local poet, Stephen Chatterton, who wrote an ode for the Musical Society which, set to music and no doubt performed by the Society, praises Walsall as the home of Mirth, Wit, Harmony, and all the Muses.

Mr. Chatterton was a clever enough poet when he went on to political topics somewhat later in life. As a young man, though, he abounded in clichés. Fortunately for my story, he had an eye for the ladies. One of his earlier effusions is entitled "The Walsall Beauties." In verse so bad one can't be sure whether it is supposed to be seriously epic or comically mock-epic, he celebrates the charms of eight young ladies, noting "bosom, neck, and arms," "killing eyes," "ruby lips," "hair of waving

Walsall (1759/60-1763)

gold," et cetera, et cetera. A few of the ladies are differentiated from the group: Miss Craddock is unusually tall, while Dolly Jones must be the prettiest, because she outdoes Helen, Clytemnestra, Juno, Venus, Athene, and all the Graces, being herself "The pride of Nature, and of Rushall-street." Before he reaches this rousing conclusion, however, Mr. Chatterton has described Miss Whateley:

> To High-street now th'unwearied muse retires,
> And WHEATLEY's praise her loftiest notes requires.
> To sing her worth she'll all her pow'rs employ,
> And fearless venture on a theme so high.
> All that can wonder raise, or awe inspire,
> Or charm the eye, or youthful bosoms fire,
> In WHEATLEY shines; a nymph beyond compare,
> So learn'd, so good, so gen'rous, and so fair.
> Thus far she sung, intending next to tell,
> How her sweet verse the Sapphic odes excell;
> When thus methought fair CRADDOCK seem'd to say,
> "Leave her to Fame, and bring the muse away."

The praise of her beauty is the usual Chatterton stereotyping—both she herself and Shenstone said she was plain—but the moral and intellectual qualities the bard mentions, unique in his catalogue of ladies, are genuinely individual. It is interesting to note that even in her early twenties she was known for such qualities and known, beyond the confines of Beoley, to be a poet. Both modest and ambitious, she must have told her new friends who "Harriot Airy" was.

The other ladies in Chatterton's effusion must have been her friends. The prettiest, Dolly Jones, and her sister Molly subscribed to Miss Whateley's 1764 book; so did three others and the father of a fourth. The remaining two may also appear in the subscription list but be unrecognizable because of married name or new dwelling place. These young women were the daughters of substantial citizens—businessmen and solicitors and town clerks, men who were active in the government of Walsall. Henry Whateley had introduced his sister to the

Walsall (1759/60-1763)

families of his own friends and associates. It is pleasant to know that, though she still missed Elizabeth Loggin, Mary had such company amid the "Crowds and Noise" of the town. Her world had widened.

The world beyond Walsall was growing better acquainted with her as well. In May 1760, "Harriet Airy" had two poems published in the short-lived *Royal Female Magazine*: "Liberty," her complaint about imprisonment, and an imitation of Anacreon. "Liberty" was preceded by her letter to Elizabeth Loggin, with the reference to December edited out for this May publication; the whole package followed a brief, anonymous note recommending the "real merit" of these "productions of a female muse." Had a friend undertaken to promote her work, or had the poet herself written the note, having grown wiser in the ways of the publishing world? I would guess the latter, because when, somewhat later, a promoter undoubtedly did appear, the pseudonym "Harriet Airy" vanished. Dr. Wall, a friend of Shenstone's, is behind a flurry of publications of "Liberty," which was printed in at least four more magazines and newspapers between December 1761 and February 1762. The author was identified variously as "the Warwickshire Poetess" or "Miss Whateley," and letters from Dr. Wall told something about her. The journals were copying from each other, as usual, and capitalizing on the popularity of *Rasselas*, but Dr. Wall had started the campaign. With his help, "Harriet Airy" vanished forever, and "Miss Whateley" took her place.

These were momentous months for Mary Whateley as both poet and woman. Her name was now before the public—and in Walsall she met the new curate of St. Matthew's, the Rev. John Darwall. With his wife Mary Fox Darwall and their two small children, he came to Walsall to take up his position early in 1762, probably in March. He must have welcomed his appointment at Walsall. A curate's life—and his income—were never secure, and this position, like his former one, was just a curacy, but the vicar was much older than John's previous superior, and the Rev. Mr. Darwall could hope to succeed to the

Walsall (1759/60-1763)

vicarage before too long. Besides, he cared about music at least as much as about theology, and Walsall had music, more music than his previous two homes, Bushbury and Trysull. He had not been totally deprived of music in those villages, however, for they were in the neighborhood of Sir Samuel Hellier of the Wodehouse, Wombourne, a contemporary of John's at Oxford and as passionately devoted to music as he was. Coming young to his inheritance, Sir Samuel gave an organ to his church, organized music meetings, supported a charity school that could train choristers, and even built a temple to Handel in his Shenstonian garden. He was indeed a congenial neighbor. But a curate could not always be visiting his friends, so John would have been glad to serve in a church and a town that had their own music.

Both the clerical profession and a love of music were something of a family tradition. John's father, Randle Darwall, who played the violin, was the rector of Haughton, Staffordshire, where John was born in 1731. The family was small: a younger brother and sister died in their teens, leaving only one sister, Honor, also younger than John. Randle sent his son to Brasenose, his own college at Oxford, where John received his B.A. in 1756. He was promptly ordained deacon, and then priest the next year, taking over the curacy at his father's church in Haughton. Sons often settled into and as it were inherited their fathers' churches, but John did not stay in Haughton long. In September 1757, he was appointed curate at Bushbury. He stayed there no longer than he had at Haughton, only a little over a year, after which he went to Trysull. Curates often moved about a great deal, but in this case a woman, Mary Fox, probably had something to do with one or both moves.

Mary Fox was the daughter of the vicar of Sheriffhales, a small town about twelve miles from both Haughton and Bushbury. And she had family, also in the church, in Wombourne, Sir Samuel Hellier's home, about seven miles from Bushbury; at some unknown time she went to live with them. Distances of twelve or seven miles were not trivial in the eigh-

Walsall (1759/60-1763)

teenth century, but they were not prohibitive, and clergymen tended to know one another. I don't know just when and how John Darwall and Mary Fox met, but they came to know one another very well indeed. When they were married in November 1758, in John's church at Bushbury, Mary Fox, who was twenty-three, had less than six weeks to wait before the birth of their first child. There had been no public calling of the banns, but secrecy was impossible in a small village. Such embarrassing circumstances for a marriage were quite common at the time, but one wonders how the Bushbury people felt when their clergyman married an obviously pregnant bride in his own church. Mrs. Darwall was no doubt glad to take her new husband and go back to her family in Wombourne after the wedding, in time for little Mary's birth on New Year's Day, 1759. Her relative there was the curate of the parish and probably helped John find another position. And perhaps Bushbury was glad to see the Darwalls go.

The Darwalls settled next door to Wombourne in Trysull where John had been appointed to the chapel, which belonged to the Wombourne parish; here the second baby, born in May 1760, was baptized John, and the third, born in June 1761, Jane. This little one died after about two months, though, so when the Darwalls went to Walsall, there were only two babies to move to the growing industrial town—but Mrs. Darwall was pregnant again.

The Rev. Mr. Darwall's clerical duties began at once. The vicar had been managing without a regular curate for some time and must have heaved a sigh of relief when help arrived. But a clergyman did not work day and night, so though Mrs. Darwall would have been busy with her new home and her babies, John would have found some time to join in the social life of the town. Devoted to music and a composer himself, he would have attended concerts and sought out the Musical Society when he was not engaged in his church duties. Mary Whateley, by now well acquainted in Walsall, could not have failed to meet him: Walsall society was a small group, she was always regular in

Walsall (1759/60-1763)

performing her own Christian duties, and she too was musical. Mary Whateley and John Darwall became friends.

Their friendship flourished warmly enough to inspire her to address a poem to him on the subject and, perhaps, warmly enough to inspire some gossip in the town. "Ode to Friendship. Inscribed to the Rev. Mr. J. Darwall" compares the dismalness of winter with the pastoral joys of other seasons and describes the importance of friendship, especially during such a season:

> In this dark Season what can chear
> The drooping Heart, or banish Fear,
>   Save *Friendship*'s placid Pow'r?
> This, like the golden Orb of Day,
> Can dart a vivifying Ray
>   To gild the gloomiest Hour.
>
> This Heart-felt Bliss, to Heav'n ally'd,
> Disclaiming *Folly*, *Noise*, and *Pride*,
>   With *Virtue* only reigns:
> And this, tho' *Envy*'s poison'd Dart
> With *Falsehood* fraught assails the Heart,
>   The *direful Blow* disdains.

The sentiments are expressed in general terms, but her disdain for the "*direful Blow*" of envy and falsehood suggests that there had been gossip. Part of the last stanza supports such a reading: "Tho' *Fortune*'s adverse Gales arise . . . / Unmov'd remains the *Friend*." Chatterton had called her both "good" and "gen'rous," but it doesn't take much to damage a young spinster's reputation. Yet Mary, courageously, proclaimed the purity of her friendship for John in print.

About her friendship with his wife one can only speculate. Much later, an unreliable piece of family gossip claims that the wife was jealous of the friend. But Miss Whateley was one of the "sureties" or sponsors at the baptism of the next Darwall baby, and the baby's mother must have had something to say about that. This fourth baby, called Randle after his grandfather, was born in September 1762—and sometime during the

Walsall (1759/60-1763)

next year, at about the age of one, he was recruited as a subscriber to Miss Whateley's book. It is not unusual to see parents and one or more children in a subscription list, but when only one appears, one would expect it to be the oldest child, or at least the oldest son. Baby Randle must have been chosen instead of Mary or young John because of a special relationship with the poet. She was his "surety," and quite possibly she had helped to care for Mrs. Darwall during her pregnancy and lying-in and to look after the newborn boy. No doubt Mrs. Darwall could have used some help. No information survives about her health, but she had only two more births to endure and about three more years to live. Quite possibly, with a yearly child and the insecurity of her husband's position, she was weakening. Certainly she was short of money and the domestic help that money can buy. Curates were notoriously underpaid at this time; at Bushbury, John had been earning just twenty-eight pounds a year. So she might have welcomed her husband's friend, good, generous, plain Miss Whateley, and the support and practical help she could offer. But one can't be sure.

Active as she probably was in the Darwalls' household, Mary Whateley did not spend all her time there. She still had her brother to attend to, her poems to write, and the larger life of the town and the world in general to observe. Her poems show that however occupied she was with personal and domestic concerns, she noticed what went on beyond her immediate horizons. During these years in Walsall, she read in *Aris's Birmingham Gazette* about the death of old King George II in October 1760 and the coronation of his young grandson, who was just her own age. A new era was beginning: the young king championed domestic virtue (which would have pleased Mary) and the nation was expanding into an empire as it took over Canada and Florida and India. The Seven Years' War that concluded in these arrangements had notable effects closer to home as well. Trade slumped in the Midlands despite the army's continuing need for Birmingham's guns, harvests were

Walsall (1759/60-1763)

poor, and food riots plagued Birmingham and other towns in the neighborhood. *Aris's Gazette* was full of bad news.

Not all of Miss Whateley's experience of a wider world was gleaned from the Birmingham newspaper, however. It was possibly during her first Walsall years that she visited Birmingham itself, a visit that produced a poem, "Rural Happiness. To a Friend." Rural happiness may seem an odd topic for a poem about troubled and industrial Birmingham, but she found it in the thirty acres of pasture and woodland that made up the park of Bordesley Hall, an elegant suburban mansion built by John Taylor. Taylor had amassed a fortune making plate, gilt buttons, and enamelled snuff-boxes; he was so rich he became the co-founder of Lloyds bank. Miss Whateley probably gained entry to the park thanks to her brother George, who, his apprenticeship long finished, was now well established in Birmingham manufacturing circles. He too worked in gold and silver plate, being, like Taylor, a "toymaker"— Birmingham was, after all, "the Toy-Shop of the World." Recently married, George was beginning to found a substantial dynasty of solid Birmingham citizens, many of whom became influential lawyers; the professional and manufacturing middle classes were indeed rising in the growing provincial towns of the eighteenth century. Perhaps Mary, with brother Henry in tow, had come the nine miles from Walsall for the christening of George's first child, John, in October 1760. The poem describes "bounteous Autumn," which need not be merely a poetic convention.

Whatever the cause of the visit, the poet was happy to be back among the fields and trees. She uses a pastoral name for the "Friend" who has asked for a poem—Evander—which gives no clue to his identity. But she is glad to answer *"Friendship's* Call," especially now that she has Nature to inspire her again. Once more she has "fair *Retirement*" in which to write and a rich harvest scene to describe, a scene surpassing in beauty those foreign scenes of the ancient poets. There is a strong tone here of pride in "Albion." Even noisy Birmingham, almost as sooty as Walsall but safely distant from Bordesley Park, is praised as

Walsall (1759/60-1763)

a fair abode "of *Freedom*, *Joy*, and *Peace!* / Where Treasure flows and useful Arts increase"—with a footnote identifying the "famous Town," perhaps in case the description sounded like some cleaner place. As the guest of manufacturers, she could hardly criticize the grubby side of Birmingham. And if she had a long enough visit, she would have found much to attract her in the famous town, with its theater and other advantages that Walsall was still to lack for many years to come. But her topic is the rural, and she returns to it, again on a patriotic note, to celebrate the peaceful security of the countryside she sees.

Next *"Borsd'ley-Hall* [sic], sweet Mansion of Delight, / In fair Proportion rises to [her] Sight," and its walks, woods, and lakes come in for their share of description. She must have grieved, remembering this beautiful scene, when Bordesley Hall was destroyed by the mobs during the Priestley riots of 1791 because its owner was a Quaker.

In the rest of the poem, three more verse paragraphs, the poet draws on two distinct traditions. First, beginning with the familiar phrase "Happy the Man," she praises "learned Leisure" in a "sweet Recess." Next comes a miniature "Vanity of Human Wishes," a small contribution to that great tradition in which the poet dismisses gold and grandeur in favor of virtue. Returning to the tradition of rural retirement, she concludes with an "unambitious Pray'r" for a "lonely Cot" in a pastoral setting, complete with Health, Freedom, and Friendship—which brings the poem nicely back full circle to *"Friendship's* Call."

This final portion of the poem suggests that Mary Whateley might have read and admired the poems of Anne Finch, Countess of Winchilsea, which were published in 1713. Miss Whateley mentions many male poets by name in her first book, but no women. She had read women poets in the *Gentleman's Magazine* and perhaps elsewhere, but she does not mention their work. By allusions and imitations and by naming names, she allies herself with Anacreon and Tibullus, Pope and Johnson, Shenstone and Langhorne—a purely male tradition. Here, however, is the only apparent link that I have been able to identify between her poems of 1764 and the mainstream of women's writing. Her "Pray'r" begins,

> "Give me, indulgent Heav'n, some lonely Cot,
> "Where I may live unenvy'd and forgot;
> "Range the sequester'd Shade with Mind serene,
> "Explore the Beauties of the Sylvan Scene. . . ."

Lady Winchilsea's "Petition for an Absolute Retreat" begins similarly:

> Give me O indulgent Fate!
> Give me yet, before I Dye,
> A sweet, but absolute Retreat,
> 'Mongst Paths so lost, and Trees so high,
> That the World may ne'er invade,
> Through such Windings and such Shade,
> My unshaken Liberty.

Mary Whateley wrote a poem called "Liberty" which shows that she too prized that quality. Both she and Lady Winchilsea chose the not uncommon terms "indulgent" and "Crowds and Noise" from the vocabulary of retirement poetry. Lady Winchilsea's "Petition" celebrates the love of the woman friend to whom it is addressed; Mary Whateley's "Rural Happiness" also addresses a friend, albeit male, but female friendship is a frequent theme in her poems. "Rural Happiness" concludes as the poet vows to "Contemn the Pomp of Courts, and pity Slaves"; in "The Petition," Lady Winchilsea finds that female friendship brings solace for her sufferings after she and her husband refused allegiance to William and Mary and were excluded from the pomp of their court. "The Petition" also has some particularly feminine touches: the poet wants light, simple, fresh clothing and "A Table spread without my Care." Miss Whateley, her brother's housekeeper, could appreciate that. Both poems, of course, express the sentiments common to the poetry of retreat, but the particular threads, however slender, that link the two

Walsall (1759/60-1763)

poems and the two poets suggest a connection. Overtly allied only with male poets and the male tradition in poetry, at least in her first book, Miss Whateley might have had this one important link with other women poets.

"Rural Happiness," like Lady Winchilsea's "Petition," celebrates the pastoral scene, but urban experience had not lessened the poet's urge to write. On the contrary, however much she had dreaded moving to town, Mary Whateley's first Walsall years were busy and productive for her as a poet. And these years were crucial in her life as a woman, as she gained new friends and new experiences.

This part of her story comes to an end sometime about the middle of 1763. The dedication to her first book is dated "Beoley, Dec. 3, 1763." Her father had died in August and her mother was now alone on the farm; all her surviving children had settled elsewhere. She must have called her daughter back, leaving Henry to manage by himself in town. Indeed, Mary might well have gone home earlier in the year if her father's health was declining. She had already lost a surrogate father that February when William Shenstone suddenly succumbed to a "putrid fever," so it was a sad year. But she had found another such father in Randle Darwall, with whom she corresponded from the isolation of Beoley. John wrote too, and told her about the birth of his fifth child, William, in October 1763. And both Darwalls, who had been bustling among their friends, reported on their success in signing up subscribers to her book. Meanwhile, Mary put the finishing touches on her manuscript. It was published in London in May 1764, followed before long by a Dublin edition. A single woman, and confined again to the country, she could not have managed such a feat without a great deal of help from her friends.

Chapter 3

Guides, Philosophers, and Friends: Shenstone, Langhorne, et al.

> Come then, my Friend, my Genius, come along,
> Oh master of the poet, and the song! . . .
> Teach me, like thee, in various nature wise,
> To fall with dignity, with temper rise. . . .
> Shall then this verse to future age pretend
> Thou wert my guide, philosopher, and friend?
>
> Pope, *Essay on Man*, IV

When her first book was published in 1764, Mary Whateley had both won and lost friends in the world of letters. Woty had apparently not lasted, or at least the friendship had been interrupted. Two others, however, were of particular and greater importance to her as she developed into a poet: William Shenstone (who died in 1763) and John Langhorne. Both were well-known men of letters, published poets with many connections in the London literary world. Other helpful and influential friends and acquaintances also did some writing, but literature was in no sense their profession. Nevertheless, they too played significant roles in Miss Whateley's venture into the world of letters. Examining the roles these men played—and all were men except for the patroness of her book—reveals something about how that world functioned and about the kinds of encouragement and discouragement she would encounter, the practical help and theoretical preconceptions she would meet.

Guides, Philosophers, and Friends

The role of her patroness was slight. She was "the Hon. Lady Wrottesley, at Perton," Frances née Grey (d. 1769), the widow of the fourth baronet. The poet probably did not know the patroness—the Dedication, properly grateful but mercifully free of the usual flattery, gives no hint of personal acquaintance. However, Miss Whateley could have met the lady's granddaughter in Shenstone's garden one summer day; they both visited there. Or John Darwall could have recruited the lady: Perton is only two miles from his former home of Bushbury, and Mr. Darwall kept up his connections in the neighborhood. However the patroness was acquired, it was useful to have one. The Wrottesley name carried a great deal of weight in the Midlands, and represented connections with the church as well as with land, money, and business. The name gave the book a respectable air and, even though the patroness and her family took only a total of five copies, undoubtedly helped its sales.

Of the men who contributed to Miss Whateley's career, the Rev. John Welchman remains the most obscure. The son of a prolific ecclesiastical writer, he had been vicar since 1726 in Tanworth, her mother's home, about three miles from Beoley; he had four daughters, all of whom subscribed to the book. He did not; he died in early May 1764, just before the book appeared. The Welchmans, then, were friends and neighbors, and perhaps even family—Whateley connections were common in that area. They certainly became family later, when Mary's nephew William married a Welchman in 1788.

One of Mary's poems is addressed to the old vicar. It reveals that he too wrote verse and that he liked hers. "To the Rev. Mr. Welchman at Tanworth" thanks him for the "Praise [his] Pen bestow'd," which warmed her heart as the "Beams of *Phoebus*" warm the "pale Bud" of "the languid *Primrose*, Winter's Child." There is a wintry atmosphere throughout this poem—the poet has been unhappy. She laments her lack of education and consequent inability to express herself as skillfully as she could wish, though she says that her obscure, rural life has been blessed. She has tried to write about "Joy and Love"

Guides, Philosophers, and Friends

as an antidote to her own "pale Care, and melancholy Gloom" but—not surprisingly—without success. But Mr. Welchman has cheered her, not only with praise of her poems but also with the more important "heav'nly Truths [his] Lays impart." His "sublime Instruction" and virtuous example have renewed her piety and her certainty of heaven. Interestingly, this poem addressed to a fatherly instructor is the only one in which, grateful for their "tender Care," she alludes to her parents. It is a poem about authority figures. Also interestingly, she goes on to give thanks that she is without the beauty which might have "tempted the Seducer's Wiles" and "betray'd [her] Heart to Pride." One can make a pretty good guess at the kind of frustration and perhaps even rejection that caused her unhappiness, and an even better guess that the Rev. Mr. Welchman, father of four daughters, had been preaching the traditional, conservative values of his faith and his social class as they apply to young women. And Mary Whateley, ambitious young woman poet though she was, submits to that discipline and professes herself grateful. Indeed, her religious and moral sentiments are always thoroughly orthodox. She strikes a rebellious note, and cautiously at that, only on the subjects of being a writer and being a woman.

Another kind of help, of a more worldly sort, came from Dr. John Wall of Worcester, whom I have mentioned before. He was a remarkable man. A practicing physician until his death in 1776, he wrote on a wide range of medical subjects, including the limitations of the popular Malvern waters. He was also both a devoted and productive painter and one of the founders of Worcester's first china factory; he combined these two talents by painting on his own porcelain and helping to invent a process for printing on it. Shenstone, who knew him well, valued both his medical skill and his conversation.

Apparently Dr. Wall had not met Miss Whateley when he first took an interest in her. Someone, perhaps Shenstone or perhaps one of the Worcester Whateleys, seems to have mentioned her, carelessly, with the result that Dr. Wall described her in his letter to a friend as a common drudge in a mean farmhouse. This letter, dated January 30, 1760, accompanied Mary Whateley's letter and poem to Miss Loggin in both the *London Chronicle* and the *Gentleman's Magazine* at the end of 1761. It was followed in the next February *Gentleman's* by a letter correcting the "injurious" picture of the poet, and since she has now "with some difficulty" been persuaded to allow her poems to be published, Dr. Wall urges the magazine's readers to support the subscription to it. A shorter version of the same letter appeared in the *London Magazine* at the same time; two of Miss Whateley's poems had appeared there the previous month (January 1762).

Shenstone was distressed. He wrote to his friend Mrs. Bennet, on March 14, 1762, "Poor Miss Whateley has been a little mauled in the Magazines through the zeal of those that *are* her Friends." Apparently his own less aggressive spirit disliked the idea of a lady being subjected to such publicity. For publicity it was. "Unlearned" poets, like Shenstone's own protégé James Woodhouse, were becoming fashionable, and energetic Dr. Wall, with his letters, his direct puffing, and his sponsorship of printings of poems, was conducting an elaborate and imaginative advertising campaign.

The Darwalls, father and son, promoted Miss Whateley's book in a more discreet and traditional fashion. A lively letter by Randle Darwall survives to tell the tale. Dated from Haughton, January 28, 1764, it addresses an unidentified "Your Worship" (seemingly an official from the bishop's seat at Lichfield) and asks him to continue the good work, begun some time before, of seeking support for Miss Whateley's book. Randle Darwall himself has collected "Eight Score Subscriptions" and reports that his son John has collected above 120. (The grand total was 761.) Randle has been convinced of Miss Whateley's merit by the zeal of other patrons who are "unquestionably good Judges" —Lord Lyttleton, Shenstone, Dr. Wall—as well as by his own acquaintance with the lady's work. He admires her a great deal: "None, undoubtedly, can be more worthy of Encouragement, than that incomparably modest and ingenious Young Lady"; to be acceptable in the eighteenth century, a woman writer had to have both talent and a proper moral character. Randle finds her letters, addressed to both John and himself, as fine as her poems: "And O!—tis Enough to puzzle a Divine . . . to say, whether she writes more charmingly in Verse or in Prose." He goes on to cite, rather smugly, some of the "Worthy Gentlemen" he has persuaded to subscribe. But he failed to persuade one "Mr. C—kes," who has "no Taste for any Thing, but Pelf, and Pettifogging." Here Randle gets sidetracked into further denunciation of yet another man who is "an odious Compound of Knave, Fool, and Clown," and loses sight of Miss Whateley completely. His rhetoric is trenchant—as his son's would later prove to be. The Darwall men had passionate spirits.

Randle Darwall did more for Miss Whateley than drum up trade. He inspired her to think seriously about the purposes of poetry. A versifier himself (some of his efforts appeared in the *London Magazine*), he apparently sent her a poem to which she responded with "Elegy on the Uses of Poetry," "inscribed" to him (see Appendix). She approaches him both as a literary critic, hoping he will approve her "faint Strokes," and as a friend. He is also a "Friend to *Virtue*, *Piety* and *Truth*," those qualities they both believe poetry should serve.

The elegy begins with a pastoral passage on contemplation at evening by the "Osier-fringed Stream," which suggests that Mary was back in Beoley, or at least remembering it vividly, when she wrote. Contemplation, Truth, Genius, Peace, and Freedom, all country dwellers, are "the Guardians of the Muse" whose task is "To harmonize, instruct, and charm Mankind":

> Her pleasing Task, thro' Nature's varied Plan,
>   To trace the Goodness of Almighty Power;
> To vindicate the Ways of God to Man,
>   Soothe *Care*'s deep Gloom, and chear the lonely Hour.

Guides, Philosophers, and Friends

Next comes a strong denunciation of poetry that is licentious, venal, or scandalous, the kind of poetry she will never write. She pronounces a curse on herself if she does; the metaphor is not entirely clear, but the curse seems to be deprivation of her poetic powers and of all friendship. A direct address to Randle Darwall on friendship and on his powers as a critic concludes the poem.

This is not mere lip service to lofty ideals. This is the ethic Langhorne espoused, the ethic Dryden praised in Anne Killigrew, though more generally and decorously stated (here there are no "steaming ordures of the stage"), the ethic suitable for all respectable poets and especially for ladies. The Dedication to the book expresses the same values. Yet Miss Whateley is not relentlessly high-minded: besides serious instruction, poetry can offer comfort, simplicity, and tenderness. Shenstone would have agreed.

By the time Miss Whateley's book appeared, Shenstone was dead. But he had been a major force in the practical business of bringing the book to publication as well as the most influential master of the young beginner. So influential was he that, as I mentioned earlier, one of the strongest tributes of the time to Mary Whateley, a passage in Mary Scott's *The Female Advocate*, hails her as "Daughter of SHENSTONE."

I also suggested earlier that this powerful influence could have begun at Mr. Loggin's when Mary was a girl. Whenever it began, the relationship was well established by 1760, when Mary was twenty-two and wrote a poem about Shenstone, the kind of poem that bespeaks the ease of long familiarity. Although it appeared in her book as "To Mr. O——y," it had begun life as "To Mr. S—— on his desiring her to paint his character"; it bears the date of December 13, 1760:

> Tho' you flatter my Genius, and praise what I write,
> Sure this whimsical Task was impos'd out of Spite.
> Because this poor Head with much scratching and thinking
> Made some idle Reflections on raking and drinking,
> To clip my weak Wings with malicious Intention,

Guides, Philosophers, and Friends

> You present me a Theme that defies all Invention.
> Your Picture! Lord bless us! where can one begin?
> To speak Truth were insipid, to lie were a Sin:
> You might think me in love should I paint your Perfections;
> Shou'd I sketch out your Faults you might make worse Objections.
> Shou'd I blend in one Piece of superlative Merit,
> Good-nature and Wit, Condescension and Spirit;
> Shou'd with Modesty, Ease and Politeness be join'd;
> Unlimited Freedom, with Manners refin'd;
> Courage, Tenderness, Honour enthron'd in one Heart;
> With Frankness, Reserve; and with Honesty, Art:
> Were these glaring good Qualities plac'd in full View,
> Do you think any Soul wou'd believe it was *you*?
> "Why then, turn t'other Side (says Illnature) and find him,
> "In some few modish Faults, leave his Sex all behind him;
> "For Levity, Flatt'ry, and so forth, he's fam'd;"—
> Prithee, Peace Fool, and let not such Trifles be named:
> If his Failings be such, Time will certainly cure 'em;
> And the *Ladies, till then,* will with Pleasure endure 'em.

It is Miss Whateley's most lighthearted and comic poem.

Why is "Mr. S———" Shenstone? After the poem was published in the *London Magazine* (January 1762), it was linked with the letter of Dr. Wall, Shenstone's friend. When it appeared in the *Annual Register* for 1761, it was printed with two poems, one by Robert Dodsley and one by "Cotswouldia," directly addressed to Shenstone; they look like a connected group. In letters to his friends Shenstone sometimes liked to pose as "raking and drinking." He himself used, and encouraged other poets to use, anapestic meter, the meter of this poem. As a young man, he himself had gone in for witty, impertinent character sketches of his friends, like that in this poem. Above all, though he nurtured Miss Whateley's genius for pastoral and thought pastoral suitable for ladies, the only poem of hers that he copied into his manuscript Miscellany was this comic one, her only poem that is *not* pastoral. Even though he altered the title, hiding modestly behind "To Mr. L———," it has to be Shenstone.

So Miss Whateley knew Shenstone well. By the fall of 1761, she had written enough poems, "a pretty Large Collection," to make him start talking about a book. He mentions her in two September letters, to Richard Graves and Thomas Percy, saying she lives in Walsall and has a "truly classical style." Yet her style needs some work, and he has already enlisted the help of a Mrs. Bennet, in London. His letter thanking Mrs. Bennet is revealing:

> I am very truly obliged to you for the pains you took at my request, to revise poor Miss Whateley's poetry. That Lady has been here [at the Leasowes] since, & esteems herself alike obliged to you. We have removed some of ye more important Objections; and I have hinted to her as particularly as I could, in what kind of manner she might improve many of the Pieces. She is neither handsome, nor, I believe, in affluent circumstances; has seen mighty Little of the world: On the other hand, she is young, unaffected, and unassuming; and that she has generous & delicate sentiments, as well as ingenuity, may, I think, be fairly concluded from the whole tenour of her Poetry.

It is possible to identify some of the revisions Miss Whateley made, apparently recommended by Shenstone and Mrs. Bennet, but it is not possible to tell which editor made which suggestions, or which changes she might have made on her own initiative. Despite these uncertainties, some of the changes seem significant.

Two poems, "An Address to my Pen" and "To my Garden," are available in two versions (1759 and 1764), and one poem, "Liberty," in three (1760, 1762, 1764). Almost no corrections were made in rhyme and meter or in grammar; Miss Whateley already had a good command of those technicalities. Indeed, Shenstone said the poems were "more correct than I almost ever saw written by a lady." Nor were the poems pruned or extended. But consistency of point of view, logic of argument, and clarity of idea—all quite good to start with—were tightened up. The editors seem to have paid most attention to diction, more than doubling the number of classical allusions in "To my Garden" and "An Address to my Pen" and frequently turning simpler terms into more formal, "poetic" words: "chearful" becomes "aetherial," "verdure" becomes "honours," "restless" becomes "flitting." Some of the changes seem to me to be improvements, some not. For this reason, and because exact attribution of the changes is impossible, and because the available samples are few, I won't draw any firm conclusions about the extent of the editors' influence, though clearly it was there. Two specific points, however, are worth mentioning.

The first version of "An Address to my Pen" concludes with a rather strange image. The scene is winter, but the pen has the power to create warmth and beauty:

> In spite of frost the bubbling fountains rise,
> And ink the absence of the stream supplies.

Inevitably, and grotesquely, the picture of a black brook crosses the mind. The idea works—both ink and stream are sources of vitality—but the picture is peculiar, apparently too peculiar for Shenstone or Mrs. Bennet. The offensive lines were replaced with the dullest of pastoral clichés:

> Where, spite of Frost, the bubbling Fountains flow,
> New *Zephyrs* soothe me, and new Roses blow.

Shenstone's own taste approved the smoothly conventional; he liked "simplicity rather than surprize" in images. One can only guess at the extent of Miss Whateley's resistance to his criteria.

That there was some resistance is demonstrated, I think, by the three versions of "Liberty." Since Shenstone died early in 1763, it seems likely that Miss Whateley alone was responsible for the second set of changes in the poem. The 1762 version is "From a corrected copy," but the final version differs significantly from it at a number of points. Many of the corrections have been retained, ten lines are identical in all three versions, and a few entirely new words and phrases are introduced in the last version, one of which ("Velvet Lawns diversify'd with Flow'rs") brings the wording closer to *Rasselas*. But in ten instances, Miss Whateley returns to her own first wording. Most often she simplifies the diction again: "wafts" and "blow" are restored to the original "breathes" and "breathe"; "bright" (applied to flowers) is restored to "sweet"; "trace" the sunburnt hill is restored to "range." Less happily, "lucid rills" is restored to the hackneyed "purling rills." More important are two changes in phrases that express her deepest feelings. Her editors thought the word "wish" was sufficient to express her frustration in her search for Variety, but she restored "hope"—a vain hope is more despairing than a vain wish. Also, "Dear Liberty—is Myra's constant theme" is restored to "Dear Liberty is wretched *Myra*'s Theme," which insists on her misery and anticipates the last line of the poem, "Here wretched *Myra*'s destin'd to remain." Her editors had not tampered with that final line, however, so they were not trying to prevent all expression of feeling. But Shenstone always advocated a combination of sincerity, modesty, and restraint, and did apparently try to tone down this poem somewhat. And he inclined toward a fashionably conventional diction. So I think the changes indicate some chafing against his taste, but for the most part that taste was accepted and Miss Whateley was, on the surface at least, a properly deferential protégée.

Her deference is most marked in her nearly total adherence to the pastoral mode. Among the poems in her first book, only the playful one, "To Mr. O———y," lacks trees and flowers. Shenstone, and many other gentlemen, believed pastoral poetry suitable for ladies because it was associated with simplicity and virtue, and therefore did not strain their limited capacities. Besides, only virtuous lady writers were acceptable. Shenstone even believed that country people really were more virtuous than city people because of the morally salutary influence of "natural objects" and the scarcity of examples of evil; he makes the point in his *Essays on Men and Manners*, and he is writing about life, not about poetic convention. His own poetry, of course, is primarily pastoral, as was his life, but he permitted

Guides, Philosophers, and Friends

himself some masculine freedoms: drinking "Florence wine" at Oxford, frequenting taverns and coffee-houses in London, and in his poetry flirting occasionally with the suggestive and the low. But this sort of thing would never do for Miss Whateley and other ladies; they are a different order of beings. Women are inferior to men and can be loved but never simply liked as friends, Shenstone believed; "genuine esteem" can be given only to equals; "affection [is] for those beneath us." However, women are superior in one respect: though they lack judgment, they have more fancy and imagination than men. Shenstone states these standard ideas directly in his *Essays* and implies them in his letters. Clearly, he cared for "poor Miss Whateley," and his own "tenderness" and "sensibility," which Dodsley so much admired, made him genuinely kind and helpful. But one can easily sense the patriarchal tone of the relationship.

She was not crushed by it. "Harriot Airy" put Woty in his place, and Miss Whateley, who praised Shenstone, also teased him, politely but pointedly, in "To Mr. O———y." When he died so suddenly, the teasing stopped and, appropriately, the praise and gratitude came to the fore:

> On the left side
> of the sole building I can call my own
> is consecrated
> A MONUMENT
> to the Memory of
> the beloved and lamented
> WILLIAM SHENSTONE:
> It is formed something like an Urn
> But of a substance so soft,
> That all his Virtues
> were with ease engraved on it;
> Yet so tenacious,
> They never can be erased:———
> It is inscribed with affection and respect
> for the gentle and elegant qualities
> of which he was
> the happy possessor;
> And stamped with the deepest gratitude,

Guides, Philosophers, and Friends

for the honour he had conferred
By his kind and condescending notice
on the
thereby dignified Owner.

The epitaph is unsigned, but Thomas Percy, the ballad collector and a close friend of Shenstone's, ascribed it to Miss Whateley. Like her Dedication, it is not effusive; it is also more personal and more balanced in its judgment of the dead than most funerary tributes. Along with the other evidence, it bespeaks a relationship that was close and warm, nurturing and fruitful, despite the limitations imposed by Shenstone's conventional views.

On the subject of publishing, those views were ambivalent. Shenstone valued modesty highly in both men and women, and he found something inherently immodest in publishing. At the same time, "A man possessed of intellectual talents would be ... blameable in confining them to his own private use." In his youth, Shenstone had published a book of poems, anonymously, and then a few individual poems, also anonymously. Dodsley had included a number of Shenstone's poems in his anthology, but Shenstone himself, though he considered the possibility and fretted over the advantages and disadvantages of asking one's friends to subscribe, had not collected his work for publication when he died. Mary Whateley, on the other hand, had publication in mind early on; devoted though she apparently was to rural solitude, she did not desire its mute, inglorious side. First as "Harriot Airy" and then, thanks to Dr. Wall, as Miss Whateley, she appeared in at least six journals before her book came out, though the *Annual Register* wrongly ascribed "To Mr. S———" to Miss Loggin. Indeed, in the Dedication to the book, Miss Whateley is conscious that she already has some "Fame to lose" and hopes the book will enable her to retain "the kind Opinion" her friends have already formed about her work. Whether Shenstone, who disapproved of ambition, attempted to quash it in Miss Whateley one cannot say; ambivalent even about a man publishing, he could well have felt strongly about such an invasion of a young lady's modesty. But on at least one occasion he had urged Lady Luxborough to allow Dodsley to include some of her songs, which were properly pastoral, in the next edition of the anthology. Despite his mixed views, at some point he decided that Mary Whateley's poems should be published. He enlisted the help of Mrs. Bennet and planned to ask Lord or Lady Dartmouth to be the patron. Before he died, he must have mentioned it as well to Robert Dodsley, his own publisher and friend—for it was Dodsley who put the book in print.

Shenstone, then, gave Mary Whateley practical help, both real and projected, and, conventional in his views of poetry and of women, acted as her "father in art." Her other major link to the world of current letters was not such an authority figure. He was more simply a friend.

John Langhorne, only three years older than Mary, liked women as people and was sensitive to their needs and disadvantages. A clergyman and man of letters, who was to be twice married and twice widowed in his relatively brief life, he considered himself "liberal" in his attitude towards women, although his ideas were not liberal in modern terms. Otherwise, he was for the most part comfortably conservative. He had a social conscience and he disliked tyranny, but he disapproved of rebellion, he championed the government in the stormy days of John Wilkes, and he served as a magistrate, praised rural retirement, and dedicated his muse to truth and freedom. His ideas accord well with those Mary Whateley expressed and implied. Despite the quantity and frequent ideological directness of his published work, however, he remains a somewhat shadowy personality. He seems to have left no body of personal letters, and no biographer has yet gone beyond the level of *The Worthies of Westmorland*, his son's introduction to his poetical works, and the *Dictionary of National Biography*. One early memoirist, even though nearly a contemporary, laments the scantiness of available information about him. But enough exists in his own and others' words to say that he liked and cared about women in a way far different from the patriarchal Shenstone.

Langhorne even believed that it was possible for men and women to be friends, a relationship Shenstone reserved for his equals. The question was controversial, and Langhorne entered the debate in a lively essay addressed to a male friend, using as an example his own friendship with a talented and interesting woman. Aware how readily love can "take root in the affection of the friend," he nevertheless insists that esteem is the basis of friendship and that he can feel esteem for a woman as well as for a man, be she a sister, a grandmother, or "any woman upon earth." The woman he describes is "neither too old to be lively, nor too young to be grave"; she sometimes has a melancholy expression, but her mind is essentially cheerful; she talks sensibly, but not brilliantly. Her taste in literature is good, but would have been better if her education had been more systematic. She reads French and Italian, writes well, practices charity, and has unusual strength as well as grace as a musician. He concludes with a description of the lady's person—even friends have physical beings—but interestingly he does not flatter or lapse into clichés. She has beautiful brown hair, a roundish face, and genteel proportions. And she looks her best in "full dress"—that is, she needs the enhancement of good, even elaborate clothes. But so do "many ladies, who are reputed handsome," he hastens to add.

The portrait is both discriminating and judicious in describing the woman's human qualities with a minimum of gender stereotyping. She is unidentified, but I suspect that she is Ann Cracroft, whom Langhorne later married: Ann loved "literary acquirements," Langhorne taught her Italian when he was tutor to her brothers, she was musical above all, and existing accounts of her make no mention of beauty. If I am right, it says a great deal about Langhorne's attitude towards women that he would marry a friend. His ideas here are quite compatible with those Mary Whateley expressed in her later poem defining married love as the highest form of friendship, thus taking sides in an ancient debate; clearly, the two poets were in some respects like-minded.

Ann Cracroft was Langhorne's most special friend, but she was not the only one. Some time after her death, he became quite close to Hannah More, so close that rumors circulated among the more conventional part of the world that he had proposed marriage—rumors denied by one of his early biographers on the simple ground that Langhorne was married to his second wife when he met Miss More. There were probably other women friends as well, unknown because there are no revealing letters. One can easily imagine the kinds of misunderstandings such friendships must have produced in a world full of Shenstones. Perhaps significantly, the poem on "Precepts of Conjugal Happiness" that Langhorne wrote for Ann Cracroft's newly married sister warns against jealousy as the great destroyer of domestic peace—and it was written well before he himself married Ann. But he persisted as a friend to women, and Mary Whateley was one of his friends.

I don't know how, or even if, they ever met. Langhorne lived in a variety of places forming a rough circle around the edges of England, and Mary Whateley never left the Midlands during Langhorne's lifetime, as far as I know. Perhaps they found each other in the pages of the *Gentleman's Magazine,* where "Harriot Airy" and "Jemmy Copywell" made contact. Somewhere in the community of letters, they came to know and admire each other's poetry, and the ideas and character expressed in that poetry. Langhorne was particularly taken with Miss Whateley's "Elegy on the Search of Happiness." Even though it was addressed to Miss Loggin, he was moved to respond to its Johnsonian moral.

The "Elegy," which has eleven quatrains, is a small "Vanity of Human Wishes" in the great Ecclesiastes/Juvenal tradition, with specific echoes of Johnson. It begins quite differently, however. The discreet young woman does not magisterially command Observation to survey the globe for her from China to

Peru. Instead, she starts by banishing Melancholy from the pastoral scene, which she describes in edenic terms:

> Hence, *Melancholy!* hence! with all thy Train
>   Of rising *Fears*, and anxious *Doubts*, remove;
> Let not thy pensive Eye deject the Plain,
>   Nor spread thy Horrors o'er the silent Grove.
>
> Far may'st thou wander from this blissful Scene,
>   Where all that's lovely decks the varied Lawn;
> Where springs the laughing Flow'r, the fragrant Green;
>   Where spreads the Lake, and skips the wanton Fawn.
>
> Now smiles the Infant *Morn* serenely gay;
>   Glitters the Dew-drop on the bending Blade;
> Now grateful Birds salute the blushing Day,
>   And Flocks unfolded seek the verdant Glade.
>
> As from the Sun Night's sable Terrors fly,
>   So these fair Scenes of Solitude, and Ease,
> Calm the rack'd Breast, repel the Heart-felt Sigh,
>   And Nature's Music tunes the Mind to Peace.

Then she calls upon "Ye gentle Pow'rs that o'er these Shades preside" to answer the question, "Say, if ye can, where *Happiness* is found?" Traditionally, grandeur, gold, learning, power, fame, and beauty are suggested, and rejected, as the source of happiness. In this comparatively brief poem, Miss Whateley provides no historical or generic examples as Johnson does, but she adopts his traditional list and his "afflictive Dart" which, in her version, brings the pain that even beauty cannot guard against:

> Can Beauty guard from Pain's afflictive Dart?
>   Can Wit or Learning give the tranquil Hour?
> Can *Fame*'s loud Clarion heal the Grief-rent Heart?
>   Or does *Contentment* fix her Seat with Pow'r?

Her true source of happiness differs somewhat from Johnson's, however: where he finds it as a by-product of right thinking,

Guides, Philosophers, and Friends

especially of prayers for love, patience, and faith, she, like some other women poets who shared the tradition, finds it in virtue and resignation:

> ... with *Virtue Happiness* is found,
>   In the calm Breast, where Resignation smiles;
> Where no vain Hopes, or wild Desires abound,
>   But sweet Content each anxious Thought beguiles.

Johnson's conclusion is sometimes called a kind of Christian stoicism; Miss Whateley's, which banishes hopes and desires, could more accurately be so called. Even her "sweet Content" is rather grim: it "beguiles" anxious thought—Johnson defines "beguile" as "delude"—and hence does not invalidate such thoughts. She is suggesting, I think, that stoicism may be useful, but she recognizes that it is essentially fraudulent. She softens the sting a little, however, with a final stanza envisioning Miss Loggin in heaven:

> Still may the blooming Goddess bless my *Friend*,
>   Reign in thy Heart, and round thy Mansion stray;
> May her kind Beams thy latest Steps attend,
>   And safe conduct thee to celestial Day.

Johnson too had envisioned a "happier seat."

Miss Whateley had taken on a major philosophical topic from the mainstream of the tradition and scaled it down to the dimensions of a lady's pastoral meditations on virtue. The poem caught Langhorne's eye, and he replied:

> TO A LADY,
> on reading an elegy written by her
> *On the Search of Happiness*

> To seek the lovely nymph you sing,
> I've wander'd many a weary mile,
> From grove to grove, from spring to spring;
> If here or there she deign'd to smile.

Guides, Philosophers, and Friends

Nay what I now must blush to say,
For sure it hap'd in evil hour;
I once so far mistook my way,
To seek her in the haunts of power.

How should success my search betide,
When still so far I wander'd wrong?
For happiness on Arrowe's side,
Was listening to Maria's song.

Delighted thus with you to stay,
What hope have I the nymph to see;
Unless you cease your magic lay,
Or bring her in your arms to me?

Clearly, he approved of the traditional sentiment and liked the pastoral picture of Mary by the river. And there is a pleasant touch of personal warmth, perhaps even intimacy, in the last line.

John Langhorne and Mary Whateley were intimate enough to know quite a lot about each other's feelings, partly through the medium of the printed word, but their poems to each other which bracket her first book suggest that they were not limited to public communication. Her poem, which ends her book, is a response to his *Visions of Fancy* (1762), a group of four elegies he wrote at the age of twenty-seven, just after he had left his position as tutor in the Cracroft family in Lincolnshire. There he had fallen in love with Ann and she had refused him, knowing that her parents would never approve his suit because of his precarious financial position. He fled to Dagenham and a curate's post. It was to be five years before his position was secure enough to make the marriage possible.

When he wrote the *Visions* he was, according to his son's memoir, "a despairing lover," and Nature provided no comfort. The poems are introduced by a French epigraph on man's need for the sweetness of Fancy even though Reason knows that such sweetness is only a dream. The elegies are primarily melancholy in tone, though the first and third offer visions of happiness. In the first, Fancy comes to the sleeping poet in a dream and promises everlasting happiness (in a pastoral setting), including what is most important, love. But in the second, the poet, now awake, recognizes the delusiveness of the vision and complains of frustrated love and frustrated desires for fame; despairing, he asks for "blest Insensibility." Elegy III is a speech by "young Delight, of Hope and Fancy born," promising happiness in rural retirement. Again the vision is denied: in the last poem, care, pain, and increasing age overcome the delusions of fancy; with the decay of youth, the pleasures of "the vernal grove" also decay.

Mary Whateley responded with "To the Rev. Mr. J. Langhorne, On reading his Visions of Fancy, &.," and placed the poem at the end of her book. Its eleven quatrains make a bleak ending, though she generously pays more attention to Langhorne than to her own sorrows. She begins by lamenting the decline of her own fancy, blighted by the pain and care that accompany ill health:

> Fraught with each Wish the friendly Breast can form,
>   A simple Muse, O! *Langhorne*, wou'd intrude;
> Her Lays are languid, but her Heart is warm,
>   Tho' not with *Fancy*'s potent Powers endu'd.
>
> *Fancy*, tho' erst she shed a glimmering Ray,
>   And op'd to fairy Scenes my Infant Eye,
> From *Pain*, and *Care*, has wing'd her chearful Way,
>   And with *Hygeia* sought a milder Sky.
>
> No more my trembling Hand attempts the Lyre,
>   Which *Shenstone* oft (sweet Bard) has deign'd to praise;
> Even tuneful *Langhorne*'s Friendship fails t'inspire
>   The Glow that warm'd my Breast in happier Days.

Despite her "cold Heart," however, she cannot "remain unmov'd" by his poem, especially as she remembers happy times in the past when she read his verse on the banks of the Arrow. She goes on to heap good wishes on him, wishes for health and fancy and fame, but most of all wishes for the rewards of love and friendship:

> On thee may faithful Friendship's cordial Smile
>   Attendant wait to soothe each rising Care;
> The Nymph thou lov'st be thine, devoid of Guile,
>   Mild, virtuous, kind, compassionate, and fair.

Ann Cracroft was being realistic, perhaps even guileful, rather than compassionate, and Miss Whateley feels for her frustrated friend. I suggest that the warmth of the sympathy expressed in this poem stems from similar feeling—John Darwall was as unattainable as Ann. Mary's ill health was probably not simply physical.

She concludes on a more professional, less personal note:

> May thy sweet Lyre still charm the generous Mind,
>   Thy liberal Muse the Patriot Spirit raise;
> While, in thy Page to latest Time consign'd,
>   *Virtue* receives the Meed of polish'd Praise.

Langhorne's "To Miss W——, Occasioned by reading some Pieces of her Poetry," which introduces Mary's book, contains a similar mixture of the personal and the professional, and addresses similar feelings. He begins by welcoming her to the company of "British *Sapphos*," of which there are many (he names Elizabeth Carter), and he goes on with good wishes for Mary. He prays that Fancy will continue to lead her with Nature, that envy and censure will leave her alone, and that general sunshine will be hers, "Till Nature claim that Being which she gave, / And Glory gild thy Passage to the Grave." Sandwiched in among these wishes is the prayer that Love will bring his rosy garlands to her "And *Hope* present Thee with eternal Spring." This can, of course, be taken as a conventional address to a young spinster, and an introductory poem serves a conventional function. But Langhorne seems to know something about the state of Mary's heart. Such a friendship would have endured.

Mary Whateley had friends, then, friends who understood her feelings, who worked with her to refine her art, who inspired particular poems, and who did a great deal to help her out of obscurity and into the public world of letters. She understood and dealt with the expectations and constraints of that world as they applied to women writers, and she must have realized how much she owed to her network of support. And yet, in her poems, she is very much her own person.

Chapter 4

Original Poems on Several Occasions
By Miss Whateley
1764

> Go, tuneful Maid, with Nature take thy Way;
> Still may'st Thou o'er her smiling Vallies stray!
>
> John Langhorne

What does a young lady who "has seen mighty Little of the world," but who wants to write, write about? Like all writers, she must express what in some sense of the word she "knows," and what she knows best are her own feelings. The "occasions" of her life are more often, and more vividly, inner events than outer, the actions of emotions rather than the actions of the world outside the self. She can, of course, also draw upon the actions of others—of family and friends, of the remote figures in newspapers—and, above all, she can draw upon whatever education she has managed to acquire, that is, upon her reading of literature. But her own feelings are central. This is true, I believe, not only of young ladies in the eighteenth century but of most young authors in most times. Their first novels are often autobiographical, their first verses therapeutic confession. It is partly for this reason that I have been using Mary Whateley's poems so freely as indicators of her life. And for another reason: despite the depersonalizing force of poetic convention and the complex, problematic matter of "persona," eighteenth-century writers were coming more and more to expect and

Original Poems on Several Occasions (1764)

assume "sincerity" in literature. Shenstone himself, in Elegy I, said good poetry "flows . . . from the heart" and urged bards to "grow sincere." Whether sincerity is even more characteristic of women's than of men's writing in this period would be difficult, perhaps impossible, to determine, given the problems of defining the term and verifying the quality it stands for. But such might well be the case. If writing sincerely about oneself derives in part from a paucity of education and of experience in the world, as the sincerity of young authors seems to suggest, women, despite their training in modesty and self-effacement, probably were more likely to be sincere. But they might well feel the need to express their truths indirectly.

Mary Whateley was not entirely without experience, and she had acquired some education, partly through her own efforts and partly under the guidance of Shenstone and perhaps others. She read widely in English literature, from Shakespeare to her own contemporaries, and she dipped into the classics. She was well enough prepared to write pastorals, for, as Dr. Johnson caustically remarked, "Pastorals . . . require no experience"; all one needs to do to be able to write pastoral poems is to read and imitate the pastoral poems of others. And it was the pastoral element in her work that her first reviewers recognized and admired.

Original Poems on Several Occasions, widely advertised from its first appearance in May 1764, promptly appeared in a Dublin edition as well, which indicates an expectation of good sales. It was soon noticed by two substantial reviews: the *Monthly Review* praised it in June, as did the *Critical Review*, though somewhat less enthusiastically, in August. The specific nature of the praise says a great deal about men's attitudes towards women's writing.

Mary Whateley's friend John Langhorne, a regular reviewer for the *Monthly Review*, wrote the first notice—anonymously, of course. He used the occasion to state his "liberal" beliefs about women writers and to define their peculiar talents as he perceived them in an interesting blend of encouragement and gender stereotyping:

Original Poems on Several Occasions (1764)

> It can never be a dispute with the liberal, whether the fine arts are the proper province for the exercise of female genius?——Nothing, certainly, but the jealousy of our sex, and the envy of their own, would urge the least pretence for excluding the Ladies from any of those elegant and happy amusements which the arts of Imitation may afford them. Some of these, however, are more generally allowed them than others——Yet, for what reason? Why allow them music, and debar them from poetry?——As well might we allow them friendship, and exclude them from love; for those arts are as much allied as these affections; and there is no more reason why a woman of genius should not be indulged with the polished amusements of poetry, than that a woman of sensibility should be refused the tender connections of love. . . .
> There are some species of poetry, in which the Ladies, from their peculiar sensibility, seem qualified to excel. Where the tender interests of the heart are the subject——in the elegant complainings of elegy——and the simplicity of pastoral imagery, they appear to have a natural superiority.

The specific poems from Mary's book that Langhorne cites illustrate these views and demonstrate that the poet "has sacrificed, in many pretty rural pieces, to the graces of simple and beautiful Nature." He quotes all ten quatrains of the "Ode to May," which concludes,

> Stranger to the Park and Play,
>   Birth-night Balls, and courtly Trains;
> Thee I woo, my gentle *May*,
>   Tune for Thee my native Strains.
>
> Blooming Groves, and wand'ring Rills,
>   Soothe thy vacant Poet's Dreams,
> Vocal Woods, and Wilds, and Hills,
>   All her unexalted Themes.

Original Poems on Several Occasions (1764)

Here indeed are "modesty" and "goodness" united, as Langhorne says. Yet the tones of Miss Whateley's poems vary, and Langhorne made some significant cuts in other poems he quotes. For example, he illustrates his author's tenderness of heart with passages from the "Elegy on a much lamented Friend," omitting the last passage in which the friend and the poet are levelled in death with Lely, Thomson, Handel, and Milton. He quotes parts of "Rural Happiness," the passages praising and praying for retirement, omitting the more patriotic descriptions and the moral teachings. From "The Pleasures of Contemplation" he quotes purely descriptive passages, not the lines where "tow'ring *Fancy* . . . leaves this Earth behind" and takes a Popeian flight "To trace th'Eternal Cause thro' all his Works"; nor does he quote the lengthy passage in which the poet condemns the excesses of drunken libertines. The closest he comes to acknowledging Miss Whateley's talent for satire is excerpting the last three verse paragraphs of "The Vanity of external Accomplishments," in which she praises learning and health as more lasting than the beauty she lacks. The earlier parts of the poem, however, are a brisk attack on the vanities of "Smarts and Belles"; there, after four silly girls have been skewered, the poet turns her weapon on men:

> Satire on Men superfluous wou'd be,
> What they approve, by our own Sex we see.
> Since Woman's Happiness depends on Man;
> 'Tis easy to conclude where first began
> This Group of Follies, that o'erspread the Earth:
> From our wise *Lords* they first receiv'd their Birth;
> These our fond Females, bent to please Mankind,
> Enlarg'd, exalted, soften'd, and refin'd.

The girls are still blameable, but men are the root cause of their follies—not a passage suitable for quotation in a review.

Langhorne concludes his review with a passage from the poem Mary addressed to him, comments (like Shenstone) that her poems "are more correct than the literary productions of Ladies

Original Poems on Several Occasions (1764)

in general," and welcomes Miss Whateley to the company of "Jones, Carter, and the rest of the British Muses."

I have lingered over this review because Langhorne, though "liberal," is either typical or keenly aware of the expectations of the book-buying public. He judges Miss Whateley's poems by the standards set for and by women writers, not by comparison with men's poetry. And by his selection and editing of examples he makes Miss Whateley's poems fit the image of the acceptable lady poet. Of course his space was limited and he could not include complete copies of many poems, but he knew Mary Whateley well, knew the less conventional side of her character and her poetry—yet he presented to the public only the "tuneful Maid." Perhaps he really considered these her best lines; perhaps he simply wanted her book to sell as widely as possible. In either case, what he wrote was intended as praise: he was notoriously partial when reviewing books by his friends. So one can see what was admired and welcomed in a lady writer.

The reviewer for the *Critical Review* had similar standards and similar perceptions. He summarizes the Dedication and concludes that Miss Whateley is a good Christian, "whatever may be her success as a poet. But we would not be supposed to intimate that this lady owes all her reputation to the motives that impelled her to write; she owes much to her execution." Then he quotes all of Langhorne's introductory poem, commenting benevolently on the mutual admiration evinced by that poem and Miss Whateley's poem to him, which stands at the end of the book. A political liberal, the reviewer compares Miss Whateley favorably with Catherine Macaulay as a defender of liberty, and quotes part of the poem "Liberty." He lists the topics of a few poems and quotes most of "Ode to Summer," an entirely conventional pastoral, which "will give the reader a sufficient idea of her manner." He likes the anapests of "To Mr. O———y," and concludes,

> From these specimens the reader will observe, that this collection is fitted rather to sooth than enlarge the mind;

Original Poems on Several Occasions (1764)

and that as it has innocently employed the poet, it may agreeably amuse the reader. The lady, with great good sense and modesty, disclaims all pretensions to force and sublimity; and we, in our turn, must make her a compliment of the softer graces; nor is this a small acquisition, since few can arrive at universal excellence: it is impossible to make a statue which shall at once unite the strength of a Farnesian Hercules to the softness of a Venus of Medicis.

The reviewer approves of the lady and therefore he can approve, mildly, of her poetry.

A number of Mary Whateley's poems are as conventionally and simply pastoral as Langhorne and the *Critical* reviewer say: the odes to May and Summer; some of those I have mentioned earlier, including passages in "Rural Happiness" and "Elegy on leaving ————"; "A Pastoral Song," in which Truth and Virtue are the nymph's best cosmetics; "Hymn to Solitude," which turns into a prayer of praise to the Creator of rural beauty; an additional handful of odes and songs full of sequestered bowers and limpid streams. A number depict forsaken maidens yearning for a faithless or otherwise unobtainable lover, "tender Pieces" that Miss Whateley, in her Dedication, claims to be the inevitable products of "the Rural Muse" rather than springing from her own experience. It is a conventional disclaimer and the poems are similarly conventional, containing nothing on which, without other evidence, one could base any sound speculation about the state of the poet's heart. A comparatively lofty Christmas pastoral, the frequent praise of virtue, the occasional melancholy, the love of solitude and retirement and contemplation, the devotion to Albion—all place these poems squarely in the mainstream of mid-century pastoral, so squarely that one cannot really point to any single specific influence on their style and contents, not even to Shenstone.

But there is more to Miss Whateley than this. The passages Langhorne omitted give some hints of her greater scope. Although all but one of the poems contain at least some

Original Poems on Several Occasions (1764)

pastoral elements, many of them are best classified as occasional poems, mostly verse letters; philosophical poems; satires; and poems that express, directly or indirectly, the plight of the poet who was also a woman. In the rest of this chapter, I will discuss the poems that fall under these headings.

One occasional poem, "Elegy written in a Garden," combines pastoral and satiric elements. It commemorates the occasion of a visit to Shenstone's Leasowes, and seems to have been written to cheer up that rather easily depressed man. Mary Whateley does not mention Shenstone or the Leasowes by name, but all the details of the poem, including some fairly obvious allusions in the final stanza, point to such an audience and such an occasion. She uses the form Shenstone prescribed for the elegy, iambic pentameter quatrains with alternating rhyme, though she did not always use it—two of her elegies are in heroic couplets. She praises the "mingled Beauties" and "varied Prospects" of the garden where "polish'd *Art* assumes fair *Nature*'s Face"— just the kind of balance Shenstone worked so hard to achieve in his landscape. The only trees she mentions are beeches, which abounded at the Leasowes. The satirical touch is light and conventional: a butterfly is sent to "gay Belinda" in town to remind her that beauty does not last, a point sure to win male approval; in a number of mottoes and inscriptions on his benches and ornamental urns, Shenstone had expressed the same point about the vanity of town ladies contrasted to the beauty and peace of the garden. In this context, Miss Whateley returns to a repeated theme, her own lack of beauty, a fact which Shenstone had noted forthrightly in his letter to Mrs. Bennet. Virtue and Health are worth more, however, and these the poet has, so she is not gloomy. She is also cheered because she can write poetry—a hint to a downcast Shenstone?—though significantly she wears only a wreath of ivy and field-flowers, not laurel. She concludes modestly that she is

> Pleas'd, while this artless rural Verse I raise,
> To see superior Merit shine confest;

Original Poems on Several Occasions (1764)

>   Supremely happy when my humble Praise
>   Can give one Transport to the gen'rous Breast.

Shenstone was generous to her, and she could expect that he would be pleased to see evidence in this poem of the skill he had helped to develop. Whether he has "superior Merit" as a poet is, however, debatable.

The other occasional poems are verse letters, to the Rev. Mr. Welchman, the two Darwalls, and John Langhorne, which I have mentioned before, poems that contain some of Mary's strongest expressions of personal feeling.

She was also capable of the relative objectivity of philosophical poetry, a kind that represents a rather daring undertaking for a woman. But she did not venture too far. In the "Elegy on the Search of Happiness" she scaled down Johnson's "Vanity of Human Wishes" to the pastoral dimension. She made similar adjustments when she took Pope as a model.

"Occasioned by reading some Sceptical Essays," like the first epistle of Pope's *Essay on Man*, attacks the "reasoning Pride" of man (a phrase she borrows from Pope) and emphasizes the narrow limitations of the human mind. Like Pope, Miss Whateley moves from the cosmic to the local: if the universe is too big for man to understand, is he any better at the how's and why's of the humblest things of the earth? Pope puts the question only once in terms of plant life: "Ask of thy mother earth, why oaks are made / Taller or stronger than the weeds they shade?" (I. 39-40). Miss Whateley, who knew that a lady's pastorals would be acceptable, casts half her poem in that mode:

>   Is this [the cosmos] too high? then say, what Parts compose
>   The blushing Texture of the vernal Rose?
>   How does the bladed Stem, and Tendril, shoot?
>   How sleeps the Blossom in the latent Root?
>   Why does the Pink a spicy Fragrance boast,
>   In which the Jasmine's fainter Sweets are lost?
>   . . . .

Original Poems on Several Occasions (1764)

> Till Nature's secret Paths thou hast explor'd,
> Say, can'st thou hope to comprehend its Lord?

Like Pope, who asked, "can a part contain the whole?" and commanded his reader to "Submit," she concludes,

> Henceforth, fond Man, thy impious Search restrain;
> Can finite Beings infinite explain?
> With vain Enquiries rack thy Thoughts no more;
> Believe, admire, love, tremble, and adore.

The orthodox conclusion, more fervently Christian than Pope's, the much greater frequency of pastoral elements, and the more limited scope of the poem in general make this philosophical poem by a lady respectably unassuming.

Her satire too is unassuming. The anapestic character sketch of Shenstone contains just a touch of it; "The Vanity of external Accomplishments" has a spirited attack on silly men, which I quoted earlier, but most of it more conventionally and more safely attacks silly girls. Silly girls are a frequent target of women poets, probably because such girls reinforced the Belinda stereotype against which their more intelligent sisters struggled. Mary Whateley shoots at that target in a number of poems, including the "Ode" which begins,

> How various is the Female Mind!
> As with the softest Breeze of Wind
>   The trembling Osiers move;
> So, as capricious *Fancy* reigns,
> We sigh in Health, we smile at Pains,
>   Admire, despise, and love.

The "Ode" goes on to two case histories. Sylvia jilts a loved youth when he loses his money and marries another for gold:

> By Pride seduc'd, she flaunts for Life
> The glitt'ring miserable Wife
>   Of an abandon'd Spouse.

Original Poems on Several Occasions (1764)

Dorinda is a high-minded young lady who reads Milton and Spenser, but even she can weep when Delia appears in a prettier necklace and smarter lace. These ladies are as changeable as those displayed in Pope's gallery, "Epistle II. To a Lady." Mary Whateley's last stanza, however, does something Pope almost never did: she puts herself, potentially at least, on a level with the objects of her satire. Pope occasionally admitted that he was imperfect, when it served his rhetorical strategy to do so, but he never went as far as Miss Whateley does:

> But why do I my Sex accuse?
> Tho' now I court the sprightly Muse,
>   Estrang'd to ev'ry Care;
> Perhaps, ere Night has drawn her Veil,
> I—all th'ideal Woes may feel—
>   Of Love and dark Despair.

She knows she is vulnerable, that her heart, like other women's hearts, can feel the pain of love. She is not above her sisters, which is to say that, despite her ventures into the genre, she did not possess the true spirit of satire. And she wrote very little of it.

One more small group of poems remains to be considered, poems that I find among Mary Whateley's best and most interesting. In them she expresses her sense of her plight as a poet who is also a woman.

In the first of these poems, "The Power of Destiny" (see Appendix), the woman poet imagines what it would be like to be a man trained to a learned profession but impelled to write instead. She knows how such a man would feel because she too is destined to write, and the destiny is an uncomfortable one:

> Sure some malignant Star diffus'd its Ray,
> When first my Eyes beheld the Beams of Day:
> Whose baleful Influence made me dip in Ink,
> And write in Rhyme before I knew to think.

Original Poems on Several Occasions (1764)

> Had Fate, propitious to my Wish, assign'd
> Me, wayward girl, of Man's *superior* kind;
> This strong Propensity had marr'd each Scheme,
> And Prudence yielded to a golden Dream.

These opening lines not only echo but also reverse a well-known passage in Pope's "Epistle to Dr. Arbuthnot":

> Why did I write? what sin to me unknown
> Dipt me in Ink, my Parents', or my own?
> As yet a Child, nor yet a Fool to Fame,
> I lisp'd in Numbers, for the Numbers came.
> I left no Calling for this idle trade,
> No Duty broke, no Father dis-obey'd.
> The Muse but serv'd to ease some Friend, not Wife,
> To help me thro' this long Disease, my Life. . . .
>
> (ll. 125-32)

Both poets find the gift of poetry uncomfortable: "sin" in Pope, "malignant" and "baleful" in Mary Whateley. But Pope, who has been passively "dipt in Ink," disclaims responsibility and presents himself as a harmless, obedient child. Not so Miss Whateley, who actively, if inevitably, dips in ink and who would leave her calling, if she had one: if she had been trained as a clergyman, doctor, or lawyer, she would read and write poetry instead. The professions are described in somewhat satirical terms: the clergyman has a head "stuff'd . . . [with] specious Lumber"; the doctor studies "the strange Effect of *Snails* and *Worms*"; the lawyer has "learnt to *baffle, bluster, bounce*, and *bawl*." (She lists a dozen authors of lawbooks the lawyer has had to study—she has been looking at her brother Henry's bookshelves.) Deserting her profession, she would seek "some Cot, retir'd from Crowd and Noise" where she would find "rural Joys" and the right atmosphere for composing elegies—a pastoral setting is required for writing, by men as well as women. As a man, she would "eternize the fav'rite Dame" in "softest Numbers." She concludes,

Original Poems on Several Occasions (1764)

> In short, whatever my Employ had been,
> It soon had yielded to this darling *Sin*:
> And nought but *Russel*'s Land, or *Gideon*'s Purse,
> Had sav'd the Poet——from——the Poet's Curse.

One can see why writing poetry is a "*Sin*" for a man trained in a profession: he probably disobeys his father, certainly betrays his calling, and faces the "Curse" of poverty. But why is the possession of the gift "baleful" and "malignant" for a woman who has no profession and is not expected to earn money? Because on a more general level, the plight of the professional man is the same as that of a woman. Her gender was expected to be her profession; she was educated to run a household, trained to serve and submit. However, this particular woman, Mary Whateley, chafes against such restriction and, by the very act of writing, rebels against the destiny prescribed by her culture and fulfills the destiny determined by her personal needs. The poem stands first in her book and serves as a brave declaration of intent, but the conflict of public and private destinies must have been painful.

Some of that conflict was mitigated or forestalled by a prudent choice of topics and modes for her poetry, especially the pastoral mode. That she wanted to write other kinds is made clear in three Anacreontics, all imitating the same model but differing somewhat from each other. Her source is Anacreon's first ode, in which the poet wants to sing of kings and heroes, but his lyre will sing only of love. Miss Whateley experiences similar frustration and, like Anacreon, reconciles herself comfortably to it in what must be the two earlier versions, one published in a magazine in 1760 and the other in her book. She has been inspired to write by the victory of Frederick the Great of Prussia over the Russians at Zorndorf (August 25, 1758), a major battle in the Seven Years' War. But when she tries to celebrate his deeds, she cannot. In the first version, her muse "insensibly declines" and says "in trembling notes," " 'What have I with War to do? / Love, my Lays belong to you.' " The

Original Poems on Several Occasions (1764)

second version is similar: the poet herself says her lays belong to love and begs Venus to become her muse.

The third version is significantly different. Here, the military references are briefer and less specific, and the poet's lyre, unlike Anacreon's, speaks directly to her:

> Fain wou'd I sing of War and Arms,
> Hostile Sounds and dire Alarms;
> Fain in nervous Verse wou'd tell,
> How *Brunswick* fought, and *Frenchmen* fell;
> How *Britannia*'s Thunders roar,
> Echoing from each distant Shore;
> I feel my glowing Heart expand,
> And strike the Strings with bolder Hand:
> But, ah! the trembling Wire resounds,
> "Murd'ring Steel and dreadful Wounds,
> "Heroes bleeding, Heaps of Slain,
> "Strew'd promiscuous o'er the Plain;
> "Foaming Billows, Seas on fire,
> "Ill become a Virgin's Lyre."
>   Convinc'd, asham'd, I leave the Field,
> Leave it to Bards in Battle skill'd;
> Pleas'd to resume my wonted Themes,
> Painted Meadows, purling Streams,
> *Cupid*'s Pow'r, *Philander*'s Eyes,
> Wreaths of Willow, Gales of Sighs:
> While spontaneous I complain,
> Echoing Rocks return the Strain;
> "*Love* shall rule these happy Fields;
> "*Mars* himself to *Cupid* yields."

The woman poet, eager to write of masculine topics, has been put firmly in her place by her own lyre. Art itself dictates what is acceptable in a woman writer; her place is the erotic pastoral. This time, the reconciliation has a hollow sound.

When I mentioned "Liberty" before, in the context of the poet's winter imprisonment in Walsall, I said it was susceptible of further interpretation; I read it as Miss Whateley's strongest statement of her frustration at being imprisoned not simply by winter but in the pastoral mode (see Appendix). The poem is,

Original Poems on Several Occasions (1764)

I believe, a personal rather than a general allegory, and the very strength of its personal statement necessitated the concealment provided by allegory, for here, instead of the obedient though specious submission seen in the third Anacreontic, is real pain and bitter resentment.

"Myra," an anagram of Mary, begins by describing the beauties of the vale of Ambara (properly, Amhara), sometimes using Johnson's own words from *Rasselas*, but from the opening lines it is clear that she is unhappy in her confinement: "Dear Liberty is wretched *Myra*'s Theme." As I mentioned before, Shenstone had changed this to "Myra's constant theme," but Mary changed it back. In this beautiful but unvarying setting, Myra's "boundless Mind" is vacant; she needs "Variety" to cheer her spirits—and pastoral poetry does indeed have a certain sameness about it. Since "Liberty" itself is cast in the pastoral mode, the poet describes the variety she craves in pastoral terms, but this is not pretty pastoral:

> Blest *Freedom!* how I long with thee to rove,
>   Where varying *Nature* all her Charms displays;
> To range the Sun-burnt Hill, the rifted Grove,
>   And trace the Silver Current's winding Maze!

Shenstone had altered the second line to "Where Nature ev'n her savage charms displays," but despite the increased clarity of "savage," "varying" was too important to give up, and Mary went back to her original wording for the final version. The other terms make the point clear enough: the hill is "Sun-burnt," the groves "rifted," the stream "winding"; the poet is sick of the boring prettiness and simplicity of pastoral and yearns for the harshness and complexity of poetry about real experience. But as a woman, with no Rasselas to set her free, she is trapped:

> Vain Wish! these Rocks, whose Summits pierce the Skies,
>   With frowning Aspect, tell me——Hope is vain:

Original Poems on Several Occasions (1764)

> 'Till, freed by Death, the purer Spirit flies;
> Here wretched *Myra*'s destin'd to remain.

The pain and bitterness speak for themselves.

"Liberty" comes right after "The Power of Destiny" in the book and is followed by the second version of the Anacreontic. If Miss Whateley was responsible for arranging the sequence herself, or if Dodsley understood what he was doing when he put the poems together, the sequence makes a clear statement of the plight of the woman poet. She does not limit herself to this topic, however; it rarely appears in the other poems. She had other topics to write about, other feelings to express. She used her art to communicate more than just ideas about that art itself. And it is this range and variety of moods and subjects, this flexibility and modulation of tone, that make *Original Poems on Several Occasions* the voice of a vividly real, and remarkable, woman.

Chapter 5

Transition (1764-November 4, 1766)

As 1764 began, Langhorne and both Darwalls, father and son, were busy among their clerical connections and other friends collecting subscriptions for Mary Whateley's book. Miss Whateley herself had cast a wide net and enlisted family both immediate and remote, from Wooton Park and Birmingham and elsewhere, as well as neighbors in Beoley. A remarkable number of her subscribers, however, were young Oxonians, suggesting that the two Loggin boys and Dr. Wall's son, all then at Oxford, had been pressed into service. A long list was finally assembled, few of name or note but enough altogether to guarantee support and sales. The poems had been polished to the poet's satisfaction. Dodsley was to bring the book out in May.

Meanwhile, Mary Whateley had little to do but wait. She looked at the bleak landscape of Beoley as winter drew slowly to an end, and thought with longing of the coming spring—and wrote a poem about it. "Written in Spring 1764" is one of only five poems in her second book that she ever dated; this particular season of this particular year was important:

> Hail, gentle SPRING! thy first approach I hail:
> Soon thy green vest shall deck the dreary dale;
> Thy genial beams shall bid the tim'rous flow'r
> Rear its fair bud, and sip the vernal show'r.
> Soon shall the purple vi'let paint the meads,
> And fragrant cowslips raise their golden heads:
> The woodbine bow'r its clust'ring sweets shall yield,
> And spicy-bosom'd blooms grace ev'ry field.
> Soon shall the sky-lark pour his various notes,

Transition (1764-November 4, 1766)

> While emulation swells a thousand throats.
> Soon shall the linnet tune his voice to love,
> And the gay goldfinch chant thro' ev'ry grove.
> Soon shall each bending branch, with chaplets hung,
> Dance to the shepherd's pipe and virgin's song.
> The limpid stream, loos'd from harsh Winter's chains,
> Shall murmur to the music of the plains.
> Dull care from Arrowe's banks shall wing her way,
> And all creation hail returning May.

This is more than a conventional pastoral. It is tense with expectation. Soon all creation will hail returning May—all creation including Mary Whateley, who was scheduled to blossom and sing in print in that enchanting month. Perhaps she whiled away the last days of waiting by reading Shenstone's collected works, which Dodsley put together and brought out shortly before her own book. But the interval no doubt seemed long.

May began with a sadness when the Rev. John Welchman died; he was buried on the tenth, but about ten days later came a cheerful event: the advertisements for Miss Whateley's book began to appear. The *London Chronicle*, *St. James's Chronicle*, *Public Advertiser*, and other journals announced the poems for five shillings sewed, "elegantly printed on royal octavo." Dodsley could, and did, produce a handsome book. I don't know when her own copy arrived in Beoley, but one can imagine the thrill she felt when she held her first book in her hand.

Now that the book was a reality, its reception was the next worry. In June, Langhorne's glowing review in the *Monthly Review* appeared, and another hurdle on the way to fame was cleared. The imitation of Anacreon, the less rebellious second version, appeared, with the poet's name, in the *London Chronicle* for June 21-22—on the front page, which was an unusual honor. July brought no reviews but two more reprints: both the *Gentleman's Magazine* and the *London Magazine* printed the complete "Ode to May," which Langhorne had singled out for special praise, and printed it with "by Miss Whateley" at the

Transition (1764-November 4, 1766)

top. August brought the *Critical Review*'s notice, which was favorable enough. Mary Whateley had arrived.

She had arrived—but where was she to go from here? She would keep on writing, but she had few if any options for a choice of life. She was twenty-six, single, not affluent. She had made some money from her book, but it could not have been much, probably about one hundred pounds. There is no firm evidence to show where she was living during this time of transition, but she was probably still at home in Beoley: the dateline on her Dedication, her spring poem, the fact that she wrote letters to John Darwall in Walsall, her mother's recent widowhood, all point in that direction. Beoley was pleasant: it could still offer the beauty and freedom of its gardens and fields, but at this stage of her life these pleasures were growing less satisfactory, as they had done for John Langhorne. And soon one of the greatest attractions of Beoley vanished—Mary's friend Elizabeth Loggin, twenty-eight years old and unmarried, was buried on October 13. The blow must have been severe, for Mary cared deeply about her women friends and Elizabeth had been her friend from the cradle. She left no poem about her loss. After the elegy on the friend who died in 1759, she never again wrote about the death of anyone close to her. Perhaps some feelings lay too deep for words.

Elizabeth's death was followed in a few days' time by a birth: Mary Fox Darwall was delivered of her sixth child, a girl, on October 25, 1764; they called her Honor after John Darwall's sister.

Much of 1765 is a blank in Mary Whateley's personal history. Two of her poems were reprinted in the *Birmingham Register*, "The Power of Destiny" and "Ode to Summer," complete with her name. Otherwise, she left no clear tracks. But the great world turned as usual, and she could read in the *Gentleman's Magazine* that King George had announced the engagement of his young sister Caroline Matilda to the prince of Denmark, and urged his loyal Commons to reduce the national debt; that West Florida wanted colonists and promised great things, but, as

Transition (1764-November 4, 1766)

another correspondent reported, Pensacola was full of drunken Indians and surrounded by sterile, engulfing sands; that Louisiana was ceded to the King of Spain; that the new stamp tax for the American colonies simply gave them financial obligations equal to those of Great Britain—but that Virginia denied England's right to impose taxes. Closer to home, "mobs and insurrections" were reported, especially in the western counties, "on account of the dearness of provisions"; a woman was burned at the stake for poisoning her elderly husband; a Birmingham boy, imprisoned for stealing a gold watch, promptly cut his throat and died.

Poems and news of poets would have attracted Miss Whateley's attention. She could read of the wicked life of the late Charles Churchill; of the death of Edward Young and the deplorable burning of his papers; of how the soul of the German poetess Anna Louisa Durbach overflowed spontaneously in verse—with two samples of her verse translated, one of which dwelt at length on the military glories and heroic death of a Brunswick prince, a masculine kind of topic that Miss Whateley had once touched on but sidestepped. Percy's *Reliques* was noticed at length and Ossian's authenticity was defended. Her friend John Langhorne's *Letters on the Eloquence of the Pulpit* won a mixture of grudging praise and a certain amount of ridicule in a long notice. In a poem on mirth, William Woty patted himself on the back for not desiring fame. And Miss Whateley's old friend from Walsall, Stephen Chatterton, had produced an elegy in which his sorrow seemed to come mainly from the frustration of his hopes for some kind of patronage from the deceased.

But all this was rather remote from the spinster in Beoley, writing her poems and watching as her twenty-eighth birthday—twenty-eight had been Elizabeth Loggin's age when she died—grew closer. It could not have been a happy period in her life. Perhaps it was this spring that she wrote the undated "Song" in which "Delia," a pastoral name she often used for herself, mourns for an unattainable lover:

Transition (1764-November 4, 1766)

Vainly bloom the sweets of spring,
    While dejected DELIA mourns,
Summer comes on rosy wing,
    But sweet peace no more returns;
Eve still hears the deep-drawn sigh,
Morn still ope's the tear-stain'd eye.

While the warblers of the grove
    Chant their wild notes thro' the dale,
I relate my hapless love
    To the breeze that fans the vale;
Or, on Arrowe's banks reclin'd,
Breathe my sorrows to the wind.

Why alas! does DAMON prove
    Faithless to my tender flame?
Why must wretched DELIA love?
    Why her heart be still the same?
While the swain inconstant flies,
Slights her tears, and mocks her sighs!

Haste, ye muses, to my aid,
    Teach me Cupid's pow'r to scorn;
Cheer a suppliant drooping maid,
    Inspire my strains, my songs adorn:
Here the cypress wreath I tear,
And henceforth the laurel wear.

Can this be no more than a conventional pastoral lament? The conclusion in which she resolves to give up Cupid and devote herself to poetry instead as a cure for love, though a central theme in the work of Theocritus, was not significant in the English pastoral tradition, so it is probably personal here rather than merely conventional. But the inconstant swain who flees from the weeping shepherdess is a purely conventional rather than a personal figure. However she may have mixed the personal and the conventional, if this poem is to any extent autobiographical it shows Mary Whateley on the banks of the River Arrow in Beoley suffering from an impossible love.

Transition (1764-November 4, 1766)

This idea is supported by a tantalizing fragment of a diary written in 1828 by John Darwall's grandson, who alleges that Mary Fox's heart was broken because John Darwall paid attentions to Miss Whateley and Miss Whateley sometimes sat on his lap. The diarist's mother had told him the story. But she could only have picked it up as family gossip, because it would have happened years before she was born. By itself, the story does not give the biographer much help, but taken in conjunction with other evidence, it looks to me as if it contains a grain of truth. Mary Whateley and John Darwall were in love.

The spring that held no "sweets" finally passed; the summer was probably no better. But then, in September, came news of an event that would change Mary Whateley's life completely. In Walsall, on the third day of that month, Mary Fox Darwall had been buried. Perhaps something had gone wrong with a seventh pregnancy or birth; the timing would suggest it. But whatever the cause of her death, Mary Whateley's friend John Darwall was now a widower with five small, motherless children to look after. No letters or other evidence survives to tell how she felt when she heard the news. But at this point, I wish I were writing a romantic novel instead of a sober biography. For while my suggestion that Mary had already fallen in love with an unattainable John may seem fanciful, she had written a poem to him about friendship and she did define married love as the highest form of friendship. Perhaps she had even sat on his lap. At any rate, after a proper interval of mourning, they were married.

The interval was considerable, slightly more than a year. John Darwall went on with his duties as curate, duties that were probably increasing as his vicar grew older. Mary Whateley prepared for her marriage, no doubt adding what she could to her stock of clothes and linens to take with her to the curate's poorly financed household. But she didn't spend all her time sewing. She must have spared a few minutes to note that one of the poems from her book, "An Invitation in Winter," was reprinted in both the *London Chronicle* for January 7-9, 1766,

Transition (1764-November 4, 1766)

and the *Gentleman's Magazine* for January—but, unfortunately, without her name. Friendship would have demanded that she take time to read John Langhorne's *Poetical Works*, published in early May, and to congratulate him on having eight books for sale all at once. Congratulations were also in order that summer for his appointment as rector of Blagdon, a position that would finally make his marriage possible. Now he could share her pleasure in an approaching wedding. She would have lingered over a poem in the *Gentleman's Magazine* for April, "To Miss Whately [sic] on her Poems," because the author, B.F., not only liked the purity and sweetness of her pastorals and "amorous strains," but recognized that she also wrote on "loftier themes," themes which would "instruct the British fair" in "the culture of the mind"; this poem reappeared in the *London Magazine* the next month. And she took time to make a new woman friend and write two poems to her.

Mrs. Hewan, Miss Whateley's new friend, is an obscure figure. The poet identifies her in a footnote as "A beautiful Scotch lady (who married an English officer)" and notes that they had a "short but agreeable intimacy in the year 1766." Perhaps the officer was quartered near Beoley in that year. What particularly attracted Miss Whateley, who was developing a fascination with things Scottish, was the fact that Mrs. Hewan wrote poetry "with great spirit and elegance." She was too modest to publish her poems and only her closest friends were allowed to see them. But those friends included Mary Whateley, whose "Ode, Addressed to Mrs. Hewan" describes a dream vision in which a slightly dishevelled muse commands her to give her lyre to her new friend. Mary, it seems, is growing too old—Phoebus favors the young, and Mrs. Hewan, for whom Scottish swains languish, is now the chosen one. And she will immortalize the silenced Mary. The muse promises,

"So shall her friendship bid thy name
"Still live in the records of fame,
 "While verse has pow'r to charm;

Transition (1764-November 4, 1766)

Banns of Marriage

Nº The Revd Mr John Darwall of the Parish of Walsall in the County of Stafford and Miss Mary Whateley of the Parish of Beoley were Married in this Church by Licence this fourth Day of November in the Year One Thousand Seven Hundred and Sixty-Six by me Edward Loggin Curate of Beoley.

This Marriage was solemnized between Us { John Darwall
Mary Whateley now Darwall

In the Presence of P. Muston
P. Douglass

Whateley/Darwall marriage signatures,
Beoley parish register.

Transition (1764-November 4, 1766)

"That potent balm of ev'ry woe,
"That source from which true pleasures flow
"Shall all thy cares disarm."

The idea that a poem immortalizes its subject is common in poetry written by men but quite rare in that written by women. It is interesting to see Miss Whateley, whose first book alludes directly only to male poets, widening her horizons to include women and claiming the same powers for their work.

Despite the muse's command, Mary did not stay silenced: she went on to write an "Elegy, Addressed to Mrs. Hewan," in which she celebrates their friendship in a pastoral setting far removed from the noisy worlds of the brave soldier, the greedy statesman, and the gay nymph. (While the other two figures are satirized, the soldier gets nothing but admiration; Mrs. Hewan's husband was an officer and Miss Whateley was always patriotic.) A "Stranger to fame's inconstant soothing tale," she leads a humble life in a pastoral setting that has its pleasures, but friendship yields "those pleasures that can never cloy"—as, apparently, the landscape no longer did. This poem makes no reference to Mrs. Hewan as a fellow poet, but it is revealing to see how close the two women poets had grown in a very short time. Despite her engagement to John Darwall, Mary Whateley still cared about women friends and about poetry.

Eventually the waiting was over and the marriage was celebrated on November 4—probably, given the English climate, a bleak, cold day with a chill pervading the ancient stone of that dark little church. Elizabeth Loggin's brother Edward, now his father's curate and just Mary's age, performed the ceremony. Afterwards, the newlyweds signed the book. First the groom, in neat, middle-sized script: John Darwall. Next, in a much larger, more dashing hand, the bride: Mary Whateley. The usual thing. But then something odd caught her eye, the unusual way Edward Loggin had recorded the name of the previous bride, an illiterate woman, before she made her mark. Mary sometimes liked the unusual. So, with the drop of ink remaining on the pen, she

Transition (1764-November 4, 1766)

went back and wrote in the word "late" between and above "Mary" and "Whateley," halfway obscuring her new husband's surname. Then, taking up all the rest of the line, she added, in her bold hand, "now Darwall." She was teasing her old friend the curate by borrowing his wording. Perhaps she was emphasizing her own literacy as well. Most important of all, she was claiming her new identity and recording it for posterity on the spot. The joy and high spirits that the gesture suggests were to continue in a happy and fulfilling marriage.

Part II

WIFE

1766-1789

Chapter 6

"Now Darwall" (1766-1775)

> Enchanting Songstress, *Darling* of the Nine,
> (Tho' not *their Darling* more than Thou art *mine*) . . . .
> John Darwall

The story of Mrs. Darwall's married life is the story of her family life: her husband's character and career, the births and deaths of children. Family had always been important in that it determined where and how she lived, as it did for most eighteenth-century women. But her early poems show that her friendships and her writing, not her family, were central to her emotional life and her sense of self. Now, however, family becomes central. Mrs. Darwall still had friends and still cared about them deeply, especially her women friends. She still wrote poetry, somehow finding the time among her many domestic duties. She was still interested in books and the theater, in the life of Walsall and the world outside. But she published almost nothing new during her twenty-three years of marriage. Her family was her career.

And yet her poems, or at least those she chose to publish, say very little directly about her family; only two unpublished poems survive, too few to tell much about what kind of work she left in manuscript (see pp. 153-54). Her second book contains two poems to her husband on domestic occasions—on an anniversary and on his request for a new poem—and a few more, about three or four, may also deal with family or related personal

"Now Darwall" (1766-1775)

concerns. But that is all. Nothing more on her husband or her marriage, nothing (except in the two poems to her husband) overtly about the children. Over half of the poems in her second book are occasional, some in the strictest sense of the word and some in a broader sense, but the occasions they speak to are the marriages and other affairs of friends, visits to Kenilworth and to a pseudo-gothic "abbey," the appearances of a favorite actress on the Walsall stage, the peace treaty of January 1783, and other such events outside the domestic circle. Some of the works which are not occasional are conventional pastorals; others include experiments in such forms as drama and ballad, a number of poems on Scottish subjects, and hymns for the Walsall church. Clearly, Mrs. Darwall had escaped from the "happy valley" of pastoral imprisonment, but she wrote and published very little about her personal life with the Rasselas who had set her free.

There are probably many reasons for this change of tone and topic in her writing. She was growing older; she had the increased status of being a married woman and a published poet; her experiences of life were more varied than they had been during her virgin years; she was out from under Shenstone's supervision; and tastes in poetry were changing. But the main reason, I think, is that she no longer needed her writing to create and fulfill a sense of self. For the young woman in Beoley, poetry was the one available outlet for her intellectual and emotional energy, and a poet was the person she wanted to be. But Mrs. Darwall, who was a much happier person than Miss Whateley had been, had other outlets for her energy and other roles to play, other people to be. Wife to a vigorous and interesting man, mother to a flock of children and stepchildren, Mary expressed her self in her domestic living and loving and apparently put very little of these intimacies into words; perhaps, as I have suggested about the deaths of people she loved, she had come to find words inadequate for her deepest feelings. She now used words, for the most part, for the expression of her less private thoughts.

"Now Darwall" (1766-1775)

From this point on, then, the relationship between the woman and the poet is rather different from what it has been, so I will use the poetry differently as I tell my story: I will draw on the poems for events in Mrs. Darwall's world more than for events in her self, though the self does not vanish. But I will still tell my story chronologically.

Every biographer faces a dilemma: the possible tedium for the reader of chronological narration versus the possible confusing of historical sequence in an organization by topics. Most biographers compromise, many placing emphasis on topics. Clarence Tracy, for example, in his biography of Mrs. Darwall's contemporary and Shenstone's good friend Richard Graves, found a point in the life of his subject when chronology no longer mattered, the point when Graves was settled in a place and a position he would occupy for the rest of his life. So Tracy then turned to a topical organization and wrote chapters on Graves's professions as clergyman and teacher, on his friends, his novels, his character. Many biographies of literary men follow this pattern. But a woman, especially a married woman in the days before birth control, was much more closely tied to chronology than a man: however cyclical and repetitious her days and years might be, her life was shaped far more than a man's by marriage, the births of children and their needs as they grew, and the life span of her spouse. So I will continue to tell my story chronologically, for the most part, and hope to avoid tedium.

There was no tedium for the newly married Darwalls. While John and Mary were getting married in Beoley on November 4, the old vicar of Walsall took over the duties of his absent curate, but on the sixth of the month, John Darwall was back at work marrying a couple there. For apparently the first and last time in his professional life, he was a bit flustered—he signed the register in the wrong place and had to scratch out his name and fill it in where it belonged. Three days later when he did another wedding he had settled down, but the mistake creates an appealing picture of an excitable, youngish man so happily

"Now Darwall" (1766-1775)

distracted by his own two-day-old marriage that he bungles the business of marrying others.

John Darwall was youngish—thirty-four—and excitable. It is impossible, of course, to discover a person's whole character from a few poems and sermons and a very few references, facts, and anecdotes. But something of John Darwall has survived in this way. Logic was not his strong suit; intense commitment to people and principles was. He was devoted to king and country. He was charitable and compassionate to the poor, but he was impractical with money and took in less from his parish than it should have yielded. He was unquestionably virile—he fathered twelve children—and energetic. Family legend has it that he composed hymns while running up and down the steps of his church—all sixty-two of them; John Langhorne's jogging around his church and churchyard every morning pales in comparison. Mr. Darwall's political and religious views were orthodox, even conservative, yet at the risk of seeming Methodistical, he introduced hymn-singing in his church. Indeed, a modern commentator on church music even goes so far as to classify him as Evangelical. Both innovative and traditional, he was a mixture of contradictions. He was also talented, lively, and passionately devoted to his wife. Perhaps not an easy man to live with in some respects, but never a dull one. He made Mary happy.

When she married him, she married a family. Overnight, she became a mother to five children, the oldest a girl of seven, the youngest just about to have her second birthday. The oldest could have helped mind the baby, but on a curate's earnings, Mrs. Darwall could not have had more than the minimum of other household help. She was busy. Yet perhaps she and John took an evening off toward the end of the November of their wedding to attend the local dancing master's exhibition of "his scholars" performing "a great Variety of Dancing ... in the newest Taste," followed by an assembly in which the audience, newlywed and otherwise, could dance—and eighteenth-century

"Now Darwall" (1766-1775)

clergymen were known to dance. At least John would have liked the music.

Almost certainly they took an evening off on another occasion that winter when a group of local amateurs got together at Wood's malt-house to perform Home's *Douglas*, with one role, probably the lead, in the relatively competent hands of young William Siddons. This extremely handsome and graceful youth soon found Walsall to be too small a pond and departed in the new year to join the Kemble family on the professional circuit; six years later he married Kemble's daughter Sarah, whose theatrical fame soon outstripped his. Walsall was not on the Kembles' circuit, so the amateur *Douglas* was probably Mrs. Darwall's one chance to see this interesting local boy perform. Certainly the play itself would have attracted her. A dazzling success in Edinburgh in 1756, this was the play that had caused a fervent Scot to stand up in the audience and exclaim, "Whar's yer Willy Shackspeare nu?" And Mrs. Darwall was devoted not only to Shakespeare but also to things Scottish.

Her taste for the Scottish and for the related modes of the primitive and the gothic shows her responsiveness to changes in taste in eighteenth-century poetry. Although her first book mentions the occasional ruined pile and screech owl at midnight, it is otherwise untouched by gothic romance or ancient ballad and never mentions Scotland. However, she had been closely associated with Shenstone, who was partial to Scots, when he was helping Percy with the *Reliques of Ancient English Poetry*; she would have known about the project, and she probably read the book when it came out in 1765. At some point in her life she read Ossian, whose work began to appear in 1760, and much later she wrote an imitation of his style. She met and admired Mrs. Hewan, the "beautiful Scotch lady." She came to admire Burns and Helen Maria Williams. And she longed in verse for the more rugged hills and more dramatic rivers of Caledonia. But I think she was doing more than just responding to changing taste in poetry. That change obviously appealed to a warm side of her temperament that had been for the most part damped

"Now Darwall" (1766-1775)

down by virgin modesty and Shenstonian strictures in her earlier work—but it was there even then. So I suspect that, with the rest of the audience, she wept at the end of *Douglas* as young Mr. Siddons gracefully died at the feet of his long-lost mother, who, all her new hopes gone, rushed off the stage (after a couple of speeches) to throw herself from the nearest precipice.

Soon, but not too soon, Mrs. Darwall had a son of her own. The first year of her marriage was not otherwise particularly eventful: in January 1767 Walsall was isolated from the world by heavy snows, but eventually the mails were restored and she learned of John Langhorne's long-delayed marriage to Ann Cracroft. The regular markets and fairs were less well stocked than usual. Harvests had been so poor that flour was scarce; even rural Beoley had to ration its supply. But the social life of Walsall went on with its occasional concerts and balls. On the domestic side, Mary's husband made music and tended his parishioners, and helped his aging vicar to count and report on the Catholics in the neighborhood. Her stepchildren grew and played and worked and squabbled as children do. Then near midnight on August 3, nine months (less one day) after her wedding, she was safely delivered of a son, and on October 22 he was christened Leicester Yonge. These were Darwall names; Mary's family names would have to wait. No doubt she was relieved that at the age of twenty-nine, her first delivery had gone well. Mrs. Langhorne was not so lucky—the next May she died in childbirth, though the baby survived. The Langhornes' long-delayed marriage was tragically brief.

September 1768 brought another son, christened Whateley. When his new son was two weeks old, John Darwall reminded his wife that she was a poet as well as a mother. On a blank leaf in a copy of her book, he inscribed a short poem to his tuneful darling:

"Now Darwall" (1766-1775)

        To Mrs. Darwall on reading Miss Whateley's
           Poems. By her Bosom-Friend.

    Enchanting Songstress, *Darling* of the Nine!
    (Tho' not *their Darling* more than Thou art *mine*)
    Queen of fair Poets, what transcendent Praise
    Is *tributary* to thy tuneful Lays!
        Smooth as the placid Stream thy Numbers flow,
    And soft and sweet as vernal Zephyrs blow.
    How musically just and pure thy Rhyme!
    How elegant thy Language and sublime!
    What powerful Sentiments thy Strains impart
    To please, melt, civilize, and mend the Heart!
    How tender, moral, good, each beauteous Line,
    Replete with Sense superlatively fine!
        Angelick Harmonist! the Trump of Fame
    Shall sound thro' Ages thy IMMORTAL NAME.
                                              J. D.

    Sept. 27th. 1768.

Not great poetry, but it is interesting to see not only his love but also his appreciation of his wife's artistic skill and good sense. The trump of fame was in fact still sounding the occasional blast, though the Darwalls could not have known that John Wesley had discovered her book earlier that same year and confided to his diary on March 22, 1768, "Some of her elegies I think quite equal to Mr. Gray's."

Perhaps it was at about this time that John asked Mary to write another poem. Most of the poems in her second book are undated, and she writes in her introduction that they were composed over a period of thirty years in intervals between "domestic duties"; to tell my story, I am taking the liberty of assigning some of them to probable times in her busy life. She had little leisure for writing, but when her husband asked for a poem, he got one:

"Now Darwall" (1766-1775)

On the Author's Husband Desiring her to Write Some Verses

Verses, my Love! as soon cou'd I
Without a wing or feather fly:
My head, with other matters fraught,
No more attempts poetic thought:—
Yet, as I hold your sov'reign sway,
In spite of genius I obey.

Ye Muses, aid me to explore
The shadowy grots, and mountains hoar,
Where ye your tuneful influence shed,—
And twine with bays your poet's head.

ERATO hears my invocation,—
My bosom glows with inspiration,—
Instant the fairy scenes appear,
Pierian sounds salute my ear:—
CONNUBIAL LOVE! enchanting theme!
Sweet subject of my muse-rapt dream,
To thee I consecrate my lays,
And thus my heart pours forth thy praise.

Blest state! by gracious heav'n design'd
   To soothe our passions into peace,
To twine in union sweet the kindred mind,
Th'endearing ties of social life to bind
   In chains so strong, yet soft, they but with life can cease.

The mutual int'rest all reserve disclaiming,
The scheme of pleasure each for other framing,
The kindling transports of parental love,
Which the sweet smiles of innocence can move,
Are thine alone, O HYMEN! to bestow,
Which hearts that do not feel them cannot know:—
   —But hark!—my darling infant cries,
   And each poetic fancy flies.

There are interesting parallels here to Lady Winchilsea's poem in praise of her husband, a radically unfashionable topic in her

"Now Darwall" (1766-1775)

day: "To Mr. F. now Earl of W. Who going abroad, had desired Ardelia to write some Verses upon whatever Subject she thought fit, against his Return in the Evening. Written in the Year 1689." Significantly, gentle Lady Winchilsea gets help with her task from the heavenly Muse, Urania, and makes Erato deny her aid; Erato gives as her reason that a spouse is a hopelessly out-of-date topic for a love poem. Mrs. Darwall, on the other hand, gets her inspiration straight from Erato; sex was important to her marriage.

The new year brought the Darwalls their first real sadness—on January 14, 1769, baby Whateley was buried. He was the only one of his mother's six to die as a child, however; John and Mary gave their children strong bodies. The father had little time to mourn. The old vicar of Walsall, Robert Felton, was suffering painfully through his final illness and John was managing all the business of the church. Felton's suffering came to an end on April 29, and it was then decent to raise the interesting question of the next vicar. The Earl of Mountrath, lord of the manor of Walsall, had the living in his gift, but he was often inclined to take the advice of his housekeeper-cum-secretary, Mrs. Preston. Even though John Darwall had made a good impression on that influential lady, the summer months must have been rather a strain, especially with Mary now expecting another child. In September, however, the strain was happily over and John Darwall was appointed vicar of Walsall. The new baby, born in October, was christened Charles Henry, which were the Earl of Mountrath's given names. Perhaps there was also a nod in the direction of Henry Whateley, Mary's lawyer brother who lived in Walsall, but gratitude to the earl was clearly uppermost.

The Darwalls had much to be grateful for. First, the new position meant, of course, moving to the vicarage house. Now Mrs. Darwall could get away from the soot and noise of town (where she had probably been living) to something like a rural retreat. A brisk five-minute walk from the church, across the face of the hillside and past the new burial ground, lay the

"Now Darwall" (1766-1775)

vicar's moor and gardens and the vicar's field with its new windmill. The house, probably built of red brick like the rest of the town, was surrounded by tall trees. Springs bubbled up not far from the doorstep, and down the slope a little farther more springs burst out so vigorously that they were called "The Spouts." These springs not only supplied Walsall with water but also fed beds of watercress and a deep, cold fishpond on the vicar's land. Mrs. Darwall, who had always loved her River Arrow, must have rejoiced at the move to these amenities. No detailed description of the house survives, but it was large—it contained "four bays of Building." Fixed to its outside wall was a curious stone tablet carved with verse using the kind of visual trickery so dear to some seventeenth-century religious poets (see opposite). I wonder what Mrs. Darwall thought of it. A barn with a threshing floor, a stable, and a cowhouse completed the establishment. It was almost like living on the farm again.

The new position also meant more money. The curate's small earnings now went into the pockets of young David Davenport, who was still single, while the Darwalls with their seven children could have been taking in anything from 130 to 300 pounds a year, the estimated value of the cure. But three years later, John wrote ruefully to his bishop that even 130 pounds "is rather more than I have hitherto made of it." Still, the fishpond and garden and cowhouse, along with the required contributions of lambs and piglets and calves from the parishioners, helped to feed the children.

Now that he occupied the vicar's chair, John Darwall needed even more of his considerable energy. Though his curate did various duties and once or twice a year a visiting clergyman preached a special sermon for charity, John was responsible for regular worship services and the Sunday morning sermon. He paid particular attention to his sermon when the bishop came from Lichfield to visit the Walsall parish, a visit before which Mr. Darwall had to fill out a detailed questionnaire on the state of his cure. These visitations were important events in the life of the church and the career of the vicar, and the improvident

"Now Darwall" (1766-1775)

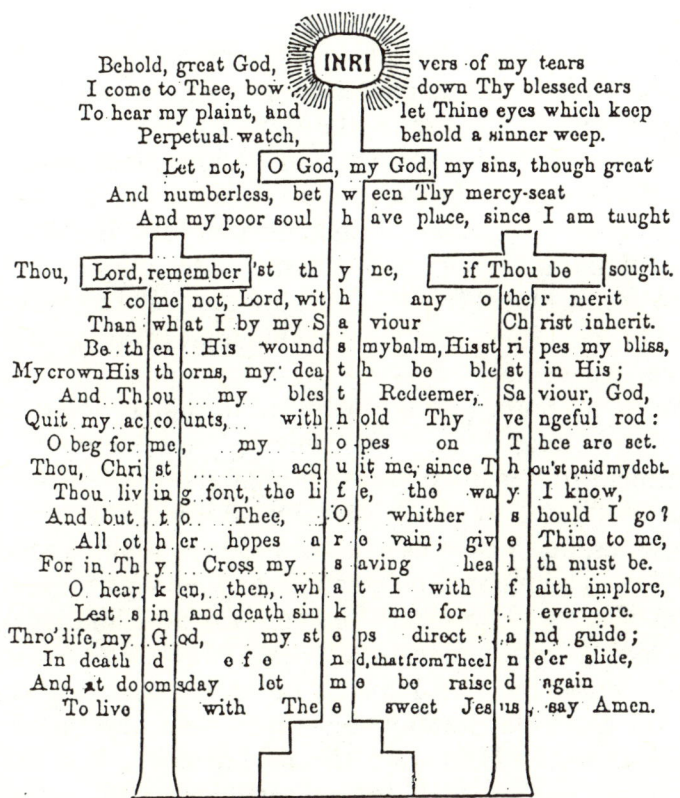

Stone tablet from the Walsall vicarage.
(From the *Trent Valley Parochial Magazine*, March 3, 1877, reproduced in Billy Meikle booklet 64; courtesy of the Walsall Local History Centre.)

"Now Darwall" (1766-1775)

Mr. Darwall had the occasional tussle with his churchwardens over the expenses involved. He also had to write up an even more detailed report or "terrier" every three years, inscribing on a gigantic sheet of parchment all the assets and appurtenances of his cure and identifying every penny owed to him from every source and every loaf of bread that was to be distributed to the poor. He shared with his curate the routine christenings, marriages, and burials, but it was his obligation alone, as a "surrogate," to provide marriage licenses for his parishioners.

He was active in the life of the town as well as the church, being involved ex officio, as it were, in various kinds of business, including the complex tangle of the Corporation's mismanaged mortgages. He also sat on formal committees, including one that was planning a sort of vigilante association of private citizens to control local crime—working-class Walsall was prone to spells of civil unrest. Henry Whateley also sat on that committee, as well as engaging actively in plans for a canal, which came to nothing, and plans to turnpike some of the dreadful local roads, which did come to pass; Henry probably consulted his brother-in-law on such matters.

One cannot say how much Mrs. Darwall was involved in all these activities, but husbands who admire their wives' good sense talk things over with them and sometimes even seek their advice. So all this was to some extent part of her life. She had other concerns too. On the domestic side, in 1770 Charles Henry was a newborn, making all the demands newborns do, to say nothing of the other children. Family obligations went beyond her own household as well. Her older sister Martha Baylies was now established in Walsall and, recently widowed, was supporting four children and probably her sister Ann by running a mercer's and draper's shop, where Mary must have done her shopping. As Mary's first year in the vicarage house unfolded, she could watch as Martha's youngest daughter, another Martha, attracted the attention of the new curate, David Davenport. Young Martha was still in her teens, and Mrs. Darwall, who was well aware of the insecurities of a curate's position, might well have

"Now Darwall" (1766-1775)

tried to discourage the match—if this poem was written to Martha Baylies. (I doubt that it was addressed at a later date to one of her own daughters; she usually called her children "young friends.")

> Lines Addressed to a Young Lady,
> On seeing her wear a Bosom Pin,
> Presented her by a Gentleman
>
> Why does this pin ELVIRA's bosom grace?
>   Is it because ALEXIS gave the toy?
> Ah! thoughtless nymph, beware, nor give it place,
>   Lest it thy sweet tranquillity destroy.
>
> The sparkling crystal may attract thine eyes,
>   But oh! the point may act as CUPID's dart,
> And, while to decency it aid supplies,
>   May thro' thy handkerchief transpierce thy heart.

But the lovers persisted. In January 1771, when Martha was just eighteen, John Darwall married them, with the consent, possibly reluctant, of the bride's widowed mother—she left the task of witnessing the marriage to another daughter instead of doing it herself.

In the Darwall household, artistic life blended with the domestic and clerical. Mrs. Darwall was writing some new poems during these years, and she saw some of her earlier work reappearing in print. "From Miss Whateley to Mr. O———y" was presented as a verse letter in Lady Dorothea DuBois's how-to book, *The Lady's Polite Secretary, or New Female Letter Writer*, in 1771. Four poems "By Miss Whateley" had been added to Pearch's *Collection of Poems*, the continuation of Dodsley's major anthology, in the 1770 edition: "The Pleasures of Contemplation," "Liberty," "Hymn to Solitude," and "Ode to May." It is encouraging to note that, except for the "Ode to May," Pearch avoided her simplest, most conventional pastorals and chose poems that carry a greater weight of meaning. And John Darwall's musical talent was recognized in that same year: his

"Now Darwall" (1766-1775)

most famous composition, usually known as "Darwall's 148th," was published for the first of many times in an anthology of psalms. He had chosen the metrical "New Version" of Psalm 148 rather than the clumsy verses of Sternhold and Hopkins and had produced a pleasing tune to go with the fervent words of praise. In the nineteenth century, as psalmody declined, other words were supplied for his tune, those of the seventeenth-century poet Richard Baxter beginning "Ye holy angels bright"; this is the version still to be found in hymnbooks today.

Psalmody had already begun declining in the eighteenth century, as church congregations either listened passively to the slow, usually amateur chanting or singing of the choir or sang themselves, without benefit of book, repeating each phrase after it was laboriously "lined out" by the clerk. John Darwall found the pace tedious and not only recommended speeding it up but also took the controversial stand that hymns, not just psalms, were permissible in the Church of England. And he wrote both, even though hymn-singing was associated with nonconformity, with the reprehensible enthusiasm of Methodists and Congregationalists and Independents. Stiff-necked Church of England clergymen, who held strictly to the old ways, hated hymns and thundered imprecations against "Dr. Watts's flights of fancy." But people found that it was a joy to sing together, and more and more were attracted to the nonconformist sects that encouraged hymns. The less stiff-necked Church of England clergymen began to bend, gradually allowing hymns to be sung by choirs of children from the charity schools and even, at last, by the whole congregation. Hymns and psalms were to be found together in anthologies from 1760, anthologies produced by the Evangelical wing of the church. In the 1770s, the matter was still highly controversial, but gradually "the hymnody, like the cuckoo, . . . ousted the psalmody" from the music books, and, though cathedral choirs still sing slow psalms at Matins and Evensong, Anglican congregations praise God together in hymn.

Mr. Darwall's manuscript book of sacred music contains not only new tunes for the 150 psalms but also three charity hymns,

"Now Darwall" (1766-1775)

one with words by his wife. These charity hymns were composed for special services, advertised in the newspaper, when sermons were preached by visiting clergymen, the children of the charity school sang, and money was collected to help finance the school. Walsall's charity school undertook the instruction of twenty-four boys and sixteen girls, who were provided with blue uniforms and taught, among other things, their Christian duties. These duties are emphasized in Mrs. Darwall's hymn: calling upon the "Daughter of celestial birth, / Bright-rob'd CHARITY," to "descend," the young singers beg the "Sons of affluence" to give so that their souls may be taught to live. Mary wrote the words and John wrote the music, an attractive example of domestic collaboration. He composed both words and music for the other two charity hymns, as well as for a hymn for Christmas Day and a "Spiritual Song on Mortality"; an Anthem based on Psalm 15 and a Hallelujah complete the collection. Some of these compositions include passages of music for the organ alone, but all except the charity hymns, Anthem, and Hallelujah are clearly intended to be sung by the congregation. Furthermore, Mrs. Darwall wrote words for a morning and an evening hymn, also to be "sung by the congregation of Walsall," as their subtitles say; John must have set these to music as well. The evening hymn itself mentions congregational song, but not as if it were a controversial issue:

> Direct our hearts to sing thy praise
>   In concert with the heav'nly choir:
> Let love divine inflame our lays,
>   And gratitude the strain inspire!

Clearly, in John Darwall's church, hymn-singing, however Evangelical it might seem, was common practice.

By 1771, the church organ, though it was not very old, was, understandably, nearly worn out and was advertised for sale. An awkward interval followed, perhaps filled in with instrumental music, but in the spring of 1773 a new organ was purchased and

"Now Darwall" (1766-1775)

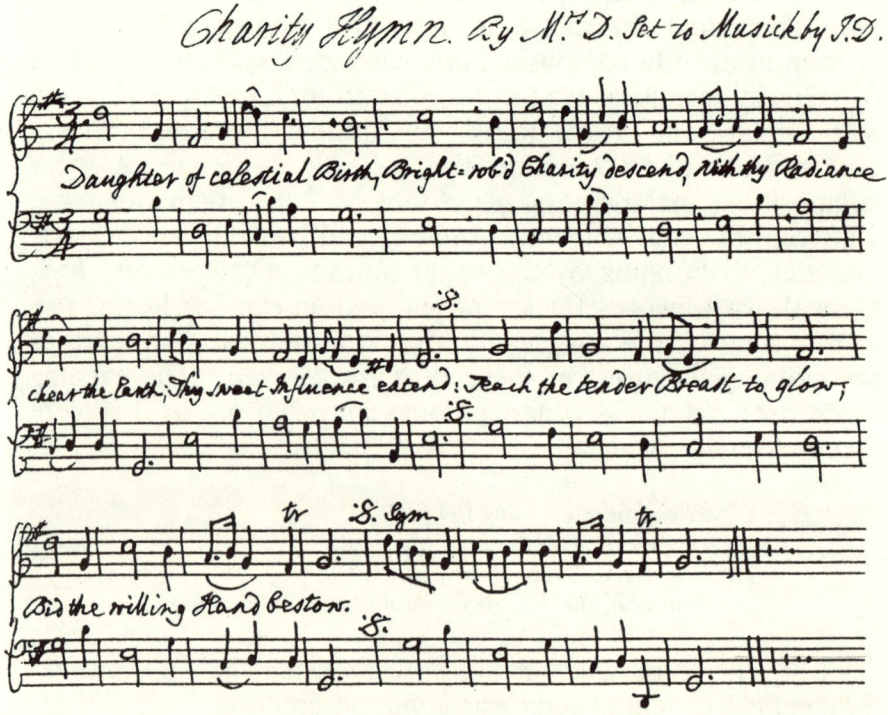

The Darwalls' Charity Hymn.
(From John Darwall's manuscript book, British Library Add. Ms. 50891 B.)

"Now Darwall" (1766-1775)

ceremoniously inaugurated in Whitsun week at a performance by Dr. Alcock of Lichfield for which one had to buy tickets. Perhaps it was not yet entirely paid for. The next Sunday afternoon, however, Mr. Balaam, the blind organist, played it for the whole congregation, and Mr. Darwall preached on a text from Psalm 150, "Praise him with stringed instruments and organs." He took this opportunity to recommend a faster tempo for the singing, as the Evangelical John Wesley had done. Mr. Balaam no doubt tried to comply. The same psalm, which Mr. Darwall had newly set to music, was sung after the sermon. It was a special occasion—the curate usually did the afternoon sermon, but music was too important to John Darwall to entrust its celebration to any hands but his own.

Mrs. Darwall would have attended this celebration even though her family duties were increasing. In December 1770 she had produced her first daughter and called her Harriet, an echo of her old pseudonym as a magazine poet. Her oldest stepchild, Mary, now had another sister to love and care for, and she was old enough to be a real help with all the children during Mrs. Darwall's confinement. But Mrs. Darwall was soon to lose that help: early in May 1772, Mary died at the age of thirteen. It was a sickly season; the parish register lists many deaths that spring, about three times the usual number, including an unusually high percentage of children. There must have been a particularly virulent disease sweeping through town. The Rev. Mr. Darwall had a great deal of work to do at the new burial ground. He had another personally sad task to perform there the next February (1773) when eight-year-old Honor died, leaving from his first marriage only the three boys. But his second marriage continued to be fruitful: in April Mary gave birth to another boy and named him Frederick. Again there were seven children in the vicarage house; little Harriet was surrounded by brothers.

Family and church were absorbing interests, but not to the exclusion of all others. Mrs. Darwall always cared about theater, and January 1774 brought Mr. Stanton's travelling company of

"Now Darwall" (1766-1775)

actors to Walsall's Green Dragon Inn for an unusually interesting season. They opened with Mrs. Centlivre's *The Wonder: A Woman Keeps a Secret*, a comedy that focusses on a friendship between two women, a topic always close to Mrs. Darwall's heart. Later in the season, the Stantons offered another play by Mrs. Centlivre, *A Bold Stroke for a Wife*, and more comedy: the Walsall premier of *She Stoops to Conquer*, and Hugh Kelly's *The School for Wives*, which had premiered at Drury Lane the previous December. Sentiment was mixed with comedy in *The West Indian*, *The Provoked Husband*, and *The Conscious Lovers*; tragedy, or rather pathos, was available in Otway's *The Orphan*. The season closed as it had begun, with a play featuring a strong female character: Arthur Murphy's recent *The Grecian Daughter*, in which a heroic princess saves her father's life twice, first by suckling him (discreetly off-stage) when he is starving, and then by stabbing the evil usurper who had imprisoned him. For some reason, it was immensely popular.

In between there was Shakespeare, *The Tempest* in February and a benefit performance of *Macbeth* in March. The latter was advertised "as altered from Shakespeare," and altered it certainly was, with a dance by the witches, songs and instrumental music here and there, and violin solos and more songs between the acts. All this was of course common practice in the eighteenth century, but this time there was even more: the final touch was an epilogue about ghosts and witches in vaguely dialectical verse composed by the indefatigable Stephen Chatterton and delivered by Mr. Holcroft, one of the beneficiaries of the whole bizarre performance.

Perhaps it was this colorful staging of Shakespeare that sent Mrs. Darwall back to the texts with a sharpened sense of the visual possibilities of the scenes and inspired her to write the Pindaric "Invocation," the poem she later used to introduce her 1794 book. The poem is a prayer to the divine nymph Imagination, asking her to visit and inspire the writer, but most of it describes the characters she inspired Shakespeare to create. The characters selected for description and the tone of the de-

"Now Darwall" (1766-1775)

scriptions themselves bring Shakespeare nicely into line with the growing taste for the gothic and the grotesque. With two exceptions, the fairies in *A Midsummer Night's Dream* and Falstaff, the characters are all tragic figures caught in their wildest moments: Lear on the stormy heath, Hamlet trembling before his father's ghost, Othello stabbing himself, Richard III in the throes of his nightmare. The sketch of Macbeth is typical:

> On the drear blasted heath
> Behold MACBETH!
> Attended by th'unhallow'd wayward crew;
> His cheek, now flush'd with hopes, now chill'd with fears,
> Now shudd'ring and dismay'd the Thane appears,
> Now grasps the airy scepter glitt'ring in his view.

Shakespeare himself has even been inspired by Imagination while reclining in a suitably gothic "grot" scooped from a rugged rock, "Adown whose steep and craggy side / . . . a foaming tide . . . rushes." Mrs. Darwall ends her poem by saying the task of describing inspired poetry is too great for her (after she has done it) and all she asks is "Shakespeare's beauties to explore"; she concludes with "reverential awe" for Imagination's "favour'd sons,—the chosen few, / by Science nurs'd, and by the Muses lov'd." She seems well aware that hers was a minor talent despite the "power of destiny" that made her write and the recognition that she achieved.

This year (1774) brought more recognition, even though it had been ten years since *Original Poems* had appeared. In April, the *Monthly Review* began its notice of Hannah More's *Inflexible Captive* with these couplets:

> To Greece no more the tuneful maids belong,
> Nor the high honours of immortal song;
> To MORE, BROOKS, LENOX, AIKIN, CARTER due,
> To GREVILLE, GRIFFITH, WHATELEY, MONTAGU!
> Theirs the strong genius, theirs the voice divine;
> And favouring Phoebus owns the BRITISH NINE.

"Now Darwall" (1766-1775)

Then, in her own bid to join the company of the British muses, Mary Scott produced *The Female Advocate*, a long poem which I have mentioned before. It names, describes, and praises an impressive list of learned and literary ladies. "Miss Wheately," so identified in a footnote, appears thus:

> Daughter of SHENSTONE hail! hail charming maid,
> Well hath thy pen fair nature's charms display'd!
> The hill, the grove, the flow'r-enamell'd lawn,
> Shine in thy lays in brightest colours drawn:
> Nor be thy praise confin'd to rural themes,
> Or idly-musing Fancy's pleasing dreams;
> But still may contemplation (guest divine!)
> Expand thy breast, and prompt the flowing line.

By singling out the philosophical "Pleasures of Contemplation," identified in a footnote, Mary Scott shows that she had grasped the full range of Miss Whateley's poetry, even though she emphasizes the indebtedness to the pastoral Shenstone.

The Female Advocate got mixed reviews. The *Gentleman's Magazine* liked it in August and listed all the ladies the poem named, singling out Elizabeth Montagu and Catherine Talbot for special attention. The *Critical Review* admired it in September but the *Monthly Review* sneered in November; neither mentioned "Miss Wheately." She was not among the best known on Miss Scott's list. But her visibility increased when Pearch's *Collection of Poems* was reprinted the next year (1775); this time Miss Whateley was correctly identified as Mrs. Darwall.

Mr. Darwall too was having a rewarding year in 1775. On May 18 he had preached a visitation sermon before the dignitaries from the cathedral at Lichfield and decided it was good enough to publish. He hired a printer in nearby Wolverhampton to set up the type. This discourse was "not intended *vainly* to *inform*" his clerical visitors of their proper duties but "*humbly* to *remind*" them, though John does not sound particularly humble as he tells his audience they must "strenuously oppose" "mixt legions of common-swearers, liars, extortioners, unjust and

"Now Darwall" (1766-1775)

covetous persons, fornicators, adulterers, men of hatred, variance, emulations, wrath, strife, seditions, heresies, envyings, murders, drunkenness, revellings, and such like,—[who] have enlisted themselves under the *Banner of Satan!*" He goes on to denounce the servants of Mammon, who, "when the *spiritual Labourer* claims his *Hire*... *keep back* the *whole*, or *part* of the *price*.... Such seldom consider, that when they defraud the ministers of God in Tithes and Offerings, they presumptuously rob God himself." Although in the introduction Mr. Darwall politely claims that his words are not intended to "*grate* the *Ears* of [his] own Parishioners," his parishioners' ears appear to have been fruitfully grated, for this year the usually impecunious vicar could afford to have the eight bells of his church recast and to add a new spire to hang them in. Perhaps there were even new shoes for the children.

John also exercised his rhetorical powers on the rebellious American colonists in a "Political Lamentation written in the year 1775," "the first essay of [his] political Pen." The poem bears no date other than the year, but it seems to have been written in reaction to the battles of Lexington and Concord (April 19, 1775): he deplores both the "ungrateful blows" that the Americans, inspired by Satan, shower on the "fost'ring Hand" of England, and their nasty habit of lurking behind trees and in ditches in order to shoot safely at their "braver Foes." Addressed to the Prime Minister, Lord North, the poem breaks into two parts: mixed denunciation and sarcasm hurled at the rebels, and a not entirely logical argument for England's right to tax her colonies. The transition between the two parts is as follows:

> But let us turn our tortur'd Eyes
>   from this affecting Scene,
> And see what Pleas these wily wights
>   for their Rebellion feign.
>
> The Question held in grand Debate,
>   which strongly they gainsay,

"Now Darwall" (1766-1775)

> Is,——Has the British Court a Right
> to tax AMERICA?

After reading this poem, one can have no doubts about the author's convictions and the intensity with which he held them, though one can have doubts about his skill as a versifier.

Whether Mrs. Darwall shared her husband's convictions is an open question. Her poems sometimes celebrate Albion and the reigning British Brunswick, though not as jingoistically as many others' poems did. But she wrote nothing specifically about the American rebellion. She might have considered the topic unsuitable for a woman, though she occasionally does touch on political matters. Or perhaps she preferred not to make poetry out of an opinion different from her husband's. Besides, she had happier topics on her mind—a few days after Lexington and Concord, her brother Henry, who had looked like being a permanent bachelor, finally married at the age of forty. He brought his bride, Margaret Clements, from her home in Worcester back to Walsall and a prosperous establishment: his law practice was flourishing and he was acquiring coal mines as well as other property. Before long, Margaret was pregnant—and so was Mary Darwall. As 1775 drew to a close, the new sisters-in-law could anticipate together the births of a first and a sixth child.

Chapter 7

Sylvia's Diary for 1776

> The business of the biographer is ... to lead the thoughts into domestic privacies, and display the minute details of daily life.
>
> Samuel Johnson

NOTE: There comes a time in biographers' lives when they feel that they know their subject so well—his or her thoughts and feelings, the routine of daily life—that they could describe all this quite accurately, even though no hard evidence exists to authenticate it. That is, biographers grow sorely tempted to be novelists. Of course, the line between the genres is fuzzy at best, and perhaps I have already overstepped it, since I have necessarily been dealing at times with probabilities rather than facts. But in this chapter I overstep deliberately—up to a point: there was a "Sylvia," younger than Mrs. Darwall, but I do not know her real name; Mrs. Darwall did write a poem inviting her to visit and she apparently came, but I don't know when—and there is no evidence whatsoever that she kept a diary. But I wanted to bring the reader closer to the life of an eighteenth-century family, and to Mrs. Darwall's life, than more conventional narration would permit. Life in any century, especially a woman's life, is largely made up of small details, domestic trivia that would be tedious to read about in impersonal narration. But that is the flavor of her life. So I have adopted this unorthodox method to try to capture some of that flavor.

Sylvia's Diary for 1776

The main incidents are still historically true, from the blizzard in January to the sermon in December. Some of the events, such as beating the bounds of the parish, occurred regularly. Others did occur, but there is no certainty that they did so in this year. Still others are merely probable, while a very few details are pure embroidery. But I think the categories to which these events belong will be self-evident, for the most part. When they are not, and when the matter is significant, the reader will find clarification in the Notes.

I have not attempted to write this diary in an eighteenth-century style, but I have tried to avoid egregious twentieth-centuryisms.

****

Invitation to the same [Sylvia],
In Winter

From regions of perpetual smoke,
    Commercia's rich domains,
Where sulph'rous streams for ever choke,
    And sooty Vulcan reigns;

Thy DELIA's muse wou'd fain take wing,
    To greet her SYLVIA's eyes;
But sure, what from such scenes can spring,
    My SYLVIA must despise.

. . . .

No blackbird swells the varied strain,
    No sky-lark wakes the morn,
But dazzling snow invests the plain,
    And nature droops forlorn.

Yet, in the dreariest wintry hour,
    The faithful heart can find
A sovereign balm, in one fair flow'r,
    To sooth the anxious mind.

Sylvia's Diary for 1776

. . . .

   Friendship, my SYLVIA, is the flow'r;
      Sometimes, to Love refin'd,
   It still exerts superior pow'r,
      To bless the kindred mind.

. . . .

   Come; tho' no vernal prospects gay
      Can here delight thy mind;
   Nor will thy favor'd youth delay,
      These distant scenes to find.

   Four guileless hearts, that, raptur'd, bend
      To love's and friendship's sway,
   Shall sprightly mirth and music blend,
      To cheer the darksome day.

   I, bless'd in my PHILANDER's love,
      With heighten'd joy shall see
   My SYLVIA, with her EDWIN, prove
      Bless'd in the same degree.

7 January (Sunday): I begin my diary for this Year of Our Lord 1776 a few days late because I have been travelling to visit my dear friend Mrs. Darwall, and when I arrived I had to spend a few more days renewing my old acquaintance with her and Mr. Darwall, and trying to learn which of the children is which. (I think I have them sorted out now.) I was considerably fatigued by my journey, especially since I have been not long recovered from my illness—I cherish Mrs. Darwall's poem that she wrote last autumn to congratulate me on my returning health. I could hardly believe my good fortune when she suggested that I come to stay with her, but when she wrote another poem on the same subject (I have copied out part of it to start this year's diary) I saw that she sincerely desired my company. But then, she is always sincere, perhaps especially in her wishes for my happiness

Sylvia's Diary for 1776

with Edwin. Her own happiness with Mr. Darwall seems complete.

About Edwin? This long time apart from him (Mrs. Darwall has made me promise to stay a whole year) will prove his constancy—and mine. My parents agreed to such a long visit partly because they do not approve of Edwin's courting me and he will not be able to visit me here, despite Mrs. Darwall's invitation. But we are permitted to write letters, and I will live for those.

This morning there is a calm in this lively house. All the family except Mrs. Darwall have gone to church despite the snow, which started last night and is still falling heavily. (She is resting—her next child is due quite soon.) I too pleaded fatigue and I am glad of the quiet in which to begin my belated diary.

The quiet is indeed unusual. No one is making music, no one is talking, no parish visitors are knocking at the door. But soon the house will be humming again. Someone always seems to be singing or playing and there is always conversation. Our talk grew particularly animated at dinner yesterday when a visitor expressed some sympathy with the colonists in North America who are attempting to gain their "liberty," as he put it. "Liberty!" Mr. Darwall snorted—I cannot begin to describe how agitated he became on this subject. Mrs. Darwall held her peace—I must ask her one day what she thinks—and after a little time turned the conversation to the topic of the rebels here in their own town of Walsall. I inquired who these might be and again the conversation grew lively. I was given to understand that the rising prices of food in the Market had so outraged some of the citizens, the poorer citizens no doubt, that they rioted until trade became impossible. Both Mr. and Mrs. Darwall deplored the high prices, but when the visitor spoke of taking on additional constables to control the rioting people, as they had done ten years before, Mr. Darwall readily agreed to the plan.

Sylvia's Diary for 1776

It is a pleasure to get acquainted with the children. John is quite grown up, nearly sixteen. He is a good student and there is talk of Oxford, but some question about the expense. He lives part of the time with his grandparents in Haughton. Randle is thirteen and will be apprenticed, though no choice of trade or master has yet been made. William, the next one, will no doubt be apprenticed as well. These are all Mrs. Darwall's stepsons; her own are too young yet for such plans, but I do not expect there will be preference given to her own blood—she is always fair and just. Charles Henry—Leicester—no, I do not yet have all her boys sorted out. But Harriet is easy—the only girl, just five years old and really quite pretty. I wonder if any of them will be poets.

The snow is coming down more heavily than ever—a genuine blizzard. I can hardly see the lofty sycamores outside my window. I hope the family find their way home safely—they should be here soon. Then farewell to peace and quiet, and to my diary. I cannot promise to write every day no matter how many thoughts I may have to record. But what I do set down will always remind me of what promises to be a remarkable year in my life.

They have returned.

14 January (Sunday): The snow continues—we are cut off from the rest of the world and it is very cold. No coaches come or go so we have no letters. I think often of Edwin.

Now I do have the children sorted out. Leicester is Mrs. Darwall's eldest—he is eight, and said to be artistic. Charles Henry is six and seems to be one of the brightest. Then Harriet, and little Frederick who is two and a half. I hope the new one will be another girl—Mrs. Darwall loves girls but says any baby is a gift of God. Mrs. Whateley, her new sister-in-law, will soon have such a gift too, I believe. We will visit when the snow permits.

Sylvia's Diary for 1776

18 January (Thursday): This was one of our musical evenings—too much snow for visitors to come, so for our family party, Mr. Darwall tried out one of the sonatas for pianoforte he has been composing. It was pleasing.

20 January (Saturday): Mrs. Darwall's new baby made her appearance yesterday morning. I had expected much more fuss, but all the rest of the household is quite accustomed to these events. Too busy to write more—I try to be useful.

26 January (Friday): A neighbor brought us some woodcocks today, which we will have roasted with claret sauce—a rare treat. Our dinners are usually quite plain.

1 February (Thursday): Mr. Darwall baptized the new baby at home today—she is named Elizabeth, in memory of her mother's girlhood friend Miss Loggin, but her mother calls her Eliza. I hope this private ceremony does not mean they fear for her life.

15 February (Thursday): Elizabeth seems quite well. The weather is a little warmer, which helps, and the post arrives regularly again. (January was dreadfully cold.) Today I slithered part way down the High Street to Mrs. Parkes's bookshop to look at the Letters of Lady Luxborough, which were published late last year but have only now arrived at the shop. Lady Luxborough was an intimate friend of Mr. Shenstone's and knew Dr. Wall, both important people in Mrs. Darwall's life. I was hoping to find some mention of "Miss Whateley"—and Mrs. Parkes allowed me to look through the book uninterrupted as long as I chose. But Lady Luxborough died in 1756, I discovered, too soon to have known Miss Whateley as a poet. And I don't think I like this lady much—even though she wrote some poetry herself she called "Poetess" a "reproachful name I would avoid," and she actually enjoyed the Memoirs of the shocking Mrs. Pilkington. I decided not to purchase the book.

Sylvia's Diary for 1776

24 February (Saturday): We have had such a complete thaw that the winter fair is taking place today as planned despite all the water that lies about. A few days ago, young John and I went on an errand for Mrs. Darwall and I thought I would have to turn back at the foot of the hill. The little river, Walsall Water, had swollen dreadfully and spread out over its banks. The footbridge across to Park Street, where our errand lay, was under some inches of water. Young John, boy-fashion, pulled off his shoes and stockings and waded across, but of course I could not do that. But people here are prepared for this flooding, which seems to be a frequent occurrence—the keeper of the New Inn across the bridge sent a pony over for me and I rode through the water in style, for a penny.

28 February (Wednesday): Today Mrs. Darwall went to be churched. I wonder if Mr. Darwall charged her sixpence for it. There are such fees, of course, and recently I overheard him lamenting the necessity of restoring the old rates. When he was appointed vicar, he reduced churchings from sixpence to fourpence, but I imagine Mrs. Darwall persuaded him that the tuppence was a necessary part of their household income. Indeed, the better I become acquainted with this household, the happier I am that my mother insisted that Mrs. Darwall accept a contribution for my maintenance during this long visit.

8 March (Friday): Now that the excitement is over I have found a few minutes to set down the story. A little more than a week ago, there was a thunderous knocking at the door when morning had just dawned. All the family were already up—some of the children were feeding the hens and the animals—but the visitor would speak only with Mr. Darwall. In a few moments, Mr. Darwall and the visitor rushed out of the house in the direction of the church. They were gone for some time, and when Mr. Darwall returned, he looked sadly distressed. He was reluctant to explain the cause of his distress but could not contain himself.

Sylvia's Diary for 1776

It seems that our dawn visitor had been crossing the churchyard on his way to work when he saw two dogs fighting over something among the graves. As he approached, the dogs snarled but backed away and he found—a dreadful sight—the mauled body of a newborn child. He covered the poor babe with his coat and weighted it down with stones to prevent the dogs doing more harm, and then he ran to the vicarage house. Mr. Darwall did what was necessary and sent the man for the constable, with whom he conferred about the possible culprit. It was a day or two before they thought of a young working woman (whose name they have not mentioned to us), unmarried but obviously with child, and together they visited her cottage. She was no longer with child, they perceived, and when they inquired, in her weakness she wept and confessed the pathetic fact: alone in the cottage when her time came, she had delivered herself of the child and then struggled to the churchyard where, in sacred ground, she dug a shallow grave and laid the little body in it. When he reported this to us, Mr. Darwall was so distressed and indignant that he never said whether the child was stillborn or whether the wretched mother had destroyed it herself. They must assume the latter because they have taken her to the old jail despite her condition. It is a sad business. We feel it deeply, especially with a new one in our own household. I cannot refrain from commenting on the difference between the two mothers: the miserable unmarried young woman, suffering alone and now in prison, and the vicar's wife, surrounded by friends and then resting comfortably after her child was born. Yet the pains of the body were the same. The difference lies in the soul. I think Mrs. Darwall feels as I do, which may be why we took Elizabeth to church for her public baptism yesterday.

In the midst of all this came news of the second Mrs. Langhorne's death in childbirth in February. (The child lived.) Poor Mr. Langhorne! To lose two wives in such a way is sad indeed. Mrs. Darwall fears for the health of her old friend under this burden of grief.

Sylvia's Diary for 1776

11 March (Monday): At Mrs. Darwall's suggestion, I have been reading Mr. Langhorne's long poem, *The Country Justice*. (Mr. Langhorne is much on our minds just now.) He does appear to care deeply about people, as she says, especially about women. At the end of Part II of the poem he describes with outrage a painful scene: a young woman dying in childbirth by the roadside because the "Ruffian officer" drove her out of town when her pains began so that her baby would not have to be supported by the parish. It is dreadful to think that such things happen in our enlightened age, yet this part of the poem was published only last year. More is yet to come, Mrs. Darwall tells me. I hope he lives to finish it.

25 March (Monday): We hear that it was agreed last week to move the Charity School classes from their present cramped quarters to the large room upstairs in the Market Cross. If there is other news, we have not heard it, being busy with all the family but especially with little Elizabeth, who seems to have a passionate temper.

9 April (Tuesday): We have seen little of Mr. Darwall these last few days except in the pulpit—Easter is one of the busiest seasons of a clergyman's year. But the service was particularly beautiful even though the dry, cold weather we have been having brought forth very few flowers for the church. I confess I have not yet grown accustomed to the singing of hymns by the congregation and still find it somewhat shocking.

17 April (Wednesday): Attended the christening of Mrs. Whateley's baby, Anna Maria. Lost sixpence at loo this evening.

2 May (Thursday): This morning Mrs. Darwall transplanted a sad little bay tree from the north side of the house to a sheltered spot on the south side, and stood looking at it for some minutes after she had fetched it water. Then she picked one or two leaves to put into the collared eels she has promised us for dinner. The weather continues dry and cold; we fear for the crops this season.

4 May (Saturday): When Elizabeth had finally gone to sleep after an angry crying spell this evening, I asked Mrs. Darwall if she regretted having no time to write poetry now that she was so much occupied with her babies and her household. She smiled, and said mysteriously, "Yes and no"—and gave me a paper of verses, which she said I might transcribe if I liked. Here it is.

> Sonnet, on Removing a Bay-Tree
> From a Northern to a Southern aspect
>
> Long, much-lov'd tree, thy tender stem has borne
>   Th'ungenial influence of the northern blast;—
> Oft the keen hail thy glossy leaves has torn,
>   No lucid beam cheer'd thee at op'ning morn;
>   Thy Winter bleak, thy Summer sunless past,
>   But in a happier scite thy lot shall now be cast.
> Shelter'd from blighting winds, on thee shall smile
>   Th'effulgent radiance of the rising day;
> Refreshing dews be thine, and richest soil,
> (O! might such blessings crown thy planter's toil)
>   And southern breezes 'mid thy foliage play,
>   Enrich thy fragrant breath and make thy green more gay;
> And lib'ral shalt thou yield th'unfading bough,
> Where genius blooms, to wreath the honor'd brow.

Perhaps I am mistaken, but I feel some unsatisfied longing in these lines, and yet I cannot doubt that she is happy in her marriage. A woman's life is not simple.

15 May (Wednesday): This is the last of three days of special supplications in church—Rogation Days—and the day when Mr. Darwall and a company of Corporation officials and other men together with a number of boys beat the bounds of the parish.

Sylvia's Diary for 1776

After prayers, they set off in high spirits. It was a cold day, but dry and bright. I rather wished I could go with them; but Mrs. Darwall explained that there were good reasons for considering it a purely masculine affair. As they walk along the boundary, they are met several times by the farmers or other inhabitants with bread and cheese and large pots of strong ale, and much ale on a cold day has its effects. There is another deterrent as well. These men carry the map of the boundary in their memories. They make great efforts to teach the younger members of their party exactly where the line runs so they will remember it, especially since they beat only one-third of the bounds each year because Walsall parish is so large. These efforts take such forms as pushing a boy into a deep pond so he will be sure to remember that point on the boundary, or beating a lad with a rod cut from a certain tree so he will remember to turn south at that tree. No doubt their tricks grow wilder as the ale goes down and they are in a fine state by the time they arrive at the Green Dragon for the splendid dinner that concludes the ceremony. I am glad not to accompany them. I will go to bed early before Mr. Darwall returns and think of Edwin.

29 May (Wednesday): Rather tired today. Yesterday was Whit-Tuesday Fair and we all went. I was not greatly interested in the farm animals on display—mostly cattle, some pigs—but was well pleased with the zebra and the he-lion. I think Randle and William slipped away to see the cock-fighting. I found the pugilists and the cudgel players bloody enough. The dairymaids for hire looked clean and neat, and some were fairly pretty. I did only a little shopping—sugar-plumbs for the children and a suit of lace ruffles for myself—luckily, without getting my pocket picked despite the press of the crowd. Everybody in Walsall seemed to be there as well as many country people. There were so many things to do and see and buy that people of all stations found much to their taste.

Sylvia's Diary for 1776

10 June (Monday): We have a printing press! I was not aware that such a purchase was being planned and Mrs. Darwall does seem somewhat concerned about the expense (but she does not discuss such private family matters with me, of course). Mr. Darwall had not been entirely pleased with the work of the Wolverhampton man who printed his *Visitation Sermon* last year and said he could do better himself. I assume he intends to try. Great to-do as he had the press set up and the cases of type installed. Then Mr. Darwall demonstrated how to mix the ink. The boys are enchanted and are already inky to the eyebrows. Mrs. Darwall is just as eager as they are to start printing something—I only hope she will do some of her own poems, and perhaps write more new ones. I'm sure she longs to. This press may be a good idea after all.

18 June (Tuesday): Mrs. Darwall entrusted me with today's marketing—I think she wanted to work with the press. The High Street was unusually busy. A man was being publicly whipped at the top of the street—they said he was a thief. I found just the right pair of buckles for the new shoes I have ordered (Walsall is famous for buckles) and a perfect piece of muslin at Mrs. Baylies's shop for a summer dress. We have had both sun and rain, and the crops have been saved.

2 July (Tuesday): It has become our custom to read passages from the *Gentleman's Magazine* aloud in the evenings when each month's issue arrives. It is a pleasing custom, but I confess that my heart sank when I saw that the Parliamentary Report for June was devoted again to trouble with the American colonies. This subject provokes great outbursts from Mr. Darwall. But tonight another article caught his eye: a Bill has been introduced that would promote the more speedy repairing of parsonage houses and their outbuildings—and his own premises are growing rather shabby. As he read on, however, he discovered that the money for repairs would not be a gift; the incumbent was only enabled to borrow and then would have to spend twenty-one years repaying the mortgage. Mrs. Darwall shook her head.

Then it was her turn to read, and she chose a letter from one "Eleonora" on the subject of marriage. The writer is twenty-nine and unmarried because she has only a small fortune. She describes what she wants from marriage—congeniality of souls—and how a widower whom she liked, and whose little girls she loved, at last rejected her because of her poverty. She had much to say about most men's preference for money rather than for domestic devotion and education in a wife. Her widower came to a sad end: he married a lady of fortune whom he did not love, and she squandered everything on equipage and visits to Bath. I was deeply moved by "Eleonora's" story, as I sat in the company of two highly congenial souls who have little money but much domestic devotion—and I thought of Edwin.

When my turn came to read, I looked first at the poetical essays and saw one by "an affectionate Husband" in celebration of his thirtieth wedding anniversary. He addressed his "Dearest Maria" in such heartfelt terms, describing their "blest state" as "preparative to that above," that I think we all had happy tears in our eyes when I had finished reading.

4 July (Thursday): One of the pieces of music the Darwalls played this evening was a gavotte by the late Mr. Avison. I danced with young William while they played. Mrs. Darwall said it was odd that there were no words for that music, because it sounded like a song. Mr. Darwall smiled and said, "Why not write some?" I hope she does.

13 July (Saturday): A few days ago there occurred an incident which I was reluctant to enter in my diary, because it put me sadly out of countenance. But Mrs. Darwall has written a poem about it, so I will tell the story. We were dining with the Whateleys, her brother and his family. Our party was large, composed mainly of Mr. Whateley's friends in the legal profession. At one point, the conversation turned to the subject of

Sylvia's Diary for 1776

love and one of the legal gentlemen began to speak of the necessity of defining one's terms in such a discussion. Soon he turned to me. "But here," he said, with an unattractive smile, "I feel sure we have an authority on the matter. She must read of it in novels, and perhaps she feels the tender passion herself. Pray, my dear, what is love? Will you give us a definition?" I know I blushed, I was covered with confusion, I could not—I would not—answer. Mrs. Darwall saw my misery and said something to the gentleman, but I was too distressed to attend to her words. Today she showed me a poem, which I asked permission to copy:

Lines addressed to a Gentleman
on hearing him ask a young lady
What Love Was
(To which she returned him no answer.)

Since Sylvia to answer your question declines,
   Permit one much older to speak in her stead,
And if you're not pleas'd with the subsequent lines,
   Say crotchets and whims have perverted her head.

In the different sexes love claims no relation;
   Tho' how to explain it, in truth, I scarce know:
In the gentlemen folly, self-love, dissipation,
   As either prevails, prompts the nonsense to flow.

You have read in romance, how poor girls have been cheated
   By lovers and heroes in authors' brains hatch'd;
By florid descriptions, and vanity heated,
   You think those exploits by your own shall be match'd.

Some nymph, whom your eye from the throng has selected,
   You fancy wou'd soften the cares of your life,
Make a good upper servant, of fraud ne'er suspected,
   Obedient and humble when once commenc'd wife.

Then you summon your forces, and open the batt'ry;
   Soft looks, kind attentions at first speak the flame;
From these you proceed to complaints, sighs and flatt'ry,
   With fifty fine things which the Muse cannot name.

Sylvia's Diary for 1776

A comical description of courtship!—as if all courtships were the same.

>By vanity dup'd, the fond nymph, all believing,
>>Thinks your peace, nay your life must depend on her eye;—
>Can those looks, sighs and tears be e'er feign'd for deceiving?
>>What pity a youth so deserving shou'd die!

I wonder if men ever do die for love.

>To be cruel and kill the dear man who adores her—
>>Ah! who to compassion cou'd be so estrang'd?
>No, she'll sooth all his sorrows next time he implores her,
>>And all his complaints shall to transports be chang'd.

>Her nature so gentle, her bosom so tender,
>>She grieves that an insect shou'd e'er suffer pain,
>And her life she will dedicate, happy to render
>>This faithful, affectionate, love-stricken swain:—

>So they wed;—she expecting that times will ne'er alter;
>>He, thinking to lord it as soon as he can,
>Begins to command,—her good purposes falter,
>>And she vows she'll ne'er give up her will to a man.

Do wives ever really give up their wills? Should they? What would it be like to be without one's own will?

>Thus cheating and cheated, they scold, storm and squabble,
>>Each cursing the day they unhappily met,
>The grief of their friends, and the jest of the rabble,
>>Now torpid with gloom, and now glowing with pet.

>Such, such is the love by which crowds are united,
>>And such are the humours that part them again,
>The pure torch of HYMEN for them was ne'er lighted
>>But PLUTUS and FOLLY constructed the chain.

>True love must be founded on virtue and reason,
>>On tempers congenial, and passions subdu'd;

Sylvia's Diary for 1776

> Then blessing and bless'd in each varying season,
> The union thro' life will with rapture be view'd.

Mrs. Darwall must have been thinking of her own marriage when she wrote that final stanza.

If this poem is printed on the press, I hope the gentleman at the dinner party receives a copy.

31 July (Wednesday): A total eclipse of the moon last night—a fearful sight. The darkness was complete for about an hour and a half. I was glad that we now understand why such things happen. An ignorant savage would be terrified, I am sure.

1 August (Thursday): From the *Gentleman's Magazine* for July: more about the great Mr. Garrick's retirement; clergymen are losing their tithes as land is sold for canals (I wonder if Mr. Darwall helped to discourage the Walsall canal plan?); a certain clergyman with two livings is said to take in 550 pounds a year (such riches!); Dr. Wall of Worcester died in June (Mrs. Darwall grieved—she told me how much he had done to bring her poems to public notice).

2 August (Friday): A letter from my mother—I am summoned home for "family reasons" but I may return in September. (No one is ill, I thank God.) Old Thomas brought the letter by hand and will accompany me on the coach. Must pack.

****

20 September (Friday): I am engaged to Edwin! The family business that required my presence at home was a change in his circumstances that smoothed away all difficulties. My own doubts had vanished long since, and now I am back in Walsall to finish out my visit. I do not know how much of a diary I can keep for the rest of this year, however, for my pen will be much employed in writing letters.

I am rather glad I was not here when the *Gentleman's Magazine* for August arrived. It contains a "Declaration by the Representatives of the United States of America [!] in General Congress assembled, July 4," a stirring piece of prose which must have stirred Mr. Darwall in a distressing direction. Mrs. Darwall was stirred by another item in the *Magazine*, she tells me—a woman in Sussex, said to be insane, was burned to death for the murder of her husband. Husbands who murder their wives are not burned, of course, only hanged. There are, I know, many different laws for the different sexes, as is only proper, but I cannot be sure that this one is right.

I am also glad I was not here when a man named Thomas Jackson nearly drowned in the vicarage fishpond. He was swimming, but the water was so cold he got a bad cramp. I think it was Randle who jumped in and pulled him out.

The next few days will be busy and entertaining. This Sunday we have the St. Matthew's Day charity sermon, to be preached by a Mr. Rutter from Wolverhampton. (He is said to be a man of ingratiating manners.) I expect the Charity Children will sing Mrs. Darwall's hymn. This is our Wake Sunday, of course, because St. Matthew is the patron saint of our church, so there will be much festivity to follow—a display of special fireworks from France, a great fair the next day with horseraces and a ball to follow, as well as the annual concert with another ball for the benefit of our organist, Mr. Alcock. But a ball without Edwin has little attraction for me. I may not go.

15 October (Tuesday): The boys have bagged some rabbits and I will cook them in a special way—mumbled, with sippets—for Charles Henry's birthday tomorrow.

29 October (Tuesday): Our mild autumn weather has tempted us all to spend as much time as possible out of doors. The little bay tree flourishes in its new spot. The children are well and lively and love to be abroad even though the evenings begin to grow damp and chilly. Mrs. Darwall is concerned for their health if they continue to play in the fields as November comes on. She has given me a copy of the cautionary poem she wrote for them on this subject; the title is "The Wood-Nymph, occasioned by a party of the author's young friends being accustomed to walk too late in the autumnal evening under a row of ancient sycamores." She pretends to be the wood-nymph "Sycamoria" and describes her beautiful grove full of music and "domestic harmony." But even she must retire when the "chilling show'r" of autumn comes down:

> Now close I shrink within my fav'rite tree,
>   Nor, tho' immortal, dare grim Winter's rage;
> Ye sons of Earth, let this a caution be;—
>   So may you haply gain a good old age.
>
>   WARNING.
>
> In wintry months ne'er breathe the morning air,
> Nor to your wonted bow'rs at eve repair;
> If noon-tide Phoebus smile, beneath his ray
> Catch the bright moment, and improve the day:
> But when dark clouds from liquid skies depend,
> When fogs arise, or freezing rimes descend;
> Then let the cheerful hearth and blazing fire
> Unbend the mind, and social mirth inspire.
> So shall succeeding springs behold you blest,
> And Sycamoria take her Winter's rest.

Sycamoria may be resting but Mrs. Darwall never seems to.

4 November (Monday): Not much of any note in October's *Gentleman's Magazine*—the usual news of the war in the colonies, or United States as they call themselves. Mrs. Darwall and I were much interested, however, in the account of the public crowning of the Italian poetess Signora Corelli. Imagine passing an "examination" in poetry (what could that be?) before a crowd of nearly four hundred people and then being crowned with laurel and saluted with one hundred cannons! England pays no such honor to her poets, and for a woman it would be unthinkable. Can this Signora Corelli be a modest woman?

8 November (Friday): The Darwalls are worried about money. I was sewing in the sitting room with Mrs. Darwall when Mr. Darwall sat down with us and, disregarding my presence, spoke for some time of the unlikelihood of being able to send young John to Oxford. He is a bright young man—loves the theater and goes about reciting Shakespeare day and night—and I think he would like to follow his father into the church. It seems a great pity. Walsall is not a rich living—the parishioners who attend regularly are few and often look quite lost in the large church—but I feel sure there must be some mismanagement or carelessness with funds here. Many clergymen, even with modest livings and large families, are able to send a son to Oxford.

When Mr. Darwall left us, Mrs. Darwall sighed and shook her head. Then she rummaged in her desk for a moment and brought out two sheets of paper which, with something like a smile, she put into my hands. At that moment there was an uproar among the children, audible even through the closed door. She hurried out and I opened the folded sheets.

Each contained a poem entitled "Hymn to Plutus," one in Mrs. Darwall's hand, the other not. I read this second poem first, saving the better one for last—and hers was better. The other was signed by her friend John Langhorne. It was good enough, but I won't copy it out. He begins by claiming he worships the god of wealth and that he is the first poet ever to do so, which seems unlikely to me. He repudiates all other values—wisdom, friendship, love, hope—and swears he will worship and love only Plutus and all he stands for. He wants a handsome country estate, "though each tree's water'd with a widow's tears." The last eight lines are enclosed with a bracket and a note in the margin says "for MW":

Sylvia's Diary for 1776

> Detested god!—forgive me! I adore.
> Great Plutus, grant me one petition more.
> Should Delia, tender, gen'rous, fair and free,
> Leave love and truth, and sacrifice to thee,
> I charge thee, Plutus, be to Delia kind,
> And make her fortunes richer than her mind.
> Be her's the wealth all heaven's broad eye can view;
> Grant her, good god, Don Philip and Peru.

Quite a challenge! I like Mrs. Darwall's answer so much that I'll copy the whole thing, if my pen lasts.

> PLUTUS! to thee I bow, to thee alone,
> And, prostrate, worship at thy splendid throne.
> To thee, great god of ocean, earth and air,
> My heart ascends, and thus prefers its pray'r.
>
> O! grant thy vot'ry wealth, howe'er 'tis gain'd,
> By murders blotted, by corruption stain'd,
> By grov'lling arts, which virtuous fools despise,
> Who wish for wealth, yet scorn the ways to rise:
> Still let them court that empty bubble, fame,
> Be self-applause their riches, peace their claim.
> Such rebels to thy sway my soul disdains,
> Theirs be the glory, Plutus! mine the gains.
> For me let Phoebus, with intenser ray,
> Pour o'er Peruvian mines the blazing day;
> Tho' Pan's fair flocks bestrew the high parch'd plains,
> Brown Ceres droop, and breathless faint the swains,
> Tho' sable slaves in countless myriads die,
> Beneath the influence of the fervid sky,
> What is't to me, who, in this temp'rate isle,
> At southern heat, and Greenland winters smile?
> To me propitious is the scorching beam,
> Tho' sick'ning nature gasp beneath the gleam;
> Since to this kind, prolific warmth I owe
> The diamond's blaze, and ruby's heighten'd glow:
> This to all-pow'rful gold matures the ore,
> For which the suppliant crowd thy shrine adore.
> Do I forget, or break a promise made,—
> Must I be tied to servile rules of trade?

Sylvia's Diary for 1776

No:——Liberty from ample fortune springs
To spurn beneath my foot such trivial things.

    Shou'd the small number, who on honor doat,
And feast on virtue in a thread-bare coat,
Say, I by falsehood and collusion gain'd
The darling end, for which each nerve was strain'd;
Whilst I enjoy the permanent delight
Of solid gold, I'll swear THEIR BLACK IS WHITE.
Tho' tongue-tied truth may blame the bold design,
The world will honor me, whilst wealth is mine:
Then, PLUTUS, grant me wealth; to thee I bend,
And my devotion but with life shall end.

I know Mrs. Darwall too well to think she really means it—she has an ironic sense of humor at times. But the world does honor the wealthy as she says, and she probably has prayed for money often. There are no dates on these poems but the paper looks worn. So is my pen!

13 November (Wednesday): Two weeks ago the King proclaimed a special Fast Day on December 13 when all his loyal subjects are to humble themselves before God and ask pardon for their sins. We are also to ask God to deliver the King's loyal North American subjects from "the violence, injustice, and tyranny of those daring rebels, who have assumed to themselves the exercise of arbitrary power," et cetera, et cetera. Mr. Darwall will be very glad indeed to compose a sermon for this occasion.

23 November (Saturday): St. Clement's Day, and the new mayor took office with considerable pomp and ceremony. Crowds of people were attracted to the show and to the shower of apples and nuts thrown to them from the windows of the Town Hall by the new mayor and other dignitaries. Bread might have been more appropriate—prices are rising again and the poor are growing increasingly restless. People fear more rioting in the Market. Walsall folk often seem to riot about something—now it is prices, but some years ago it was Methodists that incited them. They gave Mr. Wesley a rude welcome, I am told.

25 November (Monday): Mr. Darwall is busy writing up the glebe terrier and groaning about the finicking nature of the task. A huge sheet of parchment nearly covers his desk, and he laments once again the necessity of restoring the old, higher surplice fees, which he is listing along with all his other income. Where does the money go?

3 December (Tuesday): The Debating Society met last week at the Green Dragon. Now that ladies may be admitted, we had planned to go, but our plans were upset when Mr. Darwall received a letter saying that his father, who is over seventy, had been taken ill. We hadn't the heart for a debate after this sad news.

14 December (Saturday): Yesterday we had our Fast Day with the sermon that Mr. Darwall had been working on for some time. He preached on a text from Luke: "And it came to pass in those days, that there went out a decree from Caesar Augustus, that all the world should be taxed." At first I thought he was simply anticipating the Christmas season, but soon his point was clear: as Caesar Augustus had the right to tax the people of Judea, so our own King (who is not a tyrant, Mr. Darwall insisted) has the right to tax the American colonists. Even though the Blessed Virgin was "under the Inconvenience of Pregnancy" she obeyed Caesar and travelled to Bethlehem; the Americans refuse to obey even without such an excuse. We must all obey our King because he is the Lord's anointed one, Mr. Darwall explained. He called upon the Americans to turn from their adverse ways and return to their King, who is ready to forgive them. The second half of the sermon was devoted to explaining why England is afflicted with this rebellion—we are being punished for our own sins (atheism, swearing, drunkenness, chambering and wantonness, failure to attend church).

Sylvia's Diary for 1776

Only our own penitential tears will extinguish the flame of the American rebellion. Mrs. Darwall tells me that her husband has also written a poem on the subject, making the same argument for the cause of the rebellion, and he is setting it up on his press. Much as I admire him, I find the idea not quite convincing—why should my sins make an American take up his musket? Surely God will punish my sins and the sins of the whole nation, but are not the rebellious Americans also sinning? It is all very confusing.

18 December (Wednesday): My long visit to the Darwalls is drawing to a close—I am wanted at home for Christmas. I will stay for Harriet's sixth birthday on Friday and then Old Thomas will be here to take me home to Edwin, and to my parents too, of course. We will be married soon in the new year. I only wish that we may find our souls as congenial as the Darwalls'—but I confess that I also wish that we will have fewer money worries. If I had been able to keep my diary every day, I would have said much about the struggle Mrs. Darwall has to keep the household going, about the great strength of her spirit and her wonderful sense of humor, and about the richness of the life here—music, poetry, religion, friendship—despite the poverty. But even though I have set down little of all this, I will always remember.

Chapter 8

"Fond Hearts . . . Ebbing Life" (1777-1789)

>As the revolving year from out his urn
>   Casts the auspicious morn that made me thine,
>May our fond hearts with fresh affection burn,
>   Nor with our ebbing life our loves decline.
>
> Mary Darwall

1777-1781

The pattern of life in the Darwall household changed after 1776. The last child had been born, the first was going out to make his way in the world, and the older generation was dying. John's father, Randle, died in February 1777, followed by his widow in September. Randle's death meant that John inherited a substantial collection of books and some properties in Cheshire that produced a small income, but everything else went to his spinster sister, Honor. (Randle's young namesake got his silver watch, and most of the children could expect a little money when they grew up.) But even with this added income, the Darwalls' finances were tight, so young John, instead of being sent to Oxford, was apprenticed to a glover. He lasted for a month. Then he shook the dust of the Midlands from his shoes and went to London to be a clerk in the Record Office of Westminster Abbey. London had theaters and libraries; a glover's workshop did not.

Mary too lost her remaining parent—Mrs. Whateley died in Beoley early in 1780; she was eighty-three. Friends were departing as well: Elizabeth Loggin's widowed mother in 1778,

"Fond Hearts . . . Ebbing Life" (1777-1789)

and John Langhorne in 1779. He was only forty-four, and tradition has it that his grief over the deaths of his wives drove him to the dissipation that hastened his end. As the older generation faded, the younger bloomed: in 1780, young Randle was apprenticed to an ironmonger in Newport, Shropshire, where his Aunt Honor lived, and at about the same time William was sent into a haberdashery in Birmingham. Ironmongery did not suit Randle, however, or perhaps Aunt Honor didn't, and without completing his apprenticeship he too went to Birmingham and signed on with a druggist and grocer. Meanwhile, in London, young John was putting himself through a course of reading to make up for his missing university education. Mrs. Darwall could contemplate her family with some satisfaction.

John Darwall's life had some rough spots during this period. He had been busy with the printing press and produced three pieces of his own on it, the two "Political Lamentation" poems and the special Fast Day sermon, all on the subject of the American rebels. These were bound together but paginated separately, offered for sale at two shillings in April 1777, and promptly trounced by the *Monthly Review* in May. The reviewer claimed to be astonished at finding that the author meant what he said (that English sin caused American rebellion), having thought he must be in jest. The reviewer then went on to sneer at the "Sternholdian rhymes" of the "Lamentations," which must have hurt even more, since John had rejected the Sternhold and Hopkins verses when he composed his psalm music. This dismal year, which saw the deaths of John's parents as well as this painful review, concluded with the death of his curate, Charles Davenport, younger brother of the previous curate who had married Mary's niece. A new curate came but stayed only one year; he was replaced in December 1778 by John Simpson Rutter, the Wolverhampton man who had given the charity sermon two years earlier. Mr. Rutter, part of the great floating population of impoverished curates in the eighteenth-century

"Fond Hearts . . . Ebbing Life" (1777-1789)

church, had a rapidly growing family and was desperate for something like security. He will loom large later in my story.

Mr. Darwall was also deeply engaged during these years with both church and town. He took part in planning improvements for the overcrowded burial ground. His town duties involved him in the tangle of legal and personal conflicts over the Corporation's debts for mortgaged land. These disputes had been going on for fifteen years and reached a crisis in 1780 when Mr. Darwall failed to dissuade one Richard Taylor from suing the Corporation—but Taylor died before the matter came to court. The usual conflicts between the two parts of Walsall, the Borough and the Foreign, further troubled its government. Even St. Matthew's itself was not always a refuge from trouble: in May 1781 a respected old parishioner died in his pew during Sunday services, and in June everyone was nearly deafened when the bellringers rang all of Holt's peal—it took three hours and sixteen minutes. The vicar's life had its rough spots.

A number of Mrs. Darwall's poems, though undated, belong fairly definitely to this period. Perhaps, no longer producing babies, she had creative energy available for more writing. Two of these poems are connected with the theater, always a source of interest and inspiration for her. The Stantons had mounted a strong program for their 1777 season, including Lee's tragedy *Theodosius* and two plays by Congreve, *The Mourning Bride* and *Love for Love*. This last featured John Nunns as the lusty tar, Sailor Ben; he had joined the Stanton company two years earlier. It was not long after his appearance as Sailor Ben that Nunns married Miss Elizabeth Stanton, and apparently Mrs. Darwall quietly celebrated their wedding in a pair of epilogues overtly devoted to other topics: "Epilogue Written for a Favourite Actress, and spoken on her benefit night at Walsall," and "Epilogue Spoken by the Husband of the Actress who delivered the preceding one, a few nights afterwards: when a Play was performed for the benefit of a person in distress." The actress's epilogue celebrates the power women wield over men and pokes

"Fond Hearts . . . Ebbing Life" (1777-1789)

fun at miserly, misogynist bachelors who succumb to marriage at fifty:

> There is, 'tis true, a hapless stubborn race
> Of batchelors, who all our sex debase,—
> Say we are whimsical, capricious, vain;
> And paint of follies an enormous train
> Which have existence only in their brain.
> This curious system they maintain till fifty,—
> During which season they are wond'rous thrifty,—
> Count all th'expences of a married life,
> And of all animals detest a wife.
> When lo! some youthful Gillian, Madge or Betty
> Assails their doating eyes with airs so pretty,
> They quite forget the prudent youthful scheme,—
> And take a wife who breaks the golden dream.

Then the actress counsels the ladies in the audience not to presume too much and reject a genuinely loving youth, nor to give in too easily:

> Nor yet too cheaply yield the woo'd consent,
> Lest the inconstant leave you to repent:—
> But tread the middle path to HYMEN's fane,
> Where, blest and blessing, long may you remain
> Patterns of virtue,—free from care and strife,
> Possess'd of ev'ry joy that sweetens life.

Good advice from a bride, and her own marriage lasted until John Nunns's death in 1803. The husband's epilogue thanks the audience for their generosity to his wife on her benefit night (her earnings, of course, were legally his) and promises them that their charity this night will give them a "luxurious glow" and that the "person in distress" will pray heaven to bless them. It would take an attractive young man to give these platitudes much interest, but the wife's epilogue, with its vision of domestic bliss coupled with caustic descriptions of foolish men and foolish women, is a lively piece.

"Fond Hearts . . . Ebbing Life" (1777-1789)

During these years the Darwalls made at least two holiday excursions. One took them to the outskirts of Birmingham and resulted in a group of poems about an architectural phenomenon called Hockley Abbey. Bearing the date of 1473 in pebbles over the door, the abbey was created in about 1779 by Richard Ford, an "ingenious mechanic" of Birmingham. Ford, who manufactured tools and invented a variety of silver and iron products and processes, happened to notice one day that his factory hands sometimes spent rather a large part of their wages on drink (he was teetotal himself) and that neither his men nor his horse and cart were always fully employed. Putting these facts together, he formed a plan: he began to save two shillings a day, thus setting a good example for his men, and he started to use both men and cart to transport slag from the Aston blast furnace to a spot of waste ground not far off. With these small savings and his men's labor, he built a structure from the slag, a gothic pile made to look like a ruined abbey but actually functioning as a dwelling. He drained the boggy waste, planted ivy and taught it to twine over the slag, constructed gardens, moved his family in (probably in 1781), and invited the Darwalls to visit. No doubt George Whateley, a fellow worker in silver, and the Taylors of both Birmingham and Walsall came too, at some time; it was probably through these connections that the Darwalls knew the Fords.

The abbey was something of a sensation. It was written up in newspapers and local histories, and remembered in more such books long after it was demolished in the mid-nineteenth century. It stood as a kind of monument to Birmingham's industrial inventiveness and might, as well as an indicator of the popular taste for the gothic—a bizarre marriage of two late-eighteenth-century phenomena. James Bisset, who immortalized his sooty city in a lengthy "Poetic Survey Round Birmingham" (1800), was much impressed by Hockley Abbey:

> Close by yon Lake's pellucid stream, behold
> A Gothic Pile, which seems cent'ries old,

"Fond Hearts . . . Ebbing Life" (1777-1789)

Richard Ford's Hockley Abbey, c. 1780.
(From Robert K. Dent, *Old and New Birmingham* [1878-80; rpt. Wakefield: E. P. Publishing, 1972], p. 183.)

"Fond Hearts . . . Ebbing Life" (1777-1789)

> Vulcanic fancy there displayed her taste,
> And rear'd the fabric on the barren waste;
> The Forge materials for the work provides,
> Rude cinders clothe the front, compose the sides.

Mrs. Darwall, who could write better verse, merely mentioned the "feign'd time-shook walls"; she paid her tribute to the grounds and gardens rather than to the slag house. Four of her poems describe and celebrate its cold bath (apparently a sort of small swimming pool), pleasure grounds, grotto, and turf seat. Each is an occasion for meditation: the cold bath inspires thoughts on health, the pleasure grounds on the "virtue and peace" of the Fords' life together, the grotto on the pleasures of solitude as opposed to "pomp and pow'r," and the turf seat on retreat from the cares of the world. These are neat applications of pastoral convention to the specific details of the occasion—not her best poems, but the Fords must have been pleased.

Real gothic rather than industrial waste, visited on another trip, inspired a more interesting poem, "Elegy on the Ruins of Kenilworth Castle." Inscribed to the Earl of Clarendon, for whom the extinct title had been revived in 1776, this poem in nineteen quatrains describes a moonlight visit to the "gothic glories" of Kenilworth's "Stupendous walls." Appropriately, the scene makes the poet think of "the changeful state / Of sublunary grandeur, pomp and shew": medieval tournaments are now replaced by "milder sacrifice" to love, the deer park where Queen Elizabeth hunted has become farmland, the old battlefield is full of flowers and singing shepherds. In the night, imagination peoples the scene "With glimm'ring ghosts." A village maid who might wander by would fancy she saw visions and heard hollow groans; superstition would spread among the rustics to whom she told her story. The poet, however, is a rational Christian, not a gullible rustic:

> But reason's eye in other light surveys
> This mould'ring monument of earthly state,

"Fond Hearts . . . Ebbing Life" (1777-1789)

> Which, to the soul this warning truth conveys,—
> "Aspire to glories of a longer date."
>
> For when oblivion shrouds the high-arch'd dome,
> And grandeur yields to time's all-conqu'ring sway,
> The deathless soul shall find his destin'd home,—
> The cloudless regions of eternal day.

The sentiment is predictable. What is more interesting is the attitude towards the gothic. The poet clearly admires the architectural glories of Kenilworth and the colorful scene of the medieval tournament, but her admiration is untouched by nostalgia or sentimentalism: the "milder" way of modern love is better than the "dreadful, pompous sports" of the old days. Yet this is not a blind faith in progress: Queen Elizabeth and her "bevies of . . . courtly fair ones" form a rather more attractive picture than the "sun-burnt hinds" of today who "despoil / The flow'ry meads" with their ploughs. Mrs. Darwall was well aware of the realities of farming as opposed to pastoral convention. She admired the powerful Queen of the not-too-distant past but felt no yearnings for the violence of the Middle Ages. Despite its conventional imagery and predictable conclusion, the poem reveals a discriminating, individual sensibility reacting to a historic tourist attraction.

The one poem of Mary Darwall's from this period that can be dated exactly is her anniversary poem, "To Mr. D—— on his fifteenth wedding day" (November 4, 1781), one of her very few poems about her marriage. The first stanza, which is the epigraph for this chapter, sets the tone of mutual devotion; the second introduces the ever-present topic of money:

> Ne'er may ambition haunt our humble dome,
> Nor avarice her baleful influence shed,
> But sweet content and competence still roam
> Where'er our steps by providence are led.

There is a touch of the stiff upper lip here combined with the prayer for "competence." This is followed by prayers for the

"Fond Hearts . . . Ebbing Life" (1777-1789)

moral welfare of the children whatever their lots in life turn out to be. Mrs. Darwall concludes by anticipating their marriages:

> If they at H<small>YMEN</small>'s sacred altar bow,
>   May they, like her who tunes this artless lay,
> Still bless the hour when Heav'n enroll'd the vow,
>   And joyful celebrate each nuptial day.

Unless this is meaningless platitude, which I very much doubt, the Darwall marriage remained happy despite the money worries.

1782-1785

In the four years following her fifteenth anniversary celebration, the poet produced at least three more poems and the woman saw some upheavals in her family and in her town. Walsall was growing busier. The new George Hotel (1781) and the other inns developed rapidly as improved roads routed north-bound traffic from Birmingham through the town. Although innkeepers and bankers flourished as a result, some other trades slumped in 1782, and food prices rose again with the same results as in 1766—riots in the Market. This time about a hundred hungry colliers attacked an outlying mill and forced the miller to sell them his wheat at five shillings instead of the sixty he was asking; then the crowd marched on the Market and, literally holding the merchants hostage, fixed the prices for wheat for the rest of the day. No doubt everyone took advantage of the resulting bargains. The relief was temporary, however, and special collections were later taken up for the poor. In December, Lord Mountrath himself gave one hundred pounds to the cause and was thanked with a poem in *Aris's Birmingham Gazette* calling on the needy to offer grateful prayers to heaven and, which was more to the point, urging "ye

"Fond Hearts . . . Ebbing Life" (1777-1789)

GREAT" to follow Mountrath's example. The poem is unsigned; conceivably, it is Mrs. Darwall's. The more prosperous citizens attended their regular fairs and markets, benefit concerts and balls. In September 1784 they elected Mr. Rutter as mayor for a year, a post that paid only fifteen pounds and demanded considerable outlay in entertaining. The Rutters had just had yet another baby, making such a venture economically unwise, but the hopeful curate had some long-range plans in view.

Family changes included the apprenticing of Leicester, Mary's own oldest son, to Francis Eginton of Birmingham. This took place late in 1783 when Eginton was about to set up in business for himself after a varied career in Matthew Boulton's Soho factories. There, using a secret process, he had produced "polygraphs," colored reproductions of paintings by Angelica Kauffmann and other artists, which were sometimes successfully passed off as originals. When this proved unprofitable in the long run (and perhaps Boulton's company got into too much trouble?), he went back to staining and painting on glass. Some of the resulting windows graced Oxford colleges, various castles, Beckford's Fonthill, and churches as aristocratic as St. George's Chapel in Windsor Castle.

Leicester's apprenticeship to this interesting master meant a move to Birmingham, where two of his half brothers were also serving out their time. And John, his oldest half brother, was now in Birmingham as well. In March of 1783 John had convinced a board of ecclesiastical examiners that he was sufficiently educated to be ordained as a deacon; the following year he was made a priest, though it was noted on his papers that he was "literate"—that is, he did not have a university degree. Apparently this lack was not a serious handicap, because as soon as he became a deacon, he was appointed lecturer at St. Bartholomew's chapel in Birmingham, and in September 1783 he was invited home to Walsall to preach the Wake Sunday charity sermon. From glover's workshop to his father's pulpit in five years, all by his own efforts—it was a triumph.

"Fond Hearts . . . Ebbing Life" (1777-1789)

These years were productive ones for Mrs. Darwall as well. For the first and last time during her marriage, as far as I know, she published a new poem. "Female Friendship, To a Young Lady," later retitled "An Epistle to a Friend," appeared in the short-lived *British Magazine* in September 1782. It is addressed to "Monimia," a friend of long standing. The intensity of the poem, and the fact that Mrs. Darwall felt the need to publish it, suggest that she might have been responding to some recent attack on women as being incapable of friendship, rather than just addressing a topic that had long been common in misogynist satire. Or perhaps some event in her own or "Monimia's" life stirred her to action. In any event, the issue was obviously close to her heart, as a number of her poems show, and she addresses it argumentatively in this one:

> Why does vain man accuse our gentle kind
> Of pride, and weak inconstancy of mind?
> Why should he deem the female breast the seat
> Of rankling envy, and of dark deceit?
> As tyrant kings their subjects' rights invade,
> As trembling kids to lions yield the shade,
> So are we robb'd of friendship's sacred name,
> Because too timid to defend our claim.
> What, tho' no Greek or Latian bard of old
> Has female friends in deathless strains enroll'd,
> Who, like Euryalus and Nisus, dar'd
> Whatever fate their heart's lov'd partner shar'd;
> Yet equal faith and fortitude combin'd,
> They own, have oft adorn'd the female mind.

Here, in a poem apparently about friendship between women, the argument takes a somewhat surprising turn:

> Say, what is love, but friendship's brightest ray,
> Which softens woe, and cheers fate's darkest day?

The poet could have used her own marriage as an example of this kind of love, but she chose literary illustrations instead:

"Fond Hearts . . . Ebbing Life" (1777-1789)

Penelope waiting for Odysseus, Alcestis sacrificing herself for Admetus, Queen Eleanora sucking poison from her husband's wound. This last provides a transition to England's own bards —Thomson, in this instance—who credit women with being capable of friendship; Shakespeare with his Celia who follows Rosalind into exile provides the one example of love between women. Concluding the poem, a paean to "Monimia" not only proclaims her worth but also demonstrates the poet's own powers of friendship. Here she indicates that "Monimia" is as faithfully married as she is and is as true to her friendship as well. Indeed, love and friendship are so similar that they require the same kind of heart:

> The heart that to one pow'r has prov'd untrue,
> Can never pay the other homage due.

To some extent, this explains Mrs. Darwall's choice of wives as examples: she is defending woman's power of faithful commitment in general. The idea of marriage as friendship, while controversial, is not new. What is remarkable here, besides the considerable degree of equality the idea implies, is the lack of conflict between commitment to husband and to friend. Hierarchy vanishes. It is an emotional utopia—one can have it all. Could John Darwall have been so well attuned to women? At any rate, Mrs. Darwall's implication here is that women's capacity for friendship—a quality they do possess—is not a threat to men; on the contrary, it is a quality essential to the faithful wife.

Public politics rather than sexual politics soon engaged Mrs. Darwall's pen. The long siege of British Gibraltar (1779-83), the climax of centuries of such actions, was drawing to a close as she wrote "Ode on the Peace." The poem celebrates the exploits of Admiral Sir George Rodney, who had fought his way into the harbor with supplies in 1780, and the "matchless deeds" of the Rock's governor, General Sir George Augustus Elliot. "E'en a woman's heart grows bold" in the face of such heroism.

"Fond Hearts . . . Ebbing Life" (1777-1789)

These stirring tributes make up only a small part of the poem, however. The opening passage seems to deplore war in general and the American Revolution in particular:

> Long the bleeding world has groan'd,
>   Long has madd'ning discord rag'd,
> Long have Albion's sons bemoan'd
>   The hateful war with brothers wag'd.

The troubles are compounded by "faithless friends at home . . . / Disguised in patriotism's flaming robe." After praising Rodney and Elliot, Mrs. Darwall concludes with a long passage on the flight of Bellona and the appearance of "heav'n-born Peace, long wish'd for guest," who will revive commerce and heal the nation's sorrows.

A slight oddity here is that this "Ode on the Peace," celebrating the heroes of Gibraltar, is subtitled, "Written January 3rd. 1783." Even the preliminary peace treaty for Gibraltar was not signed until January 20. Clearly the poet had faith that Great Britain would be victorious, as was generally expected. But the date, the war-weary tone, and the reference to "brothers" suggest that the American Revolution was more central to her thoughts. News must just have arrived about the signing of the preliminary articles of peace between Great Britain and the United States (November 30, 1782), articles which recognized American independence and which were made official the following September. In a family where political lamentations had been loud against the rebels, there would have been much gnashing of teeth at America's victory; the glories of Gibraltar were all there was to celebrate. And it is small wonder that in the celebration poem these glories are overshadowed by the hatefulness of war and "some dark tints . . . shroud" the angelic beauties of peace.

Mrs. Darwall had recovered her fighting spirit a year later when she wrote "William and Susan, a Ballad. Written in the

"Fond Hearts . . . Ebbing Life" (1777-1789)

Year 1784." With the realities of various wars receding a little, she could turn to an experiment in form and meter and imagine a domestic conversation between a sailor and his lass. Susan has grieved for her absent William, who values honor more than love. But she learns to adopt his values:

> To love at first I gave my heart,
>   Till by thy brave example fir'd,
> I bade each selfish thought depart;
>   And, by my country's wrongs inspir'd,
> Wish'd thou victorious might'st return,
> Or I sleep with thee in the peaceful urn.

She even rejoices in his "Glorious wounds, received before," and when he returns, she is happy "to aid [his] weak limbs." Their voices unite in a particularly grisly conclusion:

> From such gallant leaders what Briton can flinch,
>   While British blood boils in each vein?
> Tho' certain his body must fall inch by inch,
>   By cannon-ball, grape-shot or chain.
> But Peace brings us rest: may prosperity show'r
>   Her blessings on each gallant soul!
> And when fresh wars burst forth, may our brave vet'rans pour
>   British thunders from thence to the pole!

What can one say about such a poem? The variety of metrical patterns would be quite interesting if set to music, for which the poem seems designed. The patriotism is unquestionable and unquestioning. The pictures of shredded bodies that the poem conjures up are horrific—I doubt that it was sung at recruiting rallies. I can only assume, or hope, that Mrs. Darwall was not thinking much beyond the technicalities of her art.

For she was still an artist and recognized as such. Her epitaph on Shenstone was reprinted in the *Gentleman's Magazine* for July 1783, and in that same year the Pearch collection was reissued with the same four poems of hers as before. And John was still an artist in music—he finished transcribing his psalms

"Fond Hearts . . . Ebbing Life" (1777-1789)

and hymns into a manuscript volume dated December 10, 1783. The creative life of the Darwall household was unquenchable.

1786-1789

Creativity continued as life itself ebbed—John Darwall's health began to decline. No information survives about the nature of his illness, but such long-drawn-out processes of dissolution were not uncommon in the eighteenth century. The parish registers show that he continued to perform his church duties, but gradually Mr. Rutter assumed more of the burden. Young John came over from Birmingham with increasing frequency to take the Sunday services, with Mr. Rutter filling in for him back at St. Bartholomew's. Young John also began to assume some of his father's tasks in the governance of Walsall; Mr. Rutter probably did too.

Like many a Christian, John Darwall meditated on the meaning of his suffering and wrote about it: his *Discourse on Spiritual Improvement from Affliction* was first printed in 1789. Sometime earlier it had been delivered as a sermon: it begins with a text from Corinthians (4:16-17) and goes on with the "first . . . secondly . . . thirdly" suitable for oral delivery. The tone is fervent, rising to a considerable height in the concluding description of Christ's sufferings, which were so much greater than any man's. Suffering on earth, endured in the proper spirit, is preparation for heaven—the theology is quite orthodox. Nothing personal marks this sermon, no reference to self, but the congregation, knowing their vicar was afflicted, would have seen the application and been the more deeply moved. A little of John Darwall comes through despite the impersonality, however. He dwells at some length on the uselessness of mere "*outward* Forms of Godliness" which "will avail us nothing *without the Religion of the Heart.*" Outward forms are still important: one must attend church (without "*indecent Whisperings*"), kneel to pray, take communion, and do good works as

"Fond Hearts . . . Ebbing Life" (1777-1789)

well. But all this is meaningless unless the inward man too is truly devoted to God. If more evidence were needed to show that the eighteenth-century Church of England was more than an affair of empty forms and ceremonies, John Darwall supplies it.

Indeed, the warmth, the fervor of his temperament is clearly evident in the rhetoric of his three published sermons. It is worth pausing here briefly to compare his tone and style—not his theology—with those of his better-known, more typical contemporaries. The subjects are the same—affliction, devotion, humility, repentance—but the rhetorical strategy and the language are not. Darwall never lingers over problems of understanding the biblical text, never balances both sides of a subtle question, never suggests that something may or may not be true. Indeed, he advises preachers to avoid speculation and unintelligible doctrine and to speak plainly. His own sermons ring, exclaim, with straightforward conviction. He threatens his listeners with hellfire and brimstone, without explaining that "fire" is merely a metaphor and "hell" simply the place of the dead. He demands of his congregation "heart-felt prayer" which can "pierce the skies," not just a "taste" for devotion. He names the ugly evils he deplores, rather than generalizing about "sin" and "vice." And while he claims to "avoid the *extravagant Heats* of *Enthusiasm*," he also claims to deliver the Word with "*burning zeal*." His spirit was passionate, his orthodoxy unquestionable. I expect that he would have agreed with Richard Graves's spokesman in *The Spiritual Quixote*, who tempered the religious excesses of young Wildgoose: "in the practice of Religion . . . nothing great can be effected without some degree of Enthusiasm; but I would not have your zeal transport you so far, as to hurry you into any irregularities. . . ."

John dedicated his last published sermon, the *Discourse on Spiritual Improvement from Affliction*, to Lord Mountrath, "from whom the author has experienced the most generous kindness, and the tenderest humanity in his *afflicted state*"; it sounds as if John's patron had sent money to his ever-needy vicar. The

"Fond Hearts . . . Ebbing Life" (1777-1789)

Discourse was very popular—it went quickly through four editions. It was printed for Mr. Darwall by Frederick Milward, who was also Walsall's bookseller in the 1780s. The Darwalls must have sold him their press in 1787: in January of that year Milward advertised in *Aris's*, calling himself a bookseller; in December, his advertisement said he was a printer and in search of a journeyman bookbinder. As John Darwall's health declined, it would have made sense to get rid of the press.

Other family affairs were being settled too—perhaps financed in part by the proceeds from the press. Charles Henry was placed with his uncle Henry Whateley to study law, though he continued to live at home. In the summer of 1788, Frederick, just fifteen years old, was apprenticed to a surgeon-apothecary in Lichfield. Randle had finished his apprenticeship and found a suitable job as a grocer-druggist in Birmingham. William had finished his with the Birmingham haberdasher and, despite his parents' opposition, went out to the West Indies to seek his fortune. The two girls, both in their teens, though they spent some time visiting family and friends, were usually at home. Harriet could look forward to a small inheritance from her grandfather, but he had died without remembering to add the two youngest, Frederick and Elizabeth, to his will. The girls' prospects were not bright. Young John's affairs, however, had improved considerably. In March 1787, still holding his post at St. Bartholomew's, he became assistant to the headmaster of the King Edward VI School in Birmingham; a John Whateley on the Board of Governors might have had something to do with the appointment. It brought in a salary of forty pounds a year. A year later, this was raised to sixty pounds, which must have seemed like affluence. Although he lacked a university degree, John was entrusted with teaching the younger boys and looking after the library. His prospects were looking up.

At least one of the older students at the school became a friend of John's and was introduced to his family. In 1787, the year John became a schoolmaster, Henry Francis Cary arrived at the King Edward VI School. This precocious lad was already,

"Fond Hearts . . . Ebbing Life" (1777-1789)

at the age of fifteen, making a start on the career in poetry that would bring him fame, especially as the translator of Dante. In the summer of his first year at Birmingham, he wrote "An Irregular Ode to General Elliot," the hero of Gibraltar (where Cary had been born) who, four years after the victorious conclusion of the siege that Mary Darwall had celebrated, had just returned to England and a tumultuous welcome. Cary's ode was modelled on Anna Seward's, written for the same occasion and published in June. The aspiring youth paid fulsome tribute to the Swan of Lichfield in his verses, which smoothed the way for a meeting with the lady after his piece was published in the spring of 1788. The admiration was mutual, and Cary gained entrée into Miss Seward's circle. He was also publishing poems in the *Gentleman's Magazine* and by the fall of 1788 had enough in hand to bring out a small book, *Sonnets and Odes*, to which Miss Seward contributed two introductory sonnets. His poems are imitative and full of adolescent sentimentalism; his prose shows more real promise. He took a lively part in critical controversy over the principles of translation, his future métier, and the relative merits of Dryden and Pope. He did not hesitate to differ from his admired Miss Seward in the pages of the *Gentleman's Magazine* on this latter question. By the time he left the Birmingham school for Oxford in April 1790, he must have considered himself a well-established figure in the literary world.

When young John Darwall brought Cary to Walsall to visit, probably on weekends when he relieved his father in the pulpit, Mrs. Darwall welcomed the promising boy. Worried about her husband's illness, she would have been glad to renew her other role, her life as a poet. It always helps to have more than one hat to wear. The two poets compared notes, read each other's poems, and became friends. Cary wrote a brief tribute to his hostess:

"Fond Hearts . . . Ebbing Life" (1777-1789)

STANZAS
Addressed to the Author,
By Mr. H. F. Cary

Doom not to dark oblivion's shade thy lays,
    Fearful of censure, or averse to fame;
In vain does genius grant her native rays,
    Unless the world behold and own the flame.

The lovliest flow'r with useless beauty glows,
    "That wastes its sweetness on the desert air,"
The public eye alone its worth bestows,
    When seen it blooms more fragrant and more fair.

It seems unlikely that he did not know of her first book; he must have seen it when he came to visit. More likely, he was aware that she was not publishing her current work. His own ambition and desire to publish are obvious. So the teenaged schoolboy graciously encouraged the fifty-year-old shrinking violet to get her own work put into print. She played up equally graciously to the role in which he had cast her:

    Thanks to the gen'rous Bard who wou'd inspire
        With confidence a timid female mind,
    Which doubts the influence of poetic fire,
        Whose traits by nature only are design'd.

She explains that she loves "sweet oblivion's peace" and is "blest" if friends, not the reading public, approve her work; she is content to be an "Uncropp'd" rose "On Tenglio's banks." After Cary's highly obvious line from Gray's "Elegy," her less obvious allusion to Thomson's "Winter" is a bit of a tease. But however amused Mrs. Darwall was by the schoolboy's pretentiousness, she treated him gently, and she included this pair of poems in her second book.

Other poets engaged her attention as well during these difficult years. In 1786, Robert Burns published his poems for the first time, and Helen Maria Williams, with two long single

"Fond Hearts . . . Ebbing Life" (1777-1789)

works already in print, brought out a collection that reprinted the long works and added some hymns and other poems. Mary Darwall's admiration of these two poets is revealing. First, though this is highly conjectural, her political attitudes could be involved. She thrilled to the "strains ecstatic" of Burns and praised his country as the homeland of "The sons of freedom." Her praise of "beauteous HELEN's sweet-ton'd lyre [which] / Breathes harmony in every gale" is less specific, but Helen Maria Williams's poems do express a notably liberal point of view: "An American Tale" is friendly to the revolutionaries and "An Epistle to Dr. Moore" lauds Swiss freedom. Indeed, Miss Williams later became an active supporter of the French Revolution, to the outrage of the British press. Mrs. Darwall never went that far, but her poem linking Burns and the beauteous Helen with the idea of freedom does suggest that her political stance, never openly stated, could have been less conservative than her husband's.

Other elements in Helen Maria Williams's poems would certainly have appealed to her. The Christian morality, the occasional pastoral setting, and the taste for the gothic resemble her own. Miss Williams's confidence in the quality of women's writing would have pleased Mrs. Darwall too. Even more suggestive about Mary Darwall's own character is Miss Williams's sometimes extreme sensibility. Many tears, both bitter and delicious, stain her pages; star-crossed lovers and alienated fathers and daughters do a great deal of swooning and dying on each other's bosoms in "Edwin and Eltruda" and elsewhere. One poem is even addressed "To Sensibility" and, after a lengthy characterization of that source of all bliss and all anguish, attacks Mrs. Greville for her rejection of emotion in her "Prayer for Indifference." From the Dedication at the beginning to the sonnet on the last page, Miss Williams's feeling heart is on display. Mary Darwall, belonging to an older generation, was less forthright in expressing her feelings, especially in her first book. But I have said that I believe she was a woman of strong passions, however decorously veiled they were; her admiration

"Fond Hearts ... Ebbing Life" (1777-1789)

for Helen Maria Williams with all her "sensibility" is another reason for my belief.

The poem in which Mary Darwall mentions Burns and Helen Maria Williams centers on Scotland, Burns's permanent and Miss Williams's temporary home. Someone had shown Mrs. Darwall a picture of a Scottish river which, together with her reading of these two interesting poets, resulted in "Lines, occasioned by seeing a beautiful print of the River Clyde." The picture included "mould'ring gothic tow'rs" as well as "rocky chasms," a rural lass doing her laundry, and the spires of Glasgow. Musing over the scene on the relatively uninteresting banks of the Tame—another name for Walsall Water and a descriptive one at that—the poet falls asleep and dreams of a beautiful naiad rising from the stream, a naiad who brings the depressing message that she, an inferior poet and hence unworthy, will never see the land of Burns and the beauteous Helen. The naiad commands,

>   "Content, amid thy native plains,
>   "Breathe to the woods thy rural strains."
>   I started, rose, and sighing cry'd,
>   Adieu, vain wish! adieu, sweet CLYDE!

The wilder glories of Scotland and the idea of its freedom might have attracted her at this time of John Darwall's illness even more than usual because they suggested escape from the increasingly oppressive cares of home.

Perhaps her sense of inferiority as a poet was eased by a tribute in the *Gentleman's Magazine* for August 1788. W. Hamilton Reed had been reading Miss Whateley's poems. He knew she was now Mrs. Darwall of Walsall, so he mentioned "the Cyclops din" of that manufacturing town, but his main emphasis is on the "flow'ry plains" where the "young adventurer" was something of a pioneer among women (apparently he had not read Duncombe's *Feminead*). It was bold, he says,

"Fond Hearts . . . Ebbing Life" (1777-1789)

> When female pow'rs were here unknown,
> To tempt the Critics wreckful strand,
> Almost defenceless and alone;
> When scarce a precedent the day could spare,
> T'assert her claim or legalize the fair.

Now, twenty-four years later, more women are writing—Reed mentions Mrs. Barbauld—but Miss Whateley merits special praise, and Langhorne showed the "finest taste" in weaving a garland for her brow. Reed's verse is undistinguished, to say the least, but his sentiments would have been welcome. And Richard Graves remembered "Miss Wheatly" when he wrote his *Recollection* of Shenstone (1788) and listed some of the poets his old friend had taken pleasure in assisting. But not everyone noticed her. When Anna Seward drew up a list of worthy female poets for the *Gentleman's Magazine* the next April, Mrs. Darwall was not included. Could there have been jealousy over Cary's divided attentions? Miss Seward did not suffer rivals gladly.

In the fall of 1788, John Darwall's health seemed for a while to take a turn for the better. The girls had been sent away to visit friends, leaving only Charles Henry at home. The relatively quiet household, which probably contributed to Mr. Darwall's improvement, was almost, but not quite, dull. On a mild, sunny afternoon—it was Halloween—Mrs. Darwall walked out into the vicarage garden where, missing her lively girls, she wrote them a verse letter describing the beauties of the season and regretting that no Harriet sits in "the osier shade" and no Eliza in the "little close sequester'd Bower." She longs for their cheerful "chat" and "artless strains," their "kind concern / [which] Consol'd [her] cares." She also misses the "animating bustle" of her Leicester, who liked to call her "old Dame."

> But 'midst these losses new delights are mine;
> How blest, supremely blest, am I to see
> In my dear Husband's eyes new Spirits shine,
> And renovated health and youthful glee!

"Fond Hearts . . . Ebbing Life" (1777-1789)

John is well enough to make music on his "accordant Lyre" while Charles Henry, "with rapid touch . . . / Unites his notes" (violin and pianoforte?)—an attractive picture of a musical family with Mary as the "raptur'd" audience. She concludes with thanks to "bounteous Providence" for these comforts.

Indeed, she was so comforted by John's improvement that her high spirits and sense of humor bubbled up irrepressibly in another verse letter to her daughters (see Appendix). This one consists of thirty doggerel couplets on the superiority of females to males in maintaining friendships, a "whimsical" epistle as she says, though as always, on the subject of friendship, bearing a core of seriousness. She never published these two verse letters. Perhaps the comic lines of the second one indicate a greater playfulness and sense of fun than she chose to reveal to the public, while the other letter may have been too personal for print. One can only wonder how many other poems like these two have vanished.

But soon her high spirits sank as the clouds returned: John's health declined once more. Clouds gathered on the national scene at the same time. In the winter of 1788-89, King George III's oddities became a serious mental disturbance, and his government and his heir wrangled over the question of a regency. But this time he recovered, and on March 12, 1789, Walsall celebrated with public dinners, a glowing speech, "illuminations," and other symbols of joy. The Darwalls, who loved their British Brunswick, no doubt joined in if they were able, happy that their king was well again even though John Darwall was not.

Increasingly dependent on his curate and his oldest son, Mr. Darwall was carrying on as best he could. Lord Mountrath, aware that his vicar was dying, sent a letter in August 1789 thanking him for his years of faithful service—and probably began to think of the question of his successor. By this time, just after the French rebels had stormed the Bastille, Mr. Darwall was almost unable to work—he performed his last

"Fond Hearts . . . Ebbing Life" (1777-1789)

marriage in that month and called banns for the last time in September. Then his name disappears from the parish register. He must have taken to his bed, and after three more months of affliction, at midday on December 18, a few days before his fifty-ninth birthday, he died. The hymn writer who had run vigorously up and down his church steps, the Rasselas who had freed Miss Whateley from the pastoral valley, was gone.

The widow dressed in black. She organized the cold meats and the cakes and wine. And on the day before Christmas, to the ringing of bells, parishioners and other friends came to pay their respects and to accompany their vicar to his grave. The life of the woman and the poet—she was just short of fifty-two years old—was profoundly changed.

Part III

WIDOW

1789-1825

Chapter 9

"The Cares of the World" (1789-1793)

> And here do see what creatures widows are in weeping for their husbands, and then presently leaving off; But I cannot wonder at it, the cares of the world taking place of all other passions.
>
> Pepys, *Diary*, October 17, 1667

As soon as the funeral was over, the grieving widow had to cope with two practical, and major, problems: how and where to live. The family's income had ceased abruptly: the bishop's office in Lichfield had sequestered her husband's salary the day after he died. And the next vicar would soon be wanting the house.

Money was the more urgent of the two problems. Besides the sequestered salary, all incidental fees, such as the odd shillings and pence paid for marrying and burying, would now go into the pockets of Mr. Rutter, the curate, who would be carrying on with the daily business of the church while the vicar's chair was empty. Mrs. Darwall had little if any cash on hand: her husband had never been prudent about money and had indeed borrowed ten guineas in the autumn from Mr. Hodgkins, the town clerk and local agent of the lord of the manor. Mr. Hodgkins despaired of ever seeing his ten guineas again, because, as he understood the situation, the Darwalls were "a large distress'd Family" and nothing had been left for their support. There wasn't even enough for a gravestone for Mr. Darwall—at least no record of a stone survives. Fortunate-

"The Cares of the World" (1789-1793)

ly, though the family was large, arrangements had been made for all the Darwall sons. But Mrs. Darwall had two daughters as well as herself to maintain, and would have been concerned about further provision for her younger sons who were just starting out. Some relief appeared in the form of a gift from young John. He made over to his stepmother the income from his grandfather's Cheshire property, which had come to him when his father died. The sum was small—forty-one pounds a year—but this mark of care and affection, as if from an "own son," made a large difference in Mrs. Darwall's finances. For the time being, she could manage.

The problem of where to live was less urgent, because custom allowed a vicar's widow to remain in the vicarage while the next vicar was being chosen, a process that usually took some months, and for another month after his formal induction. And if young John were to become the next vicar, a not uncommon form of inheritance, this problem would be solved, for he was unmarried and would need a woman to run his home. Who could be more eligible than his stepmother? But by now, Mrs. Darwall was fairly sure young John would not get the living. Indeed, it looked very much as if the next vicar would be the present curate, Mr. Rutter. And thereby hangs a tale, preserved in packets of letters among the papers of the lord of the manor of Walsall, the Earl of Mountrath, who had the living in his gift. Mrs. Darwall could not have known the whole story until later, if indeed she ever learned all the details. Her own letters show, however, that she was putting two and two together very shrewdly as events unfolded. But I will tell the story as it happened, as it can be pieced together from the surviving letters, rather than from her point of view. It is a vivid example of the struggle for survival that seethed beneath the genteel surface of eighteenth-century clerical life.

John Darwall breathed his last at "about one at noon" on December 18, 1789. He had foreseen the destiny of the vicarage, knowing his son's diffidence and Mr. Rutter's eagerness to have the position. That eagerness was understandable—Mr.

"The Cares of the World" (1789-1793)

Rutter, not a young man, was trying to support a wife and eight children on a curate's meager salary. Like Trollope's Mr. Quiverful, he seemed fated to father a baby nearly every year, nearly all of whom lived—and needed food and clothes. Yet while Mr. Rutter's desire for the vicar's position was understandable, his tactics, initiated even before Mr. Darwall's health began to decline, were distressingly crude. He made himself popular in Walsall, getting himself appointed to the governing body, the Corporation, which could be accomplished only by the influence of friends, and accepting the position of mayor for a year (1784-85). Later, as he sought security, he applied for the living at a neighboring town, Willenhall, which he failed to get, but he carefully saved the letter of recommendation written for that occasion by the sympathetic John Darwall. Apparently the letter was undated and bore a neutral heading, simply "My Lord," because that same letter was later represented as a recommendation addressed to Lord Mountrath, the patron of the Walsall living—signed, of course, by the incumbent, John Darwall.

Mr. Rutter had also prepared or had prepared for him a petition supporting his candidacy for the living; the petition, which exists among Lord Mountrath's papers, is full of the usual platitudinous testimonials to Mr. Rutter's character, and while it mentions John Darwall's death, it bears no date. The Walsall citizens who were asked to sign the petition noted that it was rather battered and old, but only one or two hesitated to sign for that reason, for Mr. Rutter was a popular man and the story had somehow gotten around that the equally popular young John Darwall was not going to apply. Mr. Rutter had got his foot in the door with questionable ethics but considerable force.

When John Darwall's eyes were closed at midday, Mr. Rutter went immediately to call on Lord Mountrath's agent, Mr. Hodgkins, to beg his assistance in getting the living. Mr. Hodgkins, ever cautious but knowing a winner when he saw one, agreed to help. Together, they travelled to London—presumably riding at a gallop most or all of the winter night or

"The Cares of the World" (1789-1793)

catching the fastest fly from Birmingham, for they arrived on the night of the nineteenth, making the journey from Walsall, roughly 120 miles, in about thirty hours. The purpose of the trip was to enlist the aid of Mr. Bradfield, Lord Mountrath's chief agent, a man of great power and influence in the affairs of the lord, the lord being something of a recluse. But Mr. Bradfield, who circulated among his lordship's estates in Ireland and England, was not in London. Mr. Hodgkins dithered, unwilling to disturb the mighty Bradfield with a letter and not quite sure where that gentleman was. One can picture Mr. Rutter fuming in the parlor of their hostelry, the Bell Inn, Cheapside, throughout the wasted Sunday. But on Monday Mr. Hodgkins took up his pen, and, in his small, finicky script, informed Mr. Bradfield of John Darwall's death and begged both his pardon for troubling him and his assistance for Mr. Rutter. He made a good case: Mr. Rutter was "respectable," had eight hungry children, and had "created a universal Friendship with the Inhabitants" of Walsall. To support his case, he enclosed not only the dubious letter of recommendation from John Darwall but also the undated petition signed by the worthies of Walsall. Either this petition had been signed and carried to London with remarkable speed, in a scant three days, or—what seems more likely—signatures had been collected while John Darwall was still alive. Even now, he was not yet in his grave.

Mr. Bradfield's reply was prompt. His lordship and Mrs. Preston, his lordship's housekeeper-cum-secretary, were distressed at the news of Mr. Darwall's death, and yes, Mr. Rutter could have the living—but only temporarily. It was, as Mr. Hodgkins already knew, promised to "a young Lad of Eleven . . . intended for the Church" when he was old enough. Meanwhile, Mr. Rutter could have it, provided that legal securities were obtained to make sure he would give it up when the time came. Mr. Bradfield outlined these arrangements, making it all appear quite simple and straightforward. What he did not mention, and perhaps did not know, was that the "young Lad,"

"The Cares of the World" (1789-1793)

Philip Pratt, was Mrs. Preston's nephew, which helps to explain Mrs. Preston's tenacity and self-interest in her dealings with the candidates for the Walsall living. (And the source of her power to control Lord Mountrath's affairs—her being the mother of his only child—was even less well known.)

No doubt Mr. Rutter was satisfied with the arrangement. He had ten or twelve years in the coveted vicarage to look forward to and anything could happen to a "young Lad" in the interim. Besides, he would then be about fifty-six years old and perhaps ready to retire. He dawdled happily in London for another two weeks, not returning to Walsall until January 4, when he visited the Widow Darwall with the news that he had Lord Mountrath's "full promise" of the living. He assured her that she was welcome to stay at the vicarage house until Midsummer. And there the matter rested for a while.

But news of the Rev. Mr. Darwall's death began to get about, and others noted the vacancy of a desirable living. One Mrs. Gaussen of Kent began to correspond with Mrs. Preston (at first under the assumption that she was the Countess of Mountrath), hoping to obtain the living for "a particular Friend." Mrs. Gaussen offered an unspecified "purchase price," assuming the living was for sale, an offer which she later promised would be "at least as much as any One Else." (It is interesting to note the approach of woman to woman on such "male" business: Mrs. Gaussen pretends that she takes the "freedom" of addressing Mrs. Preston because she does not know "how as a Female to address the Earl upon such a subject," a timidity transparently at odds with the generally commanding tone of her letters.) With this offer in hand, Mrs. Preston was in no hurry to have the impecunious Mr. Rutter confirmed in the position, whatever promise Lord Mountrath may have made, and for some time nothing was done. Mr. Rutter carried on with his duties, secure, as he thought, in Lord Mountrath's promise as relayed to him by his agents, Mr. Bradfield and Mr. Hodgkins. Quietly, he assumed the title of "minister" and began to write it

"The Cares of the World" (1789-1793)

after his name in the church records, and his signature, which had always been small and neat, grew larger and more assertive.

Not so quietly, a storm blew up over Mrs. Darwall's tenancy of the vicarage house. Except for the death in January of the little son of her friend, the bookseller and printer Frederick Milward, the winter after her husband's death had been uneventful. She was learning to live with the fact of widowhood, and no doubt worrying about money as she tried to plan for the future. She arranged to rent a house at Midsummer, when she expected to leave the vicarage, though Mr. Rutter's renovations, scheduled to begin near the end of March, might make her last months there uncomfortable. In the midst of all these plans, she was surprised and dismayed when, on March 15, Mr. Bradfield appeared on her doorstep with the news that Mr. Rutter wanted her to "remove" as soon as possible so that he and his family could move in. Mrs. Darwall let Mr. Bradfield know that she was surprised, and surprised that he should be the go-between bringing the demand, for she and Mr. Rutter had discussed the matter themselves and settled on Midsummer. But she agreed to go.

The next day both Mr. and Mrs. Rutter came to call, and Mrs. Darwall, "in the most obliging manner," let them know how hurt she was that they had sent Mr. Bradfield with their unwelcome demand. Mr. Rutter "look'd disconcerted," and not only denied asking Bradfield to deliver such a message but claimed that it was Bradfield's idea that the Rutters should move in at once to "keep people from doing trespass on the land." They discussed the matter further and concluded that nothing much could or should be done until Mr. Bradfield returned, in about six weeks, when moves and alterations might properly begin.

On the following day, March 17, Mrs. Darwall wrote to Lord Mountrath, dropping only a hint of her troubles over the vicarage house. She was ostensibly concerned instead to rectify what might have looked like a discourteous oversight. During his visit two days earlier, Mr. Bradfield had expressed surprise that she had not written to his lordship since her husband's

"The Cares of the World" (1789-1793)

death, and she hastened to explain her silence. Of course she had wanted to express her thankfulness for all his lordship's favors over the years, but "thought I might do that with more propriety when time had apply'd its lenient balm to my sorrows, than under the first impressions of grief." She prayed for his lordship's "health and happiness both Temporal and Eternal," and took the opportunity to explain why she had not written to ask for the living for young John. Both she and her husband were "fully convinced" that Mr. Rutter not only had Mr. Bradfield's support but that Mr. Bradfield had already recommended him to Lord Mountrath. And Mrs. Darwall did not want to be "despis'd as an unreasonable and obtrusive woman" for pestering his lordship on behalf of her stepson when the living was already promised. Then, almost by way of parenthesis, she concludes: "It is Mr. Bradfields advice that Mr. Rutter shou'd come into the vicarage house as soon as possible. I suppose I shall leave it in about a fortnight, but wherever I go I shall always retain the truest sense of your Lordships goodness. . . ." She has a home no longer, she might have to sleep in a haystack—genuine though her distress was, the pathos of the letter is nicely calculated.

Over the next few days, Mrs. Darwall must have been both waiting for an answer to her hint (which apparently never came) and pondering the demand—whether Bradfield's or Rutter's—that she leave the vicarage, for on March 30 she decided to approach the real source of authority and wrote a detailed letter to Mrs. Preston. She describes, briefly, her poverty and young John's generosity with his inheritance and, at greater length, the visits of Mr. Bradfield and the Rutters about the vicarage house. Then she describes her growing sense that there is something of "doubtfull . . . propriety" about the demand that she "remove" —she smelled a rat. For one thing, there is nothing on the land that trespassers could damage and hence no need to have the Rutters there to guard it. She reports that Mr. Rutter has been going about saying " 'he'll get possession, and then nobody shall root him out.' Who good Madam cou'd attempt it if he has

"The Cares of the World" (1789-1793)

indeed a promise from my Lord?" Is Mr. Rutter trying to strengthen a shaky claim to the living by establishing squatter's rights in the vicarage house? Mrs. Rutter too has been boasting to her friends that her husband could turn Mrs. Darwall out any day he likes, which causes Mrs. Darwall such distress that she writes with uncharacteristically bitter irony of Mrs. Rutter's "humanity and politeness." Furthermore, Mr. Rutter is acting as if he already owns the vicarage—exchanging plots of the glebe land, filling in ponds, cutting down trees—which would be all right if he is really going to be the next vicar, but as it is, his behavior is "misterious." One further mystery is Mr. Bradfield's insistence that he and Lord Mountrath did not know of Mr. Darwall's death until three weeks after it happened, while Mr. Rutter had announced to her his success in getting the living just two weeks and three days after that melancholy event. It doesn't add up. Mrs. Darwall refrains from calling anybody a liar and claims that "these incoherent circumstances ... perplix" her, "a poor weak woman struggling under accumulated griefs and distresses." She puts herself in Mrs. Preston's hands with apologies for the length of her letter.

The letter had the desired effect. Mrs. Preston took action, beginning by inquiring into Mr. Rutter's mysterious activities. Both Mr. Rutter and Mr. Hodgkins replied, the latter waspishly, the former humbly but defensively. Both, using various euphemisms, said Mrs. Darwall was the liar. No lands had changed hands; only one tree had been cut down; rather than destroying a pond, Mr. Rutter had drained a swampy pasture and made it usable. Furthermore, Mr. Hodgkins explained, Mr. Rutter had "Manured some part of the Land (which our late worthy Vicar never did during the whole time he occupied the Vicarage). . . ." The Darwalls had neglected more than the land, Mr. Hodgkins claimed; the vicarage, which was "all in ruins[,] . . . is now in such a Condition as to be dangerous to live in and great part must be taken down and rebuilt[. T]he late Vicar and his wife were always writing poetry or some other matter for the press instead of minding the necessary concerns of the Vicarage and

"The Cares of the World" (1789-1793)

their Family which I am afraid brought him to the poverty in which he died." Mr. Hodgkins, a legal gentleman with tidy handwriting and no doubt tidy account books, had nothing but scorn for the comparatively untidy, creative life of the Darwall household.

These contradictory versions of what was going on in Walsall must have puzzled Mrs. Preston, but her sympathies lay with the Widow Darwall—and with her self-interest. Her reply to Mrs. Darwall has not survived, but it was kind enough to make the widow's heart "glow." Canny Mrs. Preston asked for more information and on April 14 she got it: a detailed description of the ages and occupations of all the Darwall children (with emphasis on John) and a description of the Rutter family as well; a diplomatic but clear account of the misused letter of recommendation and the battered old petition; and a long argument proving, but not stating, that Mr. Bradfield had lied when he apparently told Mrs. Preston that he was unaware of any suitable young Darwall being available to take over the vicarage. Perhaps Mrs. Darwall's "glow" was enhanced by news that Mrs. Preston was holding up the appointment of Mr. Rutter, which would have made it possible for young John to apply, or perhaps Mrs. Preston made her decision to do so on the basis of Mrs. Darwall's information about the letter and the petition. In any event, make it she did. The next letter in the packet, dated April 29 and written by Mr. Hodgkins, describes "the most miserable State" of Mr. Rutter and "his whole Family"; all are "in Tears" because Mrs. Preston has perceived irregularities in the legal documents that should bind Mr. Rutter to give up the living when the "young Lad" is of age, and—the worst blow of all—Mrs. Preston now demands one thousand pounds for the living, which Mr. Rutter cannot hope to raise. With Mrs. Gaussen's offer to purchase in one hand and Mrs. Darwall's damaging information in the other, Mrs. Preston was firmly in control.

A spate of letters follows: impatient (from Mrs. Gaussen); wounded, despairing, defensive, grovelling (from Mr. Rutter);

"The Cares of the World" (1789-1793)

practical and unbending (from Mrs. Preston); busy with legal and financial details (from Mr. Hodgkins). Mr. Hodgkins is also terrified that he might have offended Mrs. Preston, he is overflowing with pity for the unhappy Rutters—and he is hardheaded enough to recommend Mr. Rutter over an unnamed younger man of thirty (John Darwall's age) because Mr. Rutter, being older, won't live as long. He even bets, "Ten to one," that Mr. Rutter will die before the "young Lad" comes of age. Accusations and counter-accusations—veiled and direct—alternate with apologies and financial bargaining. Did Lord Mountrath finally step in and put an end to it all?

It was ended, by mid-June. Mr. Rutter got the living, after a group of loyal and substantial Walsall citizens contributed six hundred pounds for Mrs. Preston. Mrs. Gaussen would have given more, but the people of Walsall liked Mr. Rutter and perhaps there had been a promise after all. They liked young John Darwall too, but he had no money and had asked for no one's help. On June 14, the bishop's office in Lichfield lifted the sequestration on the vicar's salary—it was now officially Mr. Rutter's pay. Ten days later it was Midsummer, moving day for at least three families: new tenants going into the Rutters' house, a contract that had contributed to Mr. Rutter's despair while the living was in doubt; ten Rutters going into the supposedly ruined vicarage; and the Darwalls—the widow, Harriet and Elizabeth, and presumably Charles Henry, who had been living at home while working for his lawyer uncle—going to the house Mrs. Darwall had taken from that date.

If there was a house. John Darwall had died in debt: he owed Mr. Hodgkins ten guineas and, according to that gentleman, had owed "a deal more money . . . to many other persons." Mary Darwall had almost no visible sources of income. Perhaps she should have been charged "delapidations" for the vicarage (though she denied it was in bad repair), but even Mr. Hodgkins said it would be pointless to charge her because she could not have paid. Her poverty was common knowledge. Would anyone in Walsall, however respected the

"The Cares of the World" (1789-1793)

vicar's widow was, have rented her a house? Was her claim that she "took a house for midsummer" a polite fiction, a face-saving detail to present to Mrs. Preston—and a way to set a date and thus keep the vicarage house to live in rent-free for a full six months after John Darwall's death? If so, it succeeded.

There is no evidence, in her poems or anywhere else, to show where she went on Midsummer Day. Perhaps not to a rented house, as she had little or no money. Certainly not to her widowed sister, Martha Baylies, who was nearly seventy and lived with two spinster daughters and probably her sister Ann on the proceeds from her draper's shop. It would make sense to go to her brother Henry Whateley (and perhaps the lawyer did give his apprenticed nephew a home, or perhaps Charles Henry took lodgings for himself, since he would turn twenty-one the next October and come into his inheritance of 360 pounds). And I think that Mary had expectations, or at least hopes, that Henry would take care of her; brothers often did. If so, she was disappointed. One poem, a bitter, impassioned poem, survives to support this guess. Here, Mrs. Darwall seems to be using her writing as the only available outlet for profound feelings, as she did so often in her first book.

"Elegy"—it bears no further title—begins with nostalgia for the days of plenty and hope and the "museful dream . . . on fair Arrowe's banks," a scene far different from today's:

> Now time, and grief, and cank'ring care
> (A direful train) have press'd me sore;
> And, hovering round me, black despair
> Points to some cheerless dreary shore. . . .

Happiness is gone, fancy is gone, and she longs for oblivion and the death of memory. But even in the depths, heaven can give peace, and she can be content with little:

> The clean, the homely russet stole
> Can shield me from the chilling blast;

"The Cares of the World" (1789-1793)

> The clay-form'd dish, or beechen bowl
>   Can hold my wholesome plain repast.

> What tho' the humble, thatch-roof'd cot,
>   Near some lone heath, conceal my woes;
> Be conscious rectitude my lot,
>   And sound will be my short repose.

She will earn her mite and be happy, unlike

> . . . many a gaudy child of pow'r,
> Who ne'er to misery gave a sigh,
>   Nor sought affliction's secret bow'r,

> Where the lorn widow's grief-rent breast,
>   To heav'n alone pours forth its woes,
> Where virtue droops, by wrongs oppress'd,
>   And anguish no cessation knows.

The generalities then give way to something just a little more particular: the "callous heart" of the rich man joys in gold, and "can behold without remorse / A hard-rack'd tenant's care-worn face," while he pampers his hunting dogs and horses. Amidst all his splendor, "the wretch" will suffer, however; his fine house and gardens will be dark and gloomy, domestic feuds and public strife will pursue him, and he will dread his "final hour." But the morally superior poor widow looks forward to hers:

> Be bread, content and peace my lot,
>   Till the last happy morn shall rise,
> That wafts me from my humble cot
>   To the blest regions of the skies.

Although Mrs. Darwall was not entirely without the spirit of satire, even her satirical poems have no such bitter, even vindictive tone. This one is unique. And although the description of the heartless villain is general, the generalities do fit Henry Whateley. He was doing very well indeed in his law practice and had only two children to support. He was a landlord whose

"The Cares of the World" (1789-1793)

tenants, possibly "hard-rack'd," paid him rent. He had built himself a fine country house in the still half-rural Walsall suburb of Birchills (or Birch Hills) near his coal mines; it would be possible to keep horses and hounds and a "bleating flock" in such a setting. (Mary's brother George lived in the center of Birmingham—he can't be the villain of the piece.) And there may be a specific stab at Henry's profession in these lines:

> Tho' no black-letter'd page of law
> To infamy the wretch consigns,
> Yet conscience strikes with trembling awe,
> And the sick soul 'mid splendor pines.

True, Henry had no legal obligation to his sister, even though she had worked as his housekeeper for some years, but it looks as if she had expected something, possibly a great deal, and been sorely disappointed. And yet his will, dated 1799, leaves her an annuity of twenty-one pounds a year and forgives her debts. Perhaps he had seen the error of his ways, or perhaps he had always been helpful. But I can think of no explanation for this unique poem, which seems to be autobiographical, other than the one I give here.

I would guess that after some time in limbo, or with a possibly grudging brother Henry, Mary Darwall and her girls, leaving Charles Henry in Walsall, went to Birmingham to live with young John; widows usually did move in with one of their children.

John's circumstances were improving, and he could have taken her in. By now he been appointed to the curacy of St. John's chapel in Deritend, a suburb of Birmingham, retaining his connection with St. Bartholomew's and his assistant mastership at the grammar school. Then in April 1791, the old minister of Deritend died and the congregation elected young John Darwall in his place. He was still far from well off—Deritend was a crowded, run-down old suburb, and the chapel was in such bad repair that most of the income from the attached estate, about

"The Cares of the World" (1789-1793)

eighty pounds a year, had to go to fix it up, as John was severely warned in the agreement he signed on his election. But the Deritend people promised him at least a curate's salary until the repairs were finished, and the position did include the perquisite of a large house. There was ample room for his stepmother and half sisters, he had no wife as yet, and he could use a woman's help. Besides, he had always been close to Mary. With their combined income, and family love, they would manage. Indeed, John was not penniless: determined to make up for his missing university education, he had managed to pay his first fees at Oxford and to matriculate, at the age of twenty-nine, at Magdalen Hall in March 1790, just a few months after his father's death. He was going to get those letters after his name despite the delay.

If Mrs. Darwall joined John in the minister's house in the spring of 1791—and this is still a conjecture—she would have found both advantages and disadvantages in her new urban environment. Instead of fields and gardens, trees and ponds, well above Walsall's industrial murk, she would now have been only a step away from a partially stagnant waterway, the River Rea, which was rapidly turning into a sewer and starting to breed cholera and typhus. There were still gardens leading down to the river, but no piped water (which Walsall had had for over a century) and no main drainage for the houses in the neighborhood. Workshops and barns competed with the gardens for space, and second-story dormer windows peered at each other across the narrow streets. The minister's house was next to the chapel, where the workmen hammered away at the repairs, and next to a noisy school. It was not a pretty scene.

But there was a new bridge over the Rea leading to Birmingham itself, and there Mary Darwall would have found resources to cheer her heart. There were family and friends: stepson Randle, brother George and his brood, an assortment of other Whateleys; in the suburbs were the Bordesley Hall people and other friends. And there were all the institutions that Walsall lacked: a new hospital, public libraries, regular music

"The Cares of the World" (1789-1793)

festivals (John served on the committee one year) and other concerts, and above all a real theater with a regular acting company resident in the summer season.

In 1774, Birmingham's new Theatre Royal had been opened and had competed successfully with an existing playhouse (which, oddly enough, eventually became a Methodist chapel). Embellished with a fine stone portico and boasting a handsome interior, the theater had presented some great names recently—the Kembles, Mrs. Siddons, Mr. and Mrs. Nunns—and in the 1790s that tradition of quality continued. If she was living in Deritend, Mary Darwall could have gone to a wide range of plays. (Even though the Theatre Royal burned in January 1792, the company continued to play elsewhere while it was being rebuilt.) Shakespeare, usually in drastically revised versions, was the mainstay of the repertoire, with Sheridan, Otway, Dryden, and Cibber also appearing regularly. Rowe's *Jane Shore*, always among the most popular, was mounted by particular request in 1792, and Kean himself appeared that year in a "Grand Pantomime" based on Matthew Lewis's *The Monk*. Among the other stars of the Birmingham theater was John Fawcett, Jr., who played there in July of 1790 and 1791 before launching himself on a London career. He and his parents subscribed to Mrs. Darwall's second book; it is possible that she had met him during his visits to Birmingham.

And she renewed her connection with Mrs. Nunns, who had spent some time in the Birmingham theater in the early 1780s after leaving the Walsall circuit. Now she and her husband were acting off and on at Bath, at Richmond, and on the York circuit, and had been invited to Edinburgh for the January-June season of 1793. Part of Mrs. Nunns's charm for the Edinburgh audience must have been due to the "Address" she delivered on her first appearance, written for the occasion by her old admirer, and Scotland's admirer, Mary Darwall. In her address, the actress says she hopes to please in Edinburgh, "Where judgment reigns,—where elegance and ease / Preside in ev'ry mind." Success in this theater would give her great pride, and

"The Cares of the World" (1789-1793)

if the "sweet romantic clime" of Caledonia and the muse of Robert Burns can be persuaded to inspire her, "Then shou'd I fearless meet the critic's eye, / Secure, like him, of fame and immortality." Suitably flattered, Edinburgh renewed the Nunnses' engagement for the next two seasons.

Although she was probably living in Birmingham, Mrs. Darwall kept up her links with Walsall and its occasional theater. Plans were afoot for a special benefit performance there in which young Miss Harriet Mellon was to appear. Mrs. Darwall had written an address for her to deliver at her own benefit some time earlier, probably in the 1790 season when she joined Stanton's company. That address thanks the "gen'rous fair" in the audience, recommends "health and peace" as the best cosmetics, and prays that commerce and "genuine liberty" will replace the "factious tumult" troubling Albion. Now, as the 1790s unfolded, more troubles shook England, and as the Reign of Terror swept through France, England prepared for the war that was declared on February 1, 1793. Walsall's preparations included a theatrical benefit for the expected victims; Mrs. Darwall's contribution was an "Epilogue, spoken by Miss Mellon, in the character of a British soldier's wife, after a play performed at Walsall, for the benefit of the Widows and Orphans of the soldiers and sailors who should die or be killed during the war. 1793." These verses deplore the "anarchy and dire confusion" of France and rejoice in England's superior state:

> Happy this isle! where genuine freedom reigns;
> Where genuine patriots scorn mock freedom's chains;
> Whose dauntless sons ne'er fear to meet a foe,
> Yet have a tear for ev'ry tale of woe:
> Who glow with ardor for their country's weal,
> But shrink with horror at the murd'rer's steel:
> Who'd sooner die than rear th'assassin's knife
> Against a bishop's, king's or woman's life.

"The Cares of the World" (1789-1793)

Miss Mellon, in the role of the wife of one of these dauntless heroes, recalls his parting speech and dreads the poverty of potential widowhood—but the generosity of the audience will relieve her and preserve "the wretched widow from despair."

The plight of impoverished widows was close to Mary Darwall's heart, as were the feelings of a soldier's family. Two of her own sons were serving in the Staffordshire militia when it was called up on the fateful first of February. Frederick, with four years of training behind him, signed on in January as a surgeon's mate with the rank of ensign. Leicester, Mary's oldest, was also an ensign and was later promoted to lieutenant. His career had been checkered: he had broken off his apprenticeship with the stained-glass maker for reasons of health, his mother says (though perhaps he discovered that he had no artistic talent), and had turned to clerking in a china factory, probably Dr. Wall's works in Worcester. Now the brothers were together, and, fortunately for their mother's peace of mind when the long casualty lists began to come in, in no danger of falling on "th'ensanguin'd plain" she had visualized, because the militia did not go abroad to war. The Staffordshire unit spent the 1790s moving about in England, ending up with a tour of ceremonial duty at Windsor Castle from 1798 to 1802. By then, Frederick had transferred to more dangerous duty in the 65th Foot, but Leicester was part of the corps that paraded on the king's birthday, supplied guards of honor as required, and even took part in amateur theatricals for His Majesty's amusement. George III loved his Staffordshire men dearly, and Mrs. Darwall must have been proud to have her firstborn so close to the British Brunswick's person.

Not all domestic military activity was simply ceremonial during these troubled days, however. The 1790s saw tumult at home as well as in France, such dangerous tumult that the military were called in. Just three months after John was elected minister of Deritend, the whole neighborhood was rocked by the disturbance that came to be called the Priestley riots, one manifestation of the widening gulf between conser-

"The Cares of the World" (1789-1793)

vative and radical thought in the late eighteenth century. It was the custom of a group of Birmingham men to gather for dinner on July 14, Bastille Day, to affirm their radical political faith. Joseph Priestley, chemist and Unitarian divine, intelligently absented himself from the 1791 gathering and even tried to have it cancelled because tensions were running high: during the previous winter, Richard Price's *Discourse on the Love of Our Country* had come under fierce attack by Edmund Burke in *Reflections on the Revolution in France*, which was promptly "answered" by Mary Wollstonecraft's *Vindication of the Rights of Men*; the battle raged afresh the following summer as defenders of church and king clashed with the government's critics in the public press.

But the Bastille Day dinner was scheduled and advertised, the participants gathered, and a crowd outside the hotel began smashing windows. As the evening went on, the crowd grew, and grew out of control. There were too many for the small force of constables to deal with, and the constables probably did not want to defend the radicals anyway. Soon, tiring of the hotel, the mob attacked and burned Priestley's chapel, and then devastated his house, gardens, and laboratory. The riot went on for three more days, as the houses of prominent Unitarians, other Dissenters, and even their friends were destroyed, including, on July 15, Taylor's Bordesley Hall that Mary Darwall had celebrated in her first book. This house was only about a mile away from John's establishment in Deritend. Then, on July 17, the military finally arrived and gradually restored order in the city. It was a profoundly disturbing event.

Birmingham's economy suffered as a result of the riots and rates went up to pay for damages. Food prices were rising too, and food even grew scarce at times. Trade slumped, and the music festival was cancelled in 1793. Back in Walsall, things were not much better. Trade was seriously affected by a change in fashion: shoe-buckles were going out of style and shoelaces coming in, with disastrous results for Walsall's metalworkers. They took a petition to London in 1792 begging the Prince of

"The Cares of the World" (1789-1793)

Wales to go back to wearing buckles and got Richard Brinsley Sheridan to introduce their deputation to the royal fashion-setter himself. The Prince graciously complied, decreeing that his courtiers would wear buckles henceforth, and Walsall was saved, but only temporarily. The Prince eventually tired of buckles and Walsall lost a significant part of its trade.

It was probably during these hard times that John Darwall began taking schoolboys into his house as boarders, not an uncommon way for schoolmasters to make a little more money. He needed more, because he was about to get married. During his first years in Birmingham, John had lived almost next door to Mary's brother George Whateley, the toymaker, who had five children, the youngest of whom was his only daughter, Mary. John had been a neighbor, then, all through her teens. She was nearly twenty-two when they married on January 17, 1793—another Mary Whateley/John Darwall union. He was thirty-two.

At first, all went well. With a new wife, and probably a stepmother and half sisters in residence too, John Darwall could take good care of his boarders. But soon news got about that these were not the usual boys to be found in masters' houses. Instead of boys studying at the King Edward VI School where he was employed, John Darwall had taken in others and was teaching them at home himself in his spare time. But how much time did a clergyman-schoolmaster have to spare? Complaints, in the form of anonymous letters, began to reach the governors of the school, who took note of them at their meeting on April 3. The citizens were disgruntled because their sons at the school were being cheated of their due education, and the responsive governors issued a resolution at their meeting that no assistant master should be permitted to take boarders. Governor John Whateley had removed himself from the controversy, no doubt embarrassed by his connection with the culprit; his signature does not appear under this resolution, nor does he witness the board's minutes of May 17 when John Darwall's resignation from the school was accepted, four months to the day after his wedding. The school records are silent on

"The Cares of the World" (1789-1793)

the events of the intervening six weeks, but clearly John had become persona non grata, and the pressure to resign was too great to be resisted. As soon as he went, the governors raised the salary for his position from sixty to one hundred pounds, acknowledging—too late—that it had been inadequate.

It was probably at this time, in the spring of 1793, that Mary Darwall took her two daughters and fled to Newtown, Wales. With John's income drastically reduced and a new wife added to his expenses, a stepmother and sisters would have been an impossible burden. (Even if they were not living with him, he would certainly now be unable to give them any financial assistance.) And the painful break with the school was an embarrassment for a former Whateley with a relative on the board. Whenever Mrs. Darwall left the Midlands, she was definitely living in Wales in July 1794, and must have been there long enough before that date to soak up the local atmosphere seen in two poems and establish connections with the Welsh subscribers to her book. So I guess at the spring or summer of 1793 for her move.

But why Wales? Because her interest in things Celtic, romantic, sublime, was not limited to Scotland. In a late poem she quotes with approval a line from Gray's Pindaric ode about Wales, "The Bard" (1757); she knew and liked this dramatic description of slaughtered kings and poets with its glowing tribute to Queen Elizabeth (always a favorite of hers) and its setting of the foaming rivers and craggy peaks of Snowdon. On the practical side, she must have chosen Wales because one could live there for a fraction of what it cost in England, which in the 1790s was becoming increasingly expensive. Money was very short. Harriet had inherited her 360 pounds in December 1791, but that was probably put aside for a marriage portion, and Mrs. Darwall apparently had only the yearly forty-one pounds from Randle's properties, supplemented by occasional gifts and loans—and in the 1790s even seventy-five pounds a year was a skimpy income. Mrs. Darwall's few pounds would go much farther in Wales. Newtown was particularly attractive: it

"The Cares of the World" (1789-1793)

was close to the border of England, it was still small and clean and pretty despite its growing flannel factories, and it contained friends—the thrifty Fords of Hockley Abbey retired there to be with their son, selling or leasing their peculiar slag house and exchanging the industrial murk of Birmingham for the fresh air of the pleasantly rural town. And the subscribers' lists for Mary Darwall's books suggest other possible connections with the neighborhood of Newtown as well. It was to be her home for about ten years.

Chapter 10

Poems on Several Occasions
By Mrs. Darwall
(Formerly Miss Whateley)
In Two Volumes
1794

> Erst, unarraign'd, tyrannic man confin'd
> In chains of ignorance the female mind.
> Jealous of glory, for himself alone
> The torch of science and of learning shone. . . .
> Till LIB'RAL THOUGHT chas'd error's mists away,
> And call'd those bright perfections into day.
>
> Luke Booker

Mrs. Darwall took her papers with her when she and her daughters moved to Wales, and there, after the fuss of settling in and with money still an ever-present concern, she decided to collect her poems into a book. This time she had little help: Shenstone, Langhorne, Randle and John Darwall, and Dr. Wall, all of whom had done so much to make her 1764 book a reality and a success, had all died. Her own earlier fame had faded. But she still had, or renewed, some connections with the literary and clerical worlds. No patron was found for the collection, but the Rev. Luke Booker, chaplain at Dudley near Walsall, contributed an introductory poem, the source of the epigraph for this chapter. He seems to have signed up some of the other clerical subscribers as well. Mr. Booker was an old friend, having published his own first book of poems in Wolverhampton,

Poems on Several Occasions (1794)

where he had his first clerical position, in 1785; the poetical clergyman five miles from Walsall was acquainted with the Darwalls and had preached a charity sermon for John, a kind of oration for which Booker later became famous.

Besides clerical subscribers, there were again many Oxonians, possibly recruited by Dr. Wall's son, who was practicing medicine in Oxford. There were a few noble names, a few Londoners, and a sprinkling of neighbors in Wales. The most generous of these was the Rev. Mr. Parry of Bettws, a comfortably well-off man, who agreed to take twenty books. Friends and family in Walsall subscribed, including Mary's brother Henry and his son and her aged sister Martha Baylies. Their sister Ann is not on the list—she had died in 1793—but Martha's married daughter and other Davenports chipped in. Mary's oldest brother, John, took four books, while Henry signed up for two. Brother George was probably too ill to think about it—he died the next January. There were no Darwalls on the list—money was short—but Mr. Rutter, probably making more from the Walsall vicarage than John had ever done, ordered one of the cheaper copies. In all, 359 people subscribed—not quite half as many as for the first book when Mary had had much active help, but enough.

Newtown was too small to keep a printer in business, so Mary Darwall turned to her old friend Frederick Milward in Walsall, the bookseller who had probably bought John's press. Sending a manuscript home to such a press would have stirred up a strange mixture of feelings. Milward was reasonably good at his job; he designed attractive pages and used a variety of little decorative motifs—assorted urns, a tree, a flower, a birdbath with two birds—but he was hopeless at proofreading. The book is marred by many typographical errors. He had enough material to make up two volumes, which he arranged to have offered for sale by Lowndes, a London printer. But he neglected to arrange for advertising, so the sales, apart from subscriptions, were probably small. Unsold copies would have been put to the

Poems on Several Occasions (1794)

usual uses; today the book is far scarcer than Miss Whateley's 1764 collection.

The two short notices bestowed on the book probably did little to help its sales. In July 1795, the *Critical Review* allotted it three dismissive sentences, saying curtly that "a list of subscribers prefixed to the book seems to preclude the severity of criticism." The *Monthly Review* did not get around to noticing it until September, and although the reviewer liked it, he had obviously not read it carefully. He sees in it only "the harmonious strains of a gentle muse," "the soft beauties of nature, and the tender sentiments of the heart." The poet has skill: "the poetical strings which accord with these [themes] she touches very agreeably," producing "uniform" pieces. This is untrue, but it is interesting to see the reviewer finding in a woman's poems exactly what he expected to find rather than what is really there. The stereotype of the acceptable woman poet that had shaped the thinking of her reviewers in 1764 was still alive thirty years later. Significantly, this reviewer chooses to quote as typical of the writer's talents one of the duller little pastorals. Despite the praise, he probably did not help sales much.

Yet money was clearly a motive for publishing. Lacking a patron, the book is dedicated "To her SUBSCRIBERS in general, and to those FRIENDS in particular, who have kindly interested themselves in her behalf," and the dedication is signed "their obliged, and grateful humble Servant." The general reader is informed in the Advertisement only that "Circumstances of no consequence" to him or her "induced the publication" of these "effusions"—an unusual stance; women writers often cited poverty as justification for publishing. But "interested" particular friends seem to have been assisting the widow with cash. Indeed, her brother Henry had loaned her money, knowing she could not repay him; in his will he forgave all her debts, as I mentioned earlier, without specifying how large or small they were.

Poems on Several Occasions (1794)

The Advertisement is more communicative about the contents than about the "circumstances" of the book. Whereas young Miss Whateley had been anxious to demonstrate both her modesty and her integrity in her introductory remarks, Mrs. Darwall comments succinctly that "The following pages were the effusions of a mind generally occupied in the domestic duties. When written, they were only the amusements of leisure, and were not intended to be obtruded on the public." The poems were written at intervals over thirty years and therefore contain "different subjects and sentiments." And that is just about all she has to say. The thirty years and her altered status had made a considerable difference in the poet's self-confidence, and perhaps there was now some difference in the public's willingness to accept women writers as well; so, though still modest, Mrs. Darwall felt no need to justify and explain herself at length as she had done before.

Mr. Booker's introductory poem bears witness to at least one man's opinion about women writers. "The Triumph of Liberal Sentiment" deplores the bad old days when "tyrannic man confin'd / In chains of ignorance the female mind." "Hapless woman" was kept in "dark Egyptian night" until "LIB'RAL THOUGHT" set her free and " 'Heav'n's last—best—gift' " was allowed to use her brain. If this "Bless'd revolution" had not taken place, the world would have lacked Madame Dacier's translations of the classics, Mrs. Montagu's defense of Shakespeare, Miss Seward's sublime genius—and Mrs. Darwall's "sweet strains." As the nightingale's song is dispersed and silenced by the zephyrs where there is no ear to hear it (Mr. Booker dodges the philosophical question here), woman's talents would have remained unknown. But these are "happier times," and Mrs. Darwall can expect her sweet strains to bring her "fame immortal." Somewhat less sanguine than Mr. Booker, Mrs. Darwall prays to "Bright Imagination" for help in the "Invocation" that follows his introduction.

I have mentioned, earlier in my story, not only the "Invocation" but also over half of the other pieces in these volumes, which, since occasional poems predominate, is not surprising. Those works that remain to be considered are two autobiographical poems, a few more occasional poems to which I have been unable to assign even conjectural dates, four more Scottish poems, a gothic song, a group of pastorals, and two ventures into new forms, drama and Ossianic prose.

Only rarely in this book does Mrs. Darwall use her art for autobiographical outpourings, as she often did earlier. The main example of such sometimes veiled confession here is the "Elegy" I have already discussed—assuming I am right about its application. A second, "Sonnet to Time," also expresses the sorrow of her bereavement and, like the "Elegy," deplores the painful persistence of memory.

> O Time! can e'er thy lenient hand assuage
>   The sorrows rankling in this aching breast?
>   Can'st thou e'er sooth these heart-felt pangs to rest?
> And with Lethean drop blot mem'ry's faithful page?
>
> For common griefs I know thou hast a charm,
>   And from the throbbing breast steal'st many a groan,
>   Utter'd beneath the moon's pale gleam alone;
> And many a wayward care thou canst disarm.
>
> But much I fear thy friendly pow'r will fail
>   To heal the wounds this tortur'd bosom feels;
>   For mem'ry ev'ry hour new cause reveals,
> Why woes incessant shou'd this breast assail:
>   Then how, O! how can this poor heart know peace,
>   Where sorrows with each added hour increase!

Here is none of the pious hope of comfort in heaven that marks the "Elegy." Perhaps this poem was written earlier in her widowhood, or perhaps the brief sonnet form encouraged concentration on a single emotion, which may be why the unhappy poet chose to use it. With all its restrictions, indeed because of its restrictions, the sonnet form has power. It was making a comeback in the later eighteenth century, partly thanks

Poems on Several Occasions (1794)

to Anna Seward's and Charlotte Smith's use of it. Miss Whateley had written no sonnets, but like other poets of the time, the older Mary Darwall and her daughters were finding the form increasingly attractive.

The other autobiographical poem in Mrs. Darwall's book provides some insight into her life in Newtown. "Written on walking in the Woods of Gregynog in Montgomeryshire, the seat of Arthur Blayney, Esq." is dated "1st July 1794" and concludes her second volume (see Appendix). The man whose estate is described here had clearly become a friend. Arthur Blayney, whose seat at Gregynog (about four miles from Newtown) is now part of the University of Wales, was a hospitable man of seventy-eight when this poem was written. He was a bachelor, but he liked female company and "was remarkably pleased with and pleasing to the ladies who visited him, and there were not a few." Mrs. Darwall would have enjoyed the company of Mr. Blayney's other guests, as well as approving his steady Anglicanism, large library, affable conversation, and unpretentious style of living. As a Beoley farm girl, too, she would have understood and appreciated his generosity to his tenants and his attempts to improve agricultural methods on his estate. When he died in October 1795, she lost a respected and congenial friend.

The poem not only praises the beauty of Gregynog's woods and waters but also notes the comfort for her sorrow that the poet finds there. She is still unhappy, but even "the gloomiest soul" must be charmed by the "sweetly varied scenes" of Mr. Blayney's estate. If she were not grief-stricken, the scenes would inspire her to song as cheerful as the linnet's, and even now despite her misfortunes, "fancy [may] reassume her reign"—and does, in this technically interesting poem which dramatically describes this bit of Cambria in varying pentameters and tetrameters, quatrains and couplets. Time was beginning to assuage the widow's grief.

One of the undatable occasional poems could also be classified as autobiographical, but its application to the facts of Mary Darwall's life is unclear. "Delia to Philander" is a lament

Poems on Several Occasions (1794)

for an absent lover who "Enjoy[s] a calm repose" somewhere else while Delia is left to grieve " 'mid smoke and noise." Most of the poem expresses nostalgia for happy days by the River Arrow where the poet "knew no cares but love" and listened in the poplars' shade to Philander's "mellifluous lay." Was John Darwall off on a visit to his parents in Haughton or to some other country place, leaving Mary at home in Walsall? He did write lays, though they are usually far from mellifluous. Could she have been thinking of another poetic lover? Unlikely—and John is "Philander" to her "Delia" elsewhere in her poems. The emotion seems true—loneliness and nostalgia—but the facts remain obscure.

The other occasional poems contain little personal expression. "Impromptu, on being requested to write some verses," in rather bouncy tetrameter, regrets the loss of poetic power with the increase of age, but its tone is lightened by the meter, its very existence calls its message into question—and in the book it is followed by the thirty-five-page ballad opera, "Valentine's Day," a further contradiction. If Mary Darwall was responsible for the order in which her poems appeared in these volumes, she was having a little fun with her readers here. The remaining occasional poems are quite serious. "Lines written for a young lady's sampler"—poor girl, there are twelve pentameter lines—recommends useful and virtuous employment: sewing, music, painting, and reading the Bible. "Ode Respectfully inscribed to a Young Nobleman on his return from his travels" acknowledges the pleasures of the Grand Tour but proclaims England's equal or superior merits and wishes the young nobleman well. Poems to Mrs. C—— and Mr. F—— (possibly Richard Ford's son) on their weddings express reverence for the "virtuous friendship" that is marriage. The latter rejoices that Mr. F—— has married a British beauty rather than some "foreign dame" he has seen in France; it also reveals clearly, besides her conservative patriotism, that Mrs. Darwall could play a keyboard instrument, presumably a harpsichord or piano. Otherwise, these occasional poems have no particular significance.

Poems on Several Occasions (1794)

The four poems on Scottish subjects, along with others I mentioned earlier, show not only that Mrs. Darwall was fascinated by things Caledonian but also that she was in tune with changing taste in poetry and aware of new developments. Wisely, she makes little attempt to use the language of Burns or to describe in detail scenes she had probably never seen, limiting herself to evocative place-names. These four Scottish poems are all about love. In "Down the Bourn," "Youthful Mary . . . , brae and bonny," is faithful to her Johnny despite his poverty, while "A Scotch Pastoral," Sandy's lament for a gold-digging Mary, tells the opposite story. In "The Self-Exiled Minstrel" Mrs. Darwall assumes a male persona—the only time in all her work that she does so unequivocally—to tell the story of a humble lad who became a minstrel in MacGowan's castle and, tragically, fell in love with MacGowan's high-born daughter. He rues the day when he first tuned his pipe "to OSSIAN's lays sublime" and wanders now through the stormy wilds of Scotland seeking death.

The most interesting of this group of poems is "The Death of Mary, in sequel to Mary's Dream or Sandy's Ghost." "Mary's Dream," said to be the most popular "pathetic ballad" ever to appear in Scotland, was written in 1772 by John Lowe, a gardener's son who had risen to the position of tutor to a country gentleman's family. One of the gentleman's daughters lost her lover at sea, which inspired "Mary's Dream." Lowe describes Mary going to bed and thinking of her absent Sandy; then Sandy appears to her in a dream to tell her he has been drowned after battling a raging storm for three days and nights: "cold is my clay, / It lies beneath a stormy sea." Love for Mary filled his heart despite the horrors of the gale, and he looks forward to their reunion in heaven:

> "O maiden dear, thyself prepare,
>   We soon shall meet upon that shore
> Where love is free from doubt and care,
>   And thou and I shall part no more."
> Loud crowed the cock, the shadows fled;
>   No more of Sandy could she see;

Poems on Several Occasions (1794)

> But soft the passing spirit said,
>   "Sweet Mary, weep no more for me!"

The injunction to refrain from weeping is repeated at the end of each stanza and gentles the tone of the ballad from tragedy to pathos. But when Mrs. Darwall wrote her sequel, she made Mary disregard her lover's command and, despairing, seek the beach where she had said goodbye to him:

> Unmov'd by the tempest's loud roar,
>   Or the torrents that pour'd from the sky,
> With meek resignation she cry'd;—
> "I come, my lov'd S<small>ANDY</small>, I come:
> "In death, we shall soon be ally'd,
>   "And sleep in the same wat'ry tomb."
>
> The raven with heart-chilling note
>   Shriek'd hideous, the light'ning glar'd bright;—
> When lo! on a wave came afloat
>   Her S<small>ANDY</small> all ghastly to sight:
> She bent o'er his pale breathless clay;—
> "I come, my dear S<small>ANDY</small>!" she cry'd,
> "With joy I thy summons obey."
>   Then clasp'd her cold lover and died.

John Lowe's "shore" is a metaphor for heaven, but Mary Darwall's is literal and her Mary interprets Sandy's vision of the future as a call to immediate action. Her poem goes beyond the pathetic to the gothic or horror-romantic, an increasingly popular mode. And it may not be reading too much into the poem to see here, especially in contrast with Lowe's ballad, not just changing fashion or taste but also something of the energy and passion of Mary Darwall's character.

The gothic "Song of the Sisters of Ivar" is similarly horrific. Its subtitle explains that "the thought" was taken from Thomson and Mallet's masque, *Alfred* (1740), but Mrs. Darwall's poem has only a slight connection with its source. She would have been attracted by the patriotic fervor of the masque, especially its rousing final song, "Rule Britannia." And she would have liked

Poems on Several Occasions (1794)

both the praise of Queen Elizabeth and the portrayal of Alfred's queen, Eltruda, as not only beautiful and virtuous but also devoted to England's glory. But Mrs. Darwall's poem reflects none of this. Instead, she concentrated on a brief but vivid description of the magic flag of the Danish invaders with its "pictur'd *Raven*"

> Wrought by the sisters of the *Danish* king,
> Of furious IVAR, in a midnight hour:
> While the sick moon, at their enchanted song,
> Wrapt in pale tempest, labour'd thro' the clouds.
> The *Demons* of destruction then, they say,
> Were all abroad, and mixing with the woof
> Their baleful power: The sisters ever sung;
> "Shake, standard, shake this ruin on our foes!"

Mrs. Darwall saw the possibilities for drama in this passage. Her poem has nearly as much action as the almost plotless masque and much more atmosphere:

> Loud and hollow blows the blast,
>   Thick descends the rattling hail;
> Thro' th'expanse of aether vast,
>   See the lurid light'nings trail!

The description of the chilling scene soon moves on to a "gloomy cave" in which something awful is happening, and the narrator steels herself to "watch the dread event." The event turns out to be the weaving of "a sable web" by the three sisters of Ivar, each of whom, like the witches in *Macbeth*, describes her contribution to the project in a thrilling speech. The first, promising victory to her brother, echoes the masque's line: " 'This banner, fraught with grim war's woes, / Shall shake destruction on thy foes.' " The second weaves a similar promise into the emblem of the raven, but as the third closes the charm, the moon breaks through the "friendly mists," indicating that a valorous king will rise in the west and defeat the triumphant

Poems on Several Occasions (1794)

Ivar in spite of the magic banner. This is bad news for the weavers:

> Louder howl'd the mighty wind,
>   Rending peals convuls'd the sky,
> Death-like terrors shook my mind,
>   And wild the furious sisters fly;
> Shrieking, as they leave the cell,—
>   "Danish glory, ah! farewell!"

Thomson and Mallet are tame in comparison.

The baker's dozen of pastoral poems not mentioned earlier are relatively flat compared with her gothic thrillers, and even with the tone of her other poems in general. The forms of these pastorals range from sonnets to simple lyrics to more elaborate songs with refrains; the sentiments about virtue, peace, and love are for the most part commonplace, as are the occasional references to the Creator of all nature. The dullness of these poems comes from their mere conventionality—they are exercises in the mode, not receptacles for unruly feeling as the pastorals of her first book often were. There is strong feeling in the second book, directly and indirectly expressed, but it usually appears in forms and modes other than the pastoral, probably because Mrs. Darwall had less need than Miss Whateley had to appear simple and unassuming. It is paradoxical but understandable that the older woman's pastorals should be more genuinely simple than the younger's.

Two of these simple pastorals, however, contain interesting touches. "Advice to a Young Lady" urges "Cloe" to stop pining for unrequited love—lovers who only want a girl with money are not worth languishing for. Instead of sighing, she should do as the giver of the advice herself has done: she should beguile the hours by writing poetry. In an undated but probably much earlier "Song," Mrs. Darwall had shown herself doing, or resolving to do, exactly that. There are no clues to the identity of "Cloe," the young lady in "Advice," but it could be Elizabeth,

Poems on Several Occasions (1794)

who, with no money and a passionate nature, remained a spinster and became a poet.

The other pastoral with an interesting touch is a "Song, Adapted to a favorite Gavot of Avison's." Here a forsaken maiden whose coldness discouraged her lover now longs for her Damon:

> Hapless sex! constrain'd by fashion
>   To disguise each tender thought;—
> To repress the genial passion
>   Is the art we first are taught.
>
> Hence dissembling, blushing, trembling;
>   Female wiles and airs, adieu!
> Shepherd, hear me! come and cheer me!
>   Or poor DELIA dies for you.

Although sincerity was becoming more generally valued in the eighteenth century, it was still an unusual woman who wanted to discard the protective hypocrisies she had been taught from the cradle. It couldn't be completely done, of course, and this is only a song—but the impulse to emotional honesty is there.

The same impulse and the same involvement with music appear together again in "Valentine's Day." A musical drama in the tradition of Gay's *Beggar's Opera*, though not a satire, "Valentine's Day" is made up of nine songs and a grand finale, with dialogue in anapestic couplets carrying most of the slender story. The plot, such as it is, concerns two pairs of pastoral lovers involved in romantic difficulties. Phillida is so lively and direct that Colin is rather afraid of her, but when she puts herself in his way on Valentine's Day, he confesses his love and she replies, quickly and frankly, that she loves him in return. Anna's problem, a more serious one, is just the opposite: she is so modest a maiden that Strephon thinks her indifferent, but he too gathers up his courage on Valentine's Day, asks only for pity, and both confess their love. Phillida has urged Anna to be open and sincere, but it was only on this auspicious day that the conventionally indoctrinated shepherdess could overcome her emotional hypocrisy. Despite differences in plot, the characterization bears some resemblance to that in Frances Brooke's popular comic opera *Rosina* (1783).

The story of "Valentine's Day" is padded out a bit with a long song about yet another amorous problem: four of the five shepherds in love with Bridget, "the pride of the milk-maids," had beaten each other up soundly, which she pretended to like; but she married the fifth, who was also thrashed but did not retaliate, because she felt sure that he would never beat her. The fact that the successful shepherd was the only poet-musician in the lot no doubt added to his charm. Bridget's deception here is inconsistent with the sincerity preached by Phillida but is perhaps more practical for everyday behavior. For all her moral idealism and faith in love, Mrs. Darwall was not naive.

The songs are the chief attraction of "Valentine's Day." From the deliberately "odd-measur'd verses" of Bridget's story through a variety of singable meters to the grand finale of solos and choruses, Mrs. Darwall clearly knew what she was about in these lyrics. Unfortunately, I have been unable to discover whether she was using familiar tunes as Gay had done—the meters sound practiced enough for that—or whether John Darwall composed original music for her. Nor have I found any record of a performance, though Walsall's own Musical Society could well have put it on: it requires only six singers, a couple of common props, and no particular scenery. If it was performed, it would have been a welcome addition to Walsall's limited theatrical offerings. But even if it was not, it is valuable evidence of the range of Mrs. Darwall's interests and talents.

She also ventured into another new form in her second book, an imitation of Ossian's prose poetry. Her allusion elsewhere to that misguided bard implies continued familiarity with his work. Indeed, Shenstone had received a copy of "the Erse fragments" when Macpherson first published them in 1760, which Mary could have seen. But it was not until she moved to Wales, right into the Celtic context, that she wrote her imitation. "The

Poems on Several Occasions (1794)

Moanings of Ella the Daughter of Glendalwin" was inspired, as her introductory note says, by the ruins of an ancient castle at "Dolvarwin" (Dolforwyn), about four miles down the River Severn from Newtown. Locally known as "the castle of the three virgins," its history had been lost; its name means "the maiden's meadow" and it is associated with the vengeful drowning of both Sabrina, who gave her name to the Severn, and her mother. So Mary Darwall had some ready-made atmosphere to work with, but the gaps in history left her free to invent.

And invent she did, a tragic story in the Ossianic mood of the venerable widow Edith and her three daughters: Elfrida, whose rape and murder by a "Roman knight" brought about her mother's death; and Cadina and Ella, who were abducted and escaped, but suffered so on their way home that Cadina died. Only Ella is left. She spends her time bewailing the fate of her family and of her heroic lover Cadwal, who had perished while battling her abductors. Cadwal's death is mentioned only briefly in the poem, however. Mrs. Darwall concentrates instead on the vulnerability and the courage, the mutual devotion and the suffering of the women. This emphasis on women marks a departure from her model: Macpherson, though he mentions the occasional sorrowful maiden heaving her snow-white breast, is centrally concerned with male heroism. Otherwise, "The Moanings of Ella" is quite faithful as an imitation: its broken rocks and foaming torrents, its alliteration and evocative place-names, could almost have come from Macpherson's own pen.

"The Moanings of Ella" is followed by the poem to Arthur Blayney of Gregynog; together, they bring Mary Darwall's second book to a close on a local note. On November 1, 1794, she signed and dated the dedication and sent the manuscript off to Mr. Milward in Walsall. But the book includes one more feature that I haven't mentioned yet: a group of "Sonnets, &c" marked with asterisks, which "were given to the author by two young friends, who never intended to publish in their own names, but were content to roll down the stream of time, or sink into oblivion with her they loved." These poems, similar in style

Poems on Several Occasions (1794)

to her own but more amateurish and almost all more fervid, are signed variously "Y" and "Z." They were written by Mary's two daughters, whom she often called "friends." In November 1794, Harriet was nearly twenty-four and Elizabeth nearly nineteen; sixteen years later, Elizabeth collected her own poems into a book which also includes a few by her mother and three by Harriet—so they were all poets. Internal evidence—sisterly love, mourning for a dead parent, exile from "native plains" and "parted friends"—supports the attribution as well. And I think, though I cannot be entirely sure, that Y is Harriet (she sounds older and she has a faithful lover) and Z is Elizabeth (Z expresses more of the turbulent emotions, usually unhappy, that characterize Elizabeth's book).

How far one can rely on "Sonnets, &c" for clues to the girls' lives is, as always, problematic, and I am telling Mary Darwall's story, not her daughters'. But their lives were bound together and their poems reveal a close-knit family, so I will tell a little of what Y and Z's poems suggest.

John Darwall was sorely missed. Melancholy predominates in these poems, as in much adolescent versifying, but it is quite specific in Z's "Tears of Affection" for her "sainted Parent," who she prays will become her guardian angel. When she first sees the River Severn, which runs through Newtown, Z looks forward to frequent weeping on its banks in the starlight. She longs for an absent beloved; she admires "a Gentleman going to join the army on the continent" and hopes that he and his love for her will survive the war; she loses all hope of happiness but, like her mother, knows that virtue can still "give the hour serene." Perhaps the lover did not survive the war—Elizabeth never married.

Y is a little less miserable than Z. She has her moments of "dark DESPONDENCY" but can take some comfort in the beauties of nature which she shares with a "musing, melancholy maid." She appears to have suffered from an unrequited love, which caused her to "languish like a blighted flow'r," but she still has the "guileless heart" of "faithful HENRY" and is determined to be

Poems on Several Occasions (1794)

satisfied with that. And Harriet did marry. On New Year's Day, 1795, two months after Mary Darwall signed the dedication to her book, Harriet Darwall was married in Newtown to Samuel Arrowsmith, by the minister who subscribed for twenty copies of her mother's poems. The groom was a Worcestershire man, not a Newtown resident; he must have followed the Darwall women to Wales. Charles Henry, now a budding lawyer, came from Walsall for the occasion and acted as witness along with Newtown's doctor, the son of Richard Ford. Like all weddings, this one changed the pattern of the family, and in time Samuel Arrowsmith, with his changing fortunes, became a significant influence on the course of Mary Darwall's life.

Chapter 11

Last Years (1795-1825)

... Fancy's spark has left thine eye,
And the young bloom thy cheek has flown. ...

Elizabeth Darwall

Mary Darwall had many last years, but this final chapter is not proportionately long. After her second book appeared in 1794, only a few clues survive to tell the rest of the story of her long widowhood: marriage and death dates for some of her children, two passages in Elizabeth's book of poems, dates and places of grandchildren's births, the record of a small pension, and her own obituary in the *Staffordshire Advertiser*. When a woman is not writing much and is not attached to a man with a public career or profession, she easily becomes invisible. So there are more gaps and more guesswork in this last part of the story of Mary Whateley Darwall.

She went on living in Newtown until 1803 or a little later, growing financially more comfortable after 1801 with a legacy from her brother Henry and a pension arranged by Lord Mountrath; together these resources came to thirty-one pounds a year, a significant addition to her forty-one pounds from young John's properties. In Newtown she tended Harriet when her first child, John Yerrow, was born late in 1795. Possibly she was still there to mourn the death of one or two of the Fords, the son in 1804, the father in 1806. Possibly she was not, because at about this time she joined the Arrowsmith household, now settled at Hope Mansel, Herefordshire.

Last Years (1795-1825)

Samuel Arrowsmith, Harriet's husband, remains obscure. Probably a Roman Catholic, he was not a university man; he had no public career such as the law, the church, or the military. The second son of a substantial cider merchant of Hanley Castle, Worcestershire, who had died when Samuel was nineteen, he had inherited several properties which produced rental income from agricultural land, cider works, and dwellings; these properties lay in Herefordshire, the county that had produced John Philips and his instructive poem "Cyder" (1708). But the newlyweds did not go to live on any of these properties. When they left Newtown after their first child was born, they began a series of moves, for no discoverable reason, which can be traced by the baptisms of more children: to Leominster (where Mary Elizabeth was baptized in 1798), to Hope Mansel (Louisa Ann in 1803, Charles Frederick in 1804), and finally to Brewood (Samuel in 1811). By the time the children were grown up, the Arrowsmiths had settled in Shrewsbury, where the two daughters ran private schools and the oldest son practiced medicine.

One piece of evidence for Mary Darwall's becoming part of this household when they settled in Herefordshire appears in Elizabeth's poem about leaving Hope Mansel for London, in which she regrets her separation from "the parent of [her] heart." Another poem in Elizabeth's book, written by Mrs. Darwall herself, urges Elizabeth to visit "parent" and "sister," who are clearly together. Besides, a widow commonly did live with a child, most often a daughter, and at this time Samuel Arrowsmith was prosperous enough to take his mother-in-law in; and her own finances had improved so much that she would not have been a burden. But after some time with the Arrowsmiths in Hope Mansel and then Brewood and possibly elsewhere, Mary Darwall returned to Walsall, where she died. Her last years, then, brought about a number of uprootings, more than in her maiden and married days; a widow's life at this time was quite different from a virgin's or a wife's.

Her years in Newtown and with the Arrowsmiths were eventful ones for her much-loved country. They were years of

Last Years (1795-1825)

almost unbroken and bloody war with Napoleon, of the younger Pitt's prime ministership, of the king's increasing disabilities and the eventual establishment of the Regency. John Wilkes, whose noisy political career (though quieter towards the end) had covered exactly the years of Mary's friendship and marriage with John Darwall, died peacefully in retirement in 1797. Nelson triumphed and died. Thomas Bowdler was beginning to snip away at Shakespeare. The slave trade was finally abolished. Industry expanded, despite riots and protests, which grew ever more serious. And the British Empire grew towards its nineteenth-century zenith.

These were eventful years in Mary Darwall's private world as well. In 1800, during a brief break in his military duties, Frederick married an admiral's daughter. Young John's seven children were born. Two died young, but the others survived; the oldest of the seven was born five days after Harriet's wedding, the youngest in 1805. And John's career took some unexpected turns during these years, for on November 18, 1795, Mr. Rutter died, suddenly, in the Walsall vicarage. This time John applied for the position, and although he was not the only applicant, after the usual months of negotiation he was successful. He did not move in until September 1796, having complicated arrangements to make in Deritend and at St. Bartholomew's, so perhaps the Widow Rutter had more rent-free time in the house than the Widow Darwall had had. I doubt that John invited his stepmother to join him there, however: Mrs. Preston's nephew was still hovering in the wings, so John knew his position was temporary. But it was better than Deritend (which he farmed out to a curate), and it was home.

John took an active part in Walsall life. The combination of England's increasing engagement in the war on the Continent and "the democratic spirit which is so insidiously spreading among the lower orders of people" inspired him and his fellow citizens to set up volunteer cavalry and infantry divisions in 1798. John wrote to Lord Mountrath asking for financial support; these "armed associations" were needed, he pointed out, "for the

Last Years (1795-1825)

protection of persons and property, against the assaults of Enemies either foreign or internal." He then signed on as the cavalry's chaplain and, with an appropriate sermon, consecrated their colors.

By 1803 the volunteers had disbanded, during a rare period of peace, and Mrs. Preston's nephew had grown up: the Rev. Philip Pratt took over as vicar of Walsall in December. This time, John Darwall was prepared. He had negotiated, with some difficulty, a better salary at Deritend in an attempt to equal his Walsall earnings, and, surprisingly, he had even arranged to return to his teaching job at the King Edward VI School. The school had a new headmaster who had served in Deritend's church himself and knew its poverty; he was willing to forgive and forget the incident of the boarders. As 1804 began, John was starting to do relatively well for himself. He moved his family, twice, each time farther away from the church in Deritend's busy High Street and from the noisome River Rea. His situation in life was growing increasingly comfortable and secure.

Charles Henry too had reached such a position. By 1801 he was well established as a lawyer and had settled into his own house near the bottom of Bridge Street, the new road that curved up the Walsall hill more gently than the High Street. His garden stretched down to Walsall Water where Darwall Street runs today. In January 1805, at the age of thirty-five, he married; soon his household grew as children and other family arrived. But the other family did not include his mother, at least not yet. Although these sons were doing well, Mary Darwall chose to live with Harriet.

During her Newtown and Arrowsmith years, Mary Darwall the poet was slowing down. Some of her older work was still in the public eye—Maria Riddell included "Liberty" in her *Metrical Miscellany* of 1802 and 1803. But Mary evidently wrote only a few new pieces, four of which were published in Elizabeth's book in 1810. Two other poems, published in the *Monthly Magazine and British Register* and signed "M.D.," may be hers. If there

Last Years (1795-1825)

were more, they have been lost, but perhaps her powers faded with age, as she herself had claimed in her "Impromptu." One of Elizabeth's poems also suggests such fading: "To an Old Acquaintance" addresses a woman with "furrows deep and tresses hoar" whose eye no longer beams with "Fancy's spark." But, ever patriotic, Mrs. Darwall was roused when Nelson beat the French on August 1, 1798, and she celebrated his deeds in "The Victory of the Nile." In her poem, "Old Nilus" rises from "his oozy bed" to "Hail Nelson," grateful to be delivered from the "fell barbarians" who sought to "Defile [his] mosques, and desolate [his] lands." The Sultan, equally grateful, will proclaim Nelson's "never-dying fame!" Mrs. Darwall always admired military heroes.

She also admired the author of a sonnet entitled "The Sketch" and wrote a poem praising his or her "cultur'd genius, and . . . taste refin'd." I have not found "The Sketch," which could have been published in any of dozens of magazines or newspapers, or even circulated among friends in manuscript. But it is clear from Mrs. Darwall's lines that "The Sketch" describes the modest beauty of the lily-of-the-valley and that its author is uncommonly "discriminating" in appreciating the "elegance" of the half-hidden flowers. Mrs. Darwall's response to the poem is cast in human terms: the lily is a "gentle maid," contrasting vividly with each bolder flower who "Coquets with butterflies, or smiles on bees." These "gaudy" blossoms also "expand" their petals to welcome showers and passing breezes, which is as close as Mrs. Darwall ever comes to describing sexual promiscuity. Clearly, she recognized in the author of "The Sketch" someone who shared both her own taste for restraint and, if the lily in "The Sketch" was similarly humanized, her own conservative standards for female behavior. And she took this opportunity to endorse those standards that she, like most older people, probably saw as being dangerously eroded by the younger generation.

Sometimes she admired the younger generation, however. She seems to have been particularly proud of Elizabeth, her

Last Years (1795-1825)

youngest, as a poem addressed to "Eliza" shows—assuming it is by Mary Darwall. Elizabeth, always devoted to wild mountain scenery, had gone on a tour of the Lake District in 1796 with a party of other women; she had taken notes of what she saw (and jotted down some verses) in a journal, which, probably somewhat revised, she published in 1800 in the *Monthly Magazine and British Register*. Mountains and lakes, local dialect, sunsets, weather, medieval ruins—Elizabeth loved and described it all. And "M.D." loved Eliza's journal:

> LINES *occasioned by reading in the* MAGAZINES *for* AUGUST *and* SEPTEMBER, 1800, *the* JOURNAL *of a* HASTY RAMBLE *to the* LAKES.
>
> Oh! my Eliza, could this swelling heart,
>   But paint its feelings, while with thee it strays
> O'er Nature's beauties unprofaned by art,
>   And contemplates the scenes thy hand pourtrays!
>
> Others can tamely tell me they have viewed
>   The dell abruptly sink, the mountain rise;
> Thy wand of Genius with strange powers endued,
>   Brings the whole scene to my enraptured eyes.
>
> Thus o'er the landscape veiled in partial night,
>   When the bright orb of day his radiance throws,
> A new creation bursts upon the sight,
>   And Nature's self in brighter beauty glows.
>
> March 14, 1801.   M. D.

Although she belonged to an older generation, Mary Darwall, who had written much conventional pastoral verse, shared Elizabeth's romantic enthusiasm for untamed nature.

But Elizabeth's devotion to wild scenery could be carried too far, and Mary Darwall took up her pen again when her daughter was spending some time in Wales—too much time, her neglected mother thought. "Addressed to E.D. by her Mother,

Last Years (1795-1825)

who was first known to the poetical world as *Miss Whateley*" describes the mountains and forests of "Cambria's sweet romantic scene"; the scene is somewhat less dramatic than that in "The Moanings of Ella," but it is essentially the same. The poet rejoices in the pleasure her "lov'd Eliza" takes in the familiar landscape and imagines her meditating on the ancient days of " 'high-born Hoel's harp, or soft Llewellyn's' lyre," a line adapted from Gray's "The Bard" (1757). But the former Miss Whateley goes on to tout the "Superior pleasures" of "The cheerful hearth, the social board / . . . By friendship brighten'd and with goodness join'd." She concludes with a graceful but unmistakable summons to come home and a Johnsonian wish for her daughter's happiness:

> Swift as the light-wing'd moments fly,
>   Say, can'st thou one, Eliza, spare,
> To glad an absent sister's eye,
>   Or parent's, dimm'd with age and care?
> Yes——thy own heart my advocate will prove,
> For 'tis compos'd of gratitude and love.
>
> Still be that heart by Virtue warm'd——
>   Serene and cheerful be thy mind;
> By Nature's varying beauties charm'd——
>   To Heaven's all-gracious will resigned!
> Whate'er of happiness on earth is known,
> May'st thou, Eliza, *find*——or *make* thy own!

This poem was written sometime after 1803, and the cares that dimmed the parent's eye now included the particular pain of the loss of grown-up children. Early in 1802, probably in February, at the age of thirty-four, Leicester Darwall, Mary's firstborn, had died in Hope Mansel. The Staffordshire militia in which he had been serving was soon to be disembodied; in April 1802 they left Windsor (to the king's regret—he followed them down the road for two miles waving goodbye). It looks as if Leicester had been invalided out sometime before that date. Perhaps after all he had not been strong enough to work with

Last Years (1795-1825)

stained glass, though he had survived the ceremonial duties of the militia for nearly nine years.

Except for baby Whateley, Leicester was the first of Mrs. Darwall's own children whose deaths she mourned. Frederick was the second. He had transferred from the militia to the more active 65th Foot in February 1797. He signed on as assistant surgeon and saw the world, or at least some exotic parts of it: the Lothians in Scotland in 1797-99, the Cape of Good Hope in 1800-01, Ceylon in 1802-04, and then India. His regiment went into battle when the king of Kandy objected to England's newly acquired sovereignty over Ceylon, and again when the princes of the Mahratta states objected to British rule. But disease took a higher toll than warfare, and Frederick, treating the fevers as well as the wounds of his men, probably succumbed to that. He died, aged thirty-two, on duty in Calcutta in December 1805. He was honored with an unusually long obituary in the *Staffordshire Advertiser* the following August, which noted that his "talents and humanity" were still spoken of in the militia where he had served earlier.

His younger sister Elizabeth was shattered by his death. Her poems show that she adored Frederick. The greatest "transport" of love she ever felt was caused by a letter from him "after a long silence"; she was visiting in Wales at the time and rejoices wildly because he still loves her, and longs passionately for his return. Another poem, dated November 1804, expresses her anguish as he roams "in distant climes . . . / Where Phoebus darts his fiercest ray," and recalls how as a child she followed him like his shadow. Others, though not mentioning Frederick by name, express the agony of loss. Elizabeth, born just a few years after Wordsworth and Coleridge and very much a child of the Romantic generation, poured out her heart in her poetry. Mrs. Darwall did not, despite the changed spirit of the age, or if she did she did not see fit to publish any laments for her sons.

Indeed, the mother who approved of the modest lily in "The Sketch" was rather uneasy about the fervid tones of her daughter's verse. Elizabeth's 1810 volume, dedicated to the

Last Years (1795-1825)

Prince who was about to become Regent, is introduced by a poem entitled "Author & Critic. Written for E.D. by a Friend." Although unsigned, this must be by Mary Darwall: she and her children were "friends," she refers to Shenstone, she compliments Elizabeth on the "true classic elegance" of her mind (a phrase Shenstone had used, twice, to describe Miss Whateley), and she writes in the gracefully comic anapests she had used in her poem to Shenstone. Her old guide, philosopher, and friend was much on her mind as she fulfilled a similar role for her daughter. Her authorship of this poem is most clearly evident when, speaking as "Critic," she cautions Elizabeth against wearing her heart on her sleeve, and fears lest "these tender effusions [the love poems] / Should draw from your readers ungracious conclusions." "Author" then replies, much surprised that "Critic" should think her "in earnest" and citing poets of yore, including Shenstone, whose "sorrowing hearts bled thro' pages" while their real lives were quite happy. Poets are not on oath, nor are they historians. Fiction is the muse of Fancy; "the gothic, romantic, and tender" all come from imagination. This sounds like a version of the Dedication to Miss Whateley's own poems, where the virgin author carefully explained that one cannot write pastoral without "pretending to do Homage to Cupid" at the same time. Elizabeth's poems certainly sound heartfelt, however, and both her mother and Shenstone valued sincerity. But Mrs. Darwall was trying to forestall the damage to Elizabeth's reputation such public undressing could cause for a woman even in the Romantic age.

Mrs. Darwall herself did no such undressing and, except for one early poem, did not write overtly about the deaths of those close to her. There were a number of deaths she could have written about if she had been so inclined. She had reached the age when her contemporaries were dropping off one by one. Her brother Henry died at his suburban mansion near Walsall in December 1801, and their older brother John in 1805. On the Darwall side of the family, John's sister Honor died in

Last Years (1795-1825)

Newport at the age of sixty-four on October 29, 1800, the day after her lifelong friend Jane Hewitt had died at seventy-one.

It is worth pausing for a moment over this pair of women who, less well known though probably less reclusive than the Ladies of Llangollen, had lived together with similar devotion. They were buried in one grave in the churchyard at Forton, just outside Newport, Shropshire, and memorialized at length in the *Gentleman's Magazine* as "an almost unprecedented example of sincere and affectionate friendship." For about forty-five years they had lived together "in the strictest amity," doing charitable works and were universally respected. They made their wills for each other's support. Even when one (Jane) lost her fortune and became dependent on the other, their friendship was unshaken. They dreaded the idea of separation, but, as it happened, their fears were never realized, for Honor died only a few hours after Jane:

> Their last bed of sickness exhibited a scene truly affecting and interesting to the feelings of every tender heart. She that was first taken ill, had the misfortune of breaking her leg, when both were confined: each perceived that the awful exit of one, if not both, was approaching; and as long as strength would permit, she that was most able went every day into the room of her friend to take a final adieu: and when her strength was exhausted she was carried by the attendants. At these affecting interviews they bathed each other's hands in tears, and expressed an heart-felt wish, that it might please God to permit them soon to meet again in the glorious fields of eternity. Heaven smiled and heard the pious prayer; and that angel that snatched away the soul of her that first departed, was a few hours afterwards dispatched to release the struggling soul of her absent friend, and to re-unite them in bonds of love for ever!

It is pleasing to see such love between women publicly acknowledged and respected. The Darwall family certainly admired them: when young John's wife gave birth to a daughter eleven

Last Years (1795-1825)

Honor Darwall (top) and Jane Hewitt.
(Paintings from the archives of the Darwall-Smith family.)

Last Years (1795-1825)

months later, they united the two women in the child's name, Honor Hewitt Darwall.

Since it did not have to go to Jane, virtually all of Honor's property went to her nephews and nieces. Young John got his grandfather's properties at Haughton, which added nicely to his income. All the children got cash. Elizabeth got the most—330 pounds; Honor knew a spinster needed support. Harriet's 270 pounds was carefully secured from falling under her husband's control. John was to invest and pay out most of Randle's money; after Randle broke off his apprenticeship in Newport, Aunt Honor apparently didn't quite trust him. Feather beds, books and pictures, the silver coffeepot and tea caddy, teaspoons and tablespoons, were distributed among John and the girls (he got the books, Elizabeth got most of the silver). John was to be the executor. William, Mary Fox Darwall's youngest son, the haberdasher in the West Indies, was not mentioned; presumably he had died. And Mary Whateley Darwall was not mentioned. Honor must have expected that the children would provide for her.

The network of family connections went beyond funerals and inheritances to the active world. In Birmingham, Mrs. Darwall's lawyer nephew William Whateley, one of George's sons, was appointed secretary to the King Edward VI School, just before John Darwall returned as a master; William's wife was in the midst of producing twelve children, one of whom succeeded his father as the school secretary and still stares down sternly at the boardroom table from an engraved portrait of the governors. A third John Darwall, "young" John's oldest son and a medical man of note, was one of these governors for three years while his stepcousin was secretary. In Walsall, Henry Whateley's only daughter married William Davenport, her first cousin once removed, the son of the Martha Baylies who had married John Darwall's curate. Mary's own son Charles Henry became a churchwarden under the Rev. Mr. Pratt (who had ousted "young" John) and mayor of Walsall for a year in 1814, while his cousin John Clements Whateley, Henry's only son, added the

Last Years (1795-1825)

responsibilities of a steward of the Walsall races to his other civic duties. And so the network grew—I have sketched here only a fraction of the web—with births and marriages and deaths, careers and service, making these lives still visible despite the passage of centuries, if one goes looking.

As always, however, the men are more visible than the women, and Mary Whateley Darwall disappears entirely for six years after Elizabeth's book was published. The Arrowsmiths left faint tracks: their last child was born in Brewood in 1811 and lumbered with the name Samuel Yonge Darwall Arrowsmith, and his father appears there in the poor rate book for 1814-15 occupying a house valued at £5.5. This was not the cheapest house in town—many were valued at one or two pounds—but it is hardly what one would expect for a prosperous cider merchant. Chances are, Samuel Arrowsmith's prosperity had declined by this date. Throughout Herefordshire, cider growers had been uprooting orchards and planting grain to take advantage of the highly inflated prices caused by the Napoleonic Wars. But prices of grain fell by nearly half from their peak in 1812 to their lowest point in 1815, tenant farmers failed to pay their rents, and many landowners went bankrupt. Cider itself, a famous local product that was bottled and shipped all over the world, had always been a fluctuating commodity, dependent on spring weather. Even before Waterloo, Herefordshire had suffered from failures of both wheat and cider apples in 1803 and 1804. And Samuel Arrowsmith was largely dependent on the crops. The recently instituted income tax would have taken its toll as well. So it is highly probable that the Arrowsmith fortunes sank, and the little that was left had to go to launch their first son on what would be a distinguished career as a surgeon.

After Waterloo, Mrs. Darwall must have begun to think again about where to live. Her choices were limited. Elizabeth had no fixed home; Harriet was probably in reduced circumstances; and at some unknown date, both daughters had become Roman Catholics, which could have meant friction. Both stepson

Last Years (1795-1825)

Randle (the Birmingham grocer) and his wife died in 1816; others too had died. Only stepson John and son Charles Henry were left.

Mary Darwall signed her own pension receipts in Walsall beginning in October 1817 (Charles Henry had signed them earlier) and she died in Charles Henry's house there in December 1825. These are the only facts I have found to trace the course of her life in her final few years, but clearly she went to live with her son rather than her stepson.

Her choice is understandable. John could have afforded to keep her, but there is some evidence that his wife resented her aunt/stepmother-in-law, and there could well have been ill feeling between stepmother and stepson over the old boarders scandal, which had blotted the Whateley escutcheon. And John himself was becoming a less pleasant person as he grew older. It is not surprising that he should have soured. He had been deprived of the university education he had probably expected, and only got his two Oxford degrees when he was thirty-nine and forty years old. That had involved years of juggling his commitments at the Birmingham school and at Deritend to make time for the required twelve terms of residence, which he probably kept whenever he could before he got the Walsall living. Even then he had hopes and plans for more advanced study, but he finally gave up and, with the help of chancellor's letters, got his two basic degrees. His disappointments included his first real job at Deritend, where the church was practically falling down and he had to do all the work for a curate's salary. And he was out-maneuvered when his father's living fell vacant, pushed out of his teaching job for trying to make some money, and, when he finally got the Walsall living, ousted after eight years by the nephew of his patron's mistress.

Poor John! Always conservative, he grew more narrow and more prickly. When he returned to the King Edward VI School in 1804 he was much concerned with the respectability of his students: "Children intended to work in Manufactories, and Children of the Jews" did not belong in his school, and he tried,

Last Years (1795-1825)

with limited success and in somewhat paranoid tones, to gain control over admissions. He also dug in his heels and refused to allow anything but classics to be taught in his division, though all the other masters were branching out into history and geography. He was equally rigid outside the school. Though his parish papers show that he was compassionate to the numerous poor of Deritend, he published a stern address to them threatening all the parents with hellfire if they broke the Sabbath or neglected their children. When King George III died in 1820, John Darwall, asserting his Ministerial Rights, demanded a formal request for his permission before a parishioner, who had tried to act on his own, was allowed to drape the altar in black; he even had a detailed memorandum about the affair carefully drawn up, signed, and witnessed. When George IV was crowned in July 1821, John preached a sermon demonstrating that the king derived his authority directly from God, and if his listeners wanted to go to heaven they had better not murmur against their rulers; small wonder that his doctor son became a notoriously rabid Tory. John's sermon on the coronation, despite its dogmatism, is far less emotional in tone than his father's on the American revolutionaries, but when he took up the cudgels in his own defense in a bitter pamphlet war in 1824, he nearly equalled his father's fervor. The details of the quarrel are not clear from the two pamphlets that survive, but John Darwall seems to be claiming, acrimoniously, that he did not mismanage church funds and indeed never received what was owed him over a period of ten years. His attacker calmly marshals a host of facts to refute him. I cannot tell who was right and who was wrong, but John sounds grasping and self-righteous and too, too misunderstood. Perhaps his declining health further soured his temper. He would not have been easy to live with.

Charles Henry, on the other hand, seems to have been a kindly soul with much family feeling. He had travelled to Wales for Harriet's wedding and had asked his half brother John to come over from Deritend to officiate at his own wedding early

Last Years (1795-1825)

in 1805. At some time Charles Henry gave his younger brother Frederick's widow a home; she died in his house in 1813. Perhaps she had lived there while Frederick was in India, too. Charles Henry also left an annuity for his spinster sister Elizabeth in his will. He was useful outside the family as well. Churchwarden and mayor and member of the Corporation, attorney and Master in Chancery, clerk and treasurer of Walsall's grammar school, subscriber to the charity school, Charles Henry Darwall was a solid citizen of Walsall and the father of the equally solid and much loved Charles Frederick Darwall. It was to this active and respected household that Mary Whateley Darwall came in 1817.

Walsall had changed considerably while she was away, and it continued to change. Far from the glitter of Regency London and Brighton, the sooty provincial town went in for useful improvements, for the most part. Now it boasted a public library, and there was even a proper theater, which Mrs. Darwall's friend the widowed Elizabeth Nunns had run for a while around 1810. A fine grandstand had been built for the racecourse. A less happy addition was a huge pig market in the High Street, productive of noise and smells and much legal wrangling, which involved both Charles Henry and Mary's nephew John Whateley. The old market cross, where the charity children had learned to sing Mary's hymns, had been demolished. St. Matthew's church was being almost entirely rebuilt in the early 1820s, even though its old walls were found to be so solid they had to be blasted down with gunpowder; the first new stone was laid on January 21, 1820, the same day that George IV was proclaimed king in London. The Independents and Methodists, who had been active for many years, had built alarmingly large chapels. The George Hotel got a handsome new front with classical pillars, and in 1824 the hazardous streets were finally being improved with new paving and lights. The canal, so strenuously opposed, was now a reality. Nobody beat the bounds of the parish any more, and the old churchyard, where the dogs had dug up the newborn baby, was now too full

Last Years (1795-1825)

of graves and was locked up so the public could not enter. The town that Mrs. Darwall had known was changing indeed.

And how had Mary Darwall changed? She had aged, of course—when she died in Charles Henry's house in 1825, she was just short of her eighty-eighth birthday. But she had always been a vigorous, determined woman. And her signature on her last surviving pension receipt, though her hand shook once or twice on earlier ones, is as firm and bold as it had been when she signed the book at her wedding. So, although she wrote no more poetry that I know of, I think she must have retained her other faculties until the end, and retained her vital links with her family and her world. She had had many sorrows in her long life—poverty; deaths, some painfully early, of those she loved; frustrations as a woman poet—but she had had joys as well, with her happy marriage, caring children, and modest fame.

But her fame soon faded, and she was nearly forgotten; only first editions in rare-book collections, a few poems in nineteenth-century anthologies, and a few papers in Darwall family attics and Staffordshire archives kept her from oblivion. Like so many women writers of the eighteenth century, she virtually disappeared. And yet, also like so many, she is now being restored to the light to be reread and reassessed with modern eyes. Perhaps, however modern we may be, we will come to admire both the woman and the poet as did the anonymous author of her obituary:

> DIED On the 5th Dec. at Walsall, in her 88th year, Mrs. Darwall, relict of the Rev. John Darwall, formerly vicar of Walsall, whom she survived 36 years. Her uniform piety, her mental acquirements, and the kindness of her temper and manners, commanded the veneration and love of her relatives, and the highest esteem and regard of those who knew her most.

Appendix

               Liberty, an Elegy.
              Inscrib'd to Miss Loggin.
Feigned to be written from the happy Valley of Ambara.

To you, *Eliza*, be these Lays consign'd,
    Who blest in *Freedom*'s fair Dominions live;
While I, alas! am pompously confin'd,
    Bereft of ev'ry Joy the World can give.

In vain for me the blushing Flow'rets bloom,
    And Spring eternal decks the fragrant Shade;
In vain the dewy Myrtle breathes Perfume,
    And Sounds angelic echo thro' the Glade.

The Marble Palaces, and glitt'ring Spires,
    What are they? pageant Glare, and empty Show:
Ah! how unequal to my fond Desires,
    Which tell me——Freedom makes an Heav'n below.

Pensive I range these ever verdant Groves,
    And sigh responsive to the murm'ring Stream;
While woodland Warblers chant their happy Loves,
    Dear Liberty is wretched *Myra*'s Theme.

The Velvet Lawns diversify'd with Flow'rs,
    In sweet Succession ev'ry Morn the same;
Fresh Gales that breathe thro' Amaranthine Bow'rs,
    And ev'ry Charm, inventive *Art* can frame,

Here fondly vie to crown this favour'd place:
    And here, to smooth captivity a Prey,
Each Royal Child of *Abyssinian* Race
    Consumes the vacant inauspicious Day.

Tho' festive Mirth awake the laughing Morn,
    And guiltless Revels lead the dancing *Hours*;

Appendix

Tho' purling Rills the fertile Meads adorn,
    And the wild Rock its spicy Produce pours:

Yet what are these to fill a boundless Mind?
    Tho' gay each Scene appear, 'tis still the same;
Variety——in vain I hope to find;
    Variety, thou dear, but distant Name.

With Pleasure cloy'd, and sick of tasteless Ease,
    No sweet Alternatives my Spirits chear;
Joys oft repeated lose their Pow'r to please,
    And Harmony grows Discord to my Ear.

Blest *Freedom!* how I long with thee to rove,
    Where varying *Nature* all her Charms displays;
To range the Sun-burnt Hill, the rifted Grove,
    And trace the Silver Current's winding Maze!

Free as the wing'd Inhabitants of Air,
    Who distant Climes, and various Seasons see,
Regions——tho' not, like soft *Ambara*, fair;
    Yet blest with Change, and crown'd with Liberty.

Vain Wish! these Rocks, whose Summits pierce the Skies,
    With frowning Aspect, tell me——Hope is vain:
'Till, freed by Death, the purer Spirit flies;
    Here wretched *Myra*'s destin'd to remain.

Elegy on the Uses of Poetry.
Inscribed to the Rev. Randle Darwall, M.A.

Hail! gentle *Evening*, clad in sober grey,
    Mild Mother, Thou, of *Fancy*'s airy Train;
How sweet to fly the vain Pursuits of Day,
    And range with Thee the solitary Plain!

Far from the Dome, where splendid *Anguish* weeps,
    Where *Guilt*, or *Envy*, blast the Midnight Hour;

Appendix

Lead me, where Poppy-crown'd *Contentment* sleeps,
    To the light Breeze, that fans the Dew-bath'd Flow'r.

Slow-winding near yon Osier-fringed Stream,
    On whose green Marge soft *Silence* loves to stray;
O modest *Eve!* indulge my Muse-rapt Dream,
    That breathes no light-tun'd Air, or wanton Lay.

At this still Hour oft thro' the high-arch'd Grove,
    Where dwells sage *Contemplation*, let me roam;
Where Heav'n-born *Truth*, and keen-ey'd *Genius* rove,
    Where *Peace* resides in *Freedom*'s Moss-roof'd Dome.

These Heaven ordain'd the Guardians of the Muse;
    Beneath their sacred Influence unconfin'd
She soars, superior to terrestrial Views,
    To harmonize, instruct, and charm Mankind.

Her pleasing Task, thro' Nature's varied Plan,
    To trace the Goodness of Almighty Power;
To vindicate the Ways of God to Man,
    Soothe *Care*'s deep Gloom, and chear the lonely Hour.

Nor scorn'd she mild, to sing of Swains and Flocks,
    In simple Elegance to haunt the Plains;
In *Dorian* Mood beneath impending Rocks
    To breathe the rural Reed to softest Strains;

To paint the Scenes, which sportive *Fancy* drew,
    To *Love* and *Truth* attune the tender Lyre;
While her chaste Steps fair *Virtue*'s Paths pursue,
    Scorning each sordid Wish and low Desire.

Shame to the Hand, that first *Her* Pow'r abus'd,
    And with licentious Freedom stain'd the Page;
Whose Wit infectious Poison wide diffus'd,
    Or sacrific'd to Gold the noble Rage.

When *Vice* wou'd taint the Morals of Mankind,
    When *Pride* or *Envy* wou'd debase a Name;
When *Flattery* has her venal Chaplet twin'd,
    Shall these degrade the Muse's sacred Flame?

Appendix

When *Beauty* from the chaste-rob'd *Graces* flies
    To hold light Converse with the Cyprian Queen;
While blushing *Modesty* with down-cast Eyes,
    Gives place to *Mirth*'s loud Laugh, or Jest obscene.

Shall these a Place in *Fame*'s fair Records gain,
    Who strew *Pierian* Flow'rs on *Vice*'s shrine?
No, let Oblivion shrowd each guilty Strain,
    Tho' *Wit* and *Learning* all their Pow'rs combine.

For me, the meanest of the tuneful Throng,
    If e'er to Themes like these my Voice I raise;
If venal *Flatt'ry* e'er debase my Song,
    Or aught but Merit gain my honest Praise;

Perish the Blooms, which from the Vernal Field
    This Hand has cull'd fair *Friendship*'s Brows to wreathe;
No Pleasure may the humble Off'rings yield,
    No grateful Odours, or sweet Fragrance breathe.

To *Gratitude* and *Friendship* flows this Strain;
    Accept, O *Darwall!* what your Verse inspir'd;
Else have I wak'd my Rural Reed in vain,
    Else has the Muse in vain my Bosom fir'd.

But shou'd your Eye with wonted Candour view
    This well-meant Lay, by *Truth* and *Freedom* plan'd;
Shou'd these faint Strokes, which simple *Nature* drew,
    Pass unreprov'd beneath your judging Hand;

I ask no more; *happy*, with this poor Bough,
    This tributary Strain of artless Youth,
If gracious you shall deign to bind your Brow,
    O! Friend to *Virtue*, *Piety* and *Truth!*

Appendix

The Power of Destiny

Sure some malignant Star diffus'd its Ray,
When first my Eyes beheld the Beams of Day:
Whose baleful Influence made me dip in Ink,
And write in Rhyme before I knew to think.
Had Fate, propitious to my Wish, assign'd
Me, wayward Girl, of Man's *superior* kind;
This strong Propensity had marr'd each Scheme,
And Prudence yielded to a golden Dream.
Perhaps I'd then been bred a learn'd Divine,
With *Greek* and *Hebrew* in this Head of mine;
With musty Classics stuff'd, dry Grammar Rules,
And all the specious Lumber of the Schools:
Yet had an Itch for scribbling fill'd my Brain,
This Care and Cost had been bestow'd in vain.
   Or had I, studious of the healing Art,
Been taught with Care to act old *Galen*'s Part,
Perus'd *Hippocrates*'s labour'd Page,
And thumb'd with Rev'rence each time-honour'd Sage;
Yet when from College Rules and Orders free,
My Pen had once regain'd its Liberty;
Thoughtless of Gain, and warm with fancy'd Fire,
I certainly had quitted *Mead* and *Floyer*,
For *Milton*, *Shakespear*, *Dryden*, *Pope*, and *Young*;
And left *Sanctorious* for an idle Song:
Strother, *Boerhaave*, and *Celsus*, had giv'n way
To a smart Satire or a Roundelay:
For who bemus'd, and in a rhyming Strain,
Cou'd mark the various Fibres of the Brain?
Leave all the dear Ideas Fancy forms,
To learn the strange Effect of *Snails* and *Worms*?
Try with what Qualities each Drug is fraught,
And praise the Virtues of some nauseous Draught?
   Had I been bred at *Gray*'s or *Lincoln*'s Inn,
'Mid Law-suits, empty Quibbles, Doubts, and Din,
Attended duly at the wrangling Hall,
And learnt to *baffle*, *bluster*, *bounce*, and *bawl*:
Yet with Impatience in the long Vacation,
I shou'd have left this profitable Station;
Have quitted *Salkeld* and the Lawyer's Gown,
And all the gay Amusements of the Town;

Appendix

Have fled in Raptures to the peaceful *Grange*,
And left *Coke, Carthew, Nelson, Wood*, and *Strange*,
Hughes, Hale, and *Hawkins, Bacon, King*, and *Cay*,
For *Swift, Hill, Congreve, Cowley, Garth*, and *Gay*:
And in some Cot, retir'd from Crowd and Noise,
Have sought serene Delights and rural Joys;
Mus'd by a Fountain, slept beneath a Tree;
And, 'stead of Draughts, compos'd——an Elegy.
Inspir'd by *Silvia*'s Eyes, or *Daphne*'s Air,
Or *Cynthia*'s rosy Cheeks, and curling Hair;
My most exalted Wish, and only Aim,
Had been to eternize the fav'rite Dame:
Her Charms in softest Numbers to express,
And paint my Passion in the liveliest Dress.
    In short, whatever my Employ had been,
It soon had yielded to this darling *Sin*:
And nought but *Russel*'s land, or *Gideon*'s Purse,
Had sav'd the Poet——from——the Poet's Curse.

Untitled Manuscript Poem

So wide's the diff'rence 'twixt the Sexes,
It only our poor brains perplexes
To guess at what he-creatures mean;
To think, wou'd plunge one in the spleen.
When females whether young or aged
In Friendship have their minds engaged,
Not all the bus'ness in the nation
Can make them quit the dear vocation.
If near, they chat; if absent, write
What airy fancy can indite;
And not a week, nor scarce a day
Can pass, but something's found to say;
Tho' it be simple, trite or childish,
Unmeaning, foolish, apish, wildish,
It serves to prove our heart's affection,
And Friendship ne'er can make objection.
If the free chat or artless line
Convince us of esteem, 'tis fine.

Appendix

This is the female character;
But, for the males, I dare aver
Whatever friendship they profess,
Or love, they think of nothing less.
To prove what I assert, Friend Hateley
Took a short supper with us lately:
To find some talk I was much puzzl'd;
But thought my mouth shou'd not be muzzl'd,
So ask'd him, When he heard from Steed?
He ne'er had had a line, — indeed!
And Charles had said the same before;—
Oh! how male friendship I adore!
Place the Things near to one-another,
With friendship how they keep a pother!
Ten times a day perhaps they'll meet
No doubt their Converse must be sweet.
But send them fifty miles asunder,
And what's the consequence, I wonder?
Why days, weeks, months may pass away,
And not a word have they to say;
To present objects, present friends
Th'unsteady mind alone attends;
Leaving to female breasts that lasting flame
Which only can deserve true friendship's name,
A name so dear, a flame so pleasing
May well attone for all their teazing.
They Lords of the creation! frightful!
No, female friendship's more delightful.
In female breasts sincere affection lives,
And tastes enraptur'd ev'ry joy it gives;
Prone to no change, no selfish end in view
To the heart's dictates fondly, strictly true;
Proving thro' Life and at it's awful end,
The greatest good on earth's a faithful friend.

Dear Bess, I've wrote thee many rhymes,
More than are good by twenty times;
But, as in verse I had begun,
I thought my Pen shou'd have it's run:
So fare thee well, with love and blessing
And true affection past expressing
To Harriet, thee, and all our friends
My whimsical epistle ends.

Appendix

Written on Walking in the
Woods of Gregynog
In Montgomeryshire,
the seat of
Arthur Blayney, Esq.

Ye sweetly varied scenes, that rise
   With pow'r to charm the gloomiest soul,
Ah! had ye bless'd my ravish'd eyes,
   Ere my mind bent to care's controul;
When youthful Fancy's vivid glow
Banish'd the family of woe,
Then, cheerful as the linnet's strain,
My song had echo'd o'er the plain.

   And sure these hills, these bow'rs and groves,
Where Peace resides, and Virtue roves,
Roves in their owner's form benign,
May bid misfortune cease to pine;
Give calm suspension to each care,
Cheer the dull features of despair,
Bid fancy reassume her reign,
And pleasure gild each smiling plain.

   Hail! ye majestic wilds! sweet Cambria, hail!
Music and magic float in ev'ry gale:
The mellow black-bird chants his ev'ning lay,
And the sweet red-breast warbles from the spray;
The pensive stock-dove pours his soothing tale,
And soft responses sigh thro' ev'ry vale:
Corroding grief here sinks to soft repose,
And healing balm the wounded spirit knows.

      See the mountains, tow'ring high,
      Lift their summits to the sky,
      While many a dew-charg'd, fleecy cloud,
      Brooding show'rs, their tops enshroud:
      Brown and sterile here they frown,—
      There their steepy sides adown
      Graze the shepherd's bleating care,—
      There the flow'ry pasture fair:
      Lower, down their fertile sides

Appendix

The patient hind his plough-share guides,
Where future harvests waving smile,
And health and plenty crown his toil.

Distant, the tall rock rough and hoar
　　Nods o'er Sabrina's rapid wave,
Where her shelving sedge-crown'd shore
　　Invites the blue-ey'd nymph to lave;
　　　While the whisp'ring zephyrs breathe
　　　Thro' the woody dell beneath.

　　　Now the placid orb of night
　　Sheds o'er the grove her soften'd light,
　　Gilds the smooth lake with silv'ry beam,
　　And adds new beauties to the stream,
　　As murm'ring to the breeze it flows,
　　And sooths all nature to repose.

O! Care, when with thy train I've toil'd all day,
Give me at eve thro' these lov'd haunts to stray,—
Woo peace and contemplation to my breast,
While ev'ry jarring thought is charm'd to rest.

　　　　　　　　　　　　　　　　M.D.
　　　　　　　　　　　　　　1st. July 1794.

Appendix

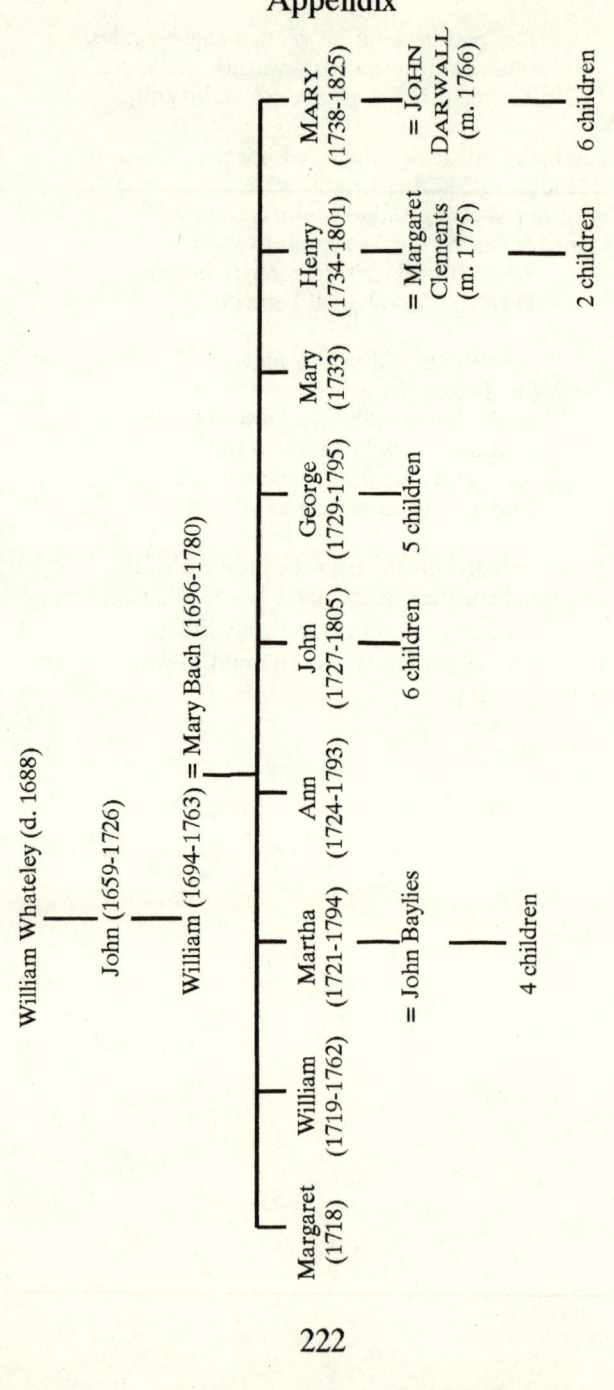

Appendix

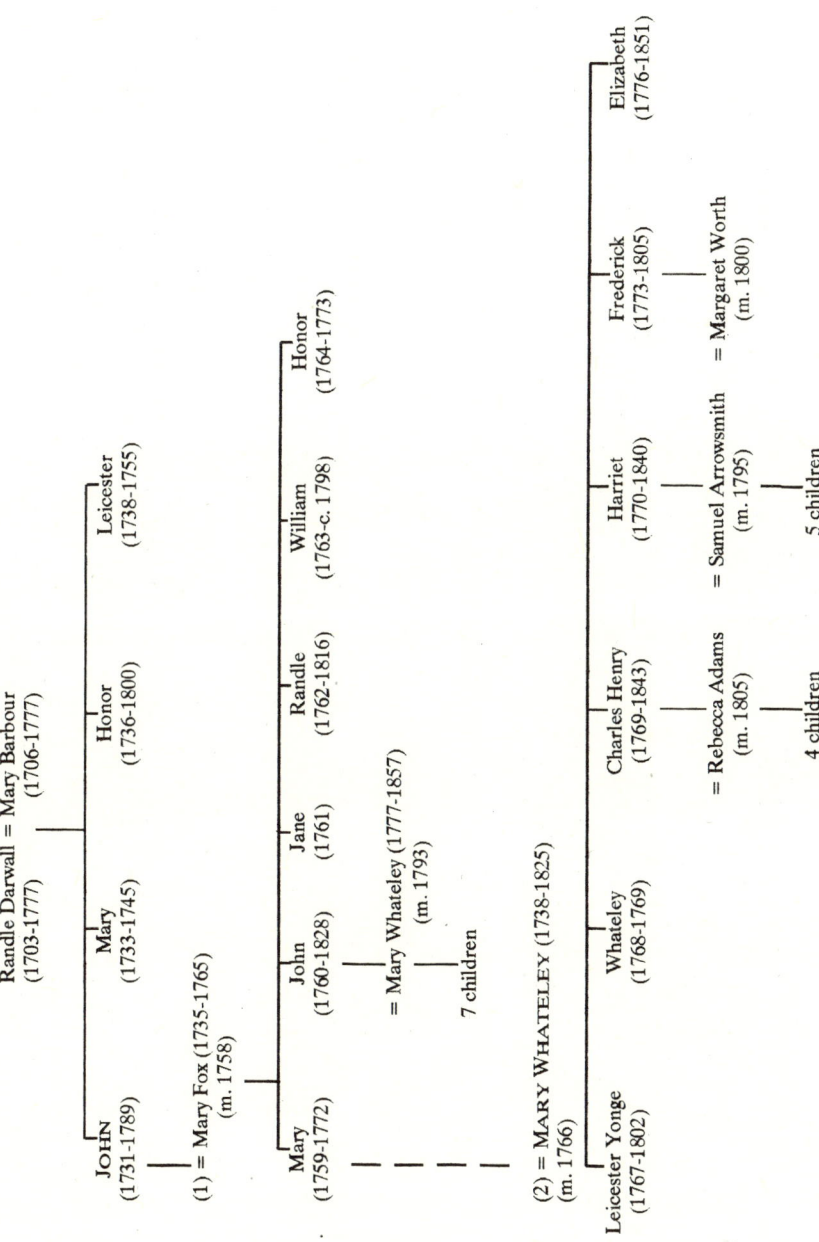

223

References

Abbreviations frequently used:

1764: [Mary Whateley], *Original Poems on Several Occasions by Miss Whateley* (London: R. and J. Dodsley, 1764).

1794:1, 2: [Mary Darwall], *Poems on Several Occasions by Mrs. Darwall (Formerly Miss Whateley)*, 2 vols. (Walsall: F. Milward, 1794).

1810: Elizabeth Darwall, *The Storm with Other Poems* (London: Ridgway, 1810).

Aris: *Aris's Birmingham Gazette*; references taken from manuscript notebooks by Henry Somerfield in Walsall Local History Centre, which reproduce most articles referring to Walsall.

BRL: Birmingham Reference Library.

Diary: extracts from manuscript diary by Dr. John Darwall, 1828 (Darwall-Smith family archives).

DNB: *Dictionary of National Biography*.

GM: *Gentleman's Magazine*.

LJRO: Lichfield Joint Record Office.

PRO: Public Record Office (London and Kew).

Salt: William Salt Library, Stafford.

SRO: Staffordshire County Record Office.

VH: *Victoria History of the Counties of England*.

References

WLHC: Walsall Local History Centre.

Sources for genealogical data:

Alumni Oxonienses.

Aris obituary index, manuscript, BRL (Local Studies).

Darwall-Smith family archives: manuscript genealogical trees (Whateley and Darwall); manuscript list of John Darwall's twelve children (birth dates, times, and places; christening dates; names of sureties).

International Genealogical Index and individual parish registers, especially those of Beoley, Worcs.; Walsall, Staffs.; Deritend, War. These parish registers also contain data on the clergymen's careers, including dated signatures.

Scrapbooks of *Staffordshire Advertiser* announcements of births, marriages, and deaths, 1795-1840 (Salt).

Notes

Introduction

1. "the BRITISH NINE"—*Monthly Review*, April 1774, p. 243; see p. 105 below.

1. Anna Seward's list—GM April 1789, p. 292.

Chapter 1

9. did not own the farm . . . ninety-nine years—Indenture between John Whateley and Ralph Sheldon, dated September 20, 1698; I thank Philip Mortiboy and BRL for a copy of this document.

9. William . . . go into farming—Whateley is a common name in the Midlands. The William Whateley of Wooten Wawen (d. in Wooten Wawen 1762) is the most likely one of that name to be the poet's brother. John, her second brother, was married there in 1755; his wife and two children subscribed to 1764 from "Wooton Park."

9. taking with her the third child, Ann—Probable, given the Martha Baylies and Ann Whateley residing in Walsall in the early 1790s.

10. 360 pounds—Will of John Whateley (d. 1726; Hereford and Worcester County Record Office, Ref. No. 008.7 BA3585).

10. major crops in Beoley—All information about Beoley, its Hall, and its church, from VH *Worcestershire*, primarily Vol. 4, 12-19; *Worcestershire Directory for 1820*, compiled by S. Lewis (Stourbridge: Heming [1820]); *Noake's Guide to Worcestershire* (London: Longman, 1868); and a personal visit.

10. 1720 . . . William Whateley himself—Noted in the parish register.

11. a humble house—E. A. B. Barnard, "Some Beoley Parish Accounts 1656-1700," rpt. from *Transactions of the Worcestershire Archaeological*

Notes

Society for 1948 (BRL Local Studies), pp. 38-39, lists Beoley householders in 1674; William Whateley's house with one hearth put him in the lower half of the economy of the parish, where thirty-two out of sixty houses had more than one hearth.

The ranks and properties of the Whateley family come from various indentures (1683, 1694, 1698, 1704, 1728, 1735), and the Returns for Papist Estates (1717 and 1737); I thank Philip Mortiboy and BRL for copies of these documents.

13. Lawrence Stone—*The Family, Sex and Marriage in England 1500-1800* (London: Weidenfeld and Nicolson, 1977).

13. George ... apprenticed to a "toymaker" ... gold and silver—Apprenticeship records, Society of Genealogists (London), p. 6293 (17/159, 1745). I thank S. C. van Dulken of the British Library for information about George's patents.

14. Henry ... to ... Walsall ... to read law—Law List for 1777 but practicing in 1760s (WLHC deeds, etc.); not a member of the Inns of Court, so trained under apprenticeship system. I thank Mrs. M. Harrod of the Law Society, London, for this and other information about the List.

14. sent each other verses—GM Supplement 1761, p. 635.

14. Dr. John Wall ... two letters—GM Supplement 1761, p. 635; GM February 1762, p. 84.

15. encouraged her to persevere—For the GM's mixed but primarily supportive attitude toward women, see Jean E. Hunter, "The 18th-Century Englishwoman: According to the Gentleman's Magazine," in *Woman in the 18th Century and Other Essays*, ed. Paul Fritz and Richard Morton (Toronto and Sarasota: Stevens and Hakkert, 1976), pp. 73-88.

15. "a parcell of old watches"—John Whateley's will.

15. "Well, Mrs. Loggin"—For this anecdote, I am indebted to Mrs. D. M. Manson, Bordesley Historical Society, Redditch.

Notes

15-16. Shenstone ... wrote her a letter—*Letters of William Shenstone*, ed. Duncan Mallam (Minneapolis: Univ. of Minnesota Press, 1939), p. 115.

16. cousins in Tardebigge—Marjorie Williams, *William Shenstone: A Chapter in Eighteenth-Century Taste* (Birmingham: Cornish Brothers, 1935), p. 138.
Conjecture about an early Whateley/Shenstone connection is strengthened by the fact that William and John Whateley went to farm in Wooten Wawen, and Barrels, the home of Shenstone's friend Lady Luxborough from 1736, is "part of Wooten Wawen" (Helen S. Hughes, *The Gentle Hertford: Her Life and Letters* [New York: Macmillan, 1940], p. 441).

16. "Daughter of SHENSTONE"—Mary Scott, *The Female Advocate* (1774), intro. Gae Holladay, Augustan Reprint Society Publication No. 224 (Los Angeles: William Andrews Clark Memorial Library, 1984), p. 26.

16. Delia for Strephon ... Sylvia's sighs—1764, pp. 45-47, 60-61.

16. a plain girl—1764, pp. 58, 93, 105; unpublished letter from Shenstone to Mrs. Bennet, October 30, 1761 (BRL Archives).

17. "Elegy on a much lamented Friend"—1764, pp. 23-25.

19. "To my Garden" ... "To Mr. Copywell"—GM June 1759, p. 282.

19. "Harriott Airy"—I thank Roger Lonsdale for calling "Harriott" to my attention and for identifying her as Mary Whateley. Two of "Harriott's" poems appear, revised, in 1764, which makes the identification firm.

20. another poem by "Harriot Airy"—"An Address to my Pen"; see pp. 46-47 below.

21. "Ode to Truth"—GM November 1759, p. 538.

22. "Harriot" ... disappears—She reappeared briefly in *Memoirs of a Coquet; or, The History of Miss Harriot Airy* (London: Hoggard, 1765),

Notes

an anonymous novel in which the heroine, who has a turn for writing verses, remains unmarried as punishment for her coquetry; the impermanence of female friendship is also derided. Could this be Copywell's revenge on Mary Whateley?

22. "Copywell" . . . William Woty—DNB. For bankruptcy, see *London Gazette*, September 10, 1757; I thank Betty Rizzo for this information.

Chapter 2

24. year of 1759 was ending—"Ode to Truth" is dated from Beoley, November 14, 1759; and see p. 26 below and note.

24. real estate . . . debts—*Aris*, August 4, 1760; November 1, 1762; etc.

24. "Elegy on leaving ———"—1764, pp. 34-35.

25. Lady Luxborough had used the name—"Written at Ferme Ornee, near Birmingham; August 7th, 1749," in *A Collection of Poems in Six Volumes by Several Hands* (London: J. Dodsley, 1770), 4, 310-11; for the attribution of this and her other poems, see Shenstone, *Letters*, p. 307 note. See also Ian A. Gordon, ed., *Shenstone's Miscellany 1759-1763* (Oxford: Clarendon Press, 1952), p. 144, where he identifies, among others, Lady Luxborough as "Asteria" and Shenstone as "Cynthio."

26. Walsall had no library—Major sources for Walsall's history and geography: VH *Staffordshire*, Vol. 17; E. L. Glew, *History of the Borough and Foreign of Walsall* (Walsall: Robinson, 1856); Ernest James Homeshaw, *The Corporation of the Borough and Foreign of Walsall* (Walsall: County Borough, 1960); Herbert Lee, *A Short History of Walsall* (Walsall: Kirby, 1927); Marilyn Lewis and David Woods, *The Book of Walsall* (Buckingham: Barracuda Books, 1987); Thomas Pearce, *History and Directory of Walsall* (Birmingham: Thomson and Wrightson, 1813); Frederic W. Willmore, *A History of Walsall* (Walsall and London: Robinson and Simpkin, Marshall, 1887); Richard D. Woodall, *Walsall Milestones* (Sutton Coldfield: Tector, [1951]); eighteenth- and nineteenth-century maps from WLHC; personal observation.

Notes

26. "Now as the depth of *December* . . ."—GM Supplement 1761, p. 635; "Beoley" is misspelled "Berty" but glossed in a footnote as her home. Her letter introduced by a letter from Dr. Wall dated January 30, 1760.

26. "Liberty"—1764, pp. 17-20.

26. then steeply—So steeply that today the top of the High Street is a flight of steps preventing traffic from making the perilous turn into the crossbars of the T which it made in the eighteenth century.

28. *The Spaniard Outwitted*—*Aris*, September 22, 1760. Probably the anonymous farce *The Intriguing Footman, or, The Spaniard Outwitted* (1742); possibly George Downing's pantomime, *The Tricks of Harlequin; or, The Spaniard Outwitted* (1739).

28. Stephen Chatterton—*Poems by the Late Mr. Stephen Chatterton* (London: Printed for the author's widow, 1795); "Walsallia, an Ode. For the Musical Society at Walsall" (pp. 41-42); "The Walsall Beauties" (pp. 12-15). Chatterton is usually dubbed "of Willenhall," but when he contributed a poem to GM in 1765, he gave his address as Walsall.

30. at least four more—*London Chronicle*, December 26-29, 1761, p. 628; GM Supplement 1761, p. 636; *Royal Magazine*, January 1762, pp. 9-10; *London Magazine*, January 1762, p. 46.

30. Dr. Wall had started—The earliest publication, in the *London Chronicle*, is introduced by a letter from "A.W." saying he has had Dr. Wall's letter (dated January 30, 1760) and the poem "for some time." "A.W." may be a fiction. The particulars cannot be reconstructed, but it is clear that one way or another Dr. Wall was promoting Mary Whateley's work.

31. Sir Samuel Hellier—VH *Staffordshire*, Vol. 20, 201, 204-06, 220; *Alumni Oxonienses*.

31. Randle Darwall—*Alumni Oxonienses*; *Notes and Queries* Series 3, Vol. 12 (August 3, 1867), 96-97.

31. ordained deacon, and then priest—Ordination papers (B/A/10, LJRO).

Notes

31. curate at Bushbury—On his marriage bond and allegation he is noted as curate of Bushbury (B/C/6,7, LJRO).

32. Trysull where John had been appointed—He signs himself "clerk" in the parish register.

33. "Ode to Friendship"—1764, pp. 100-01.

33. piece of family gossip—Diary.

34. notoriously underpaid—Norman Sykes, *Church and State in England in the Eighteenth Century* (Cambridge: Cambridge Univ. Press, 1934), Chapter 5, "The Clerical Subalterns." Richard Graves paid his curate thirty pounds (Clarence Tracy, *A Portrait of Richard Graves* [Toronto: Univ. of Toronto Press, 1987], p. 86). Parson Woodforde, with an income of four hundred pounds, "lived in some style" (Ronald Blythe, intro. to *A Country Parson: James Woodforde's Diary 1759-1802* [Oxford: Oxford Univ. Press, 1985], p. 12).

34. Bushbury . . . twenty-eight pounds—Letter of appointment, Jeremiah Whitehouse to the Bishop of Lichfield and Coventry, September 2, 1757 (B/A/10/1757, LJRO).

34-35. Trade slumped . . . food riots—Conrad Gill, *History of Birmingham*, Vol. 1 (London, New York, and Toronto: Oxford Univ. Press, 1952), 128, 447.

35. "Rural Happiness"—1764, pp. 29-33.

35. Bordesley Hall . . . John Taylor—VH *Warwickshire*, Vol. 7, 63, 89, 95; Victor Skipp, *The Centre of England* (London: Eyre Methuen, 1979), p. 217; John Morris Jones, *Memoirs of Aston Parish* (Birmingham: City Education Department, 1978), p. 37.

35. "the Toy-Shop of the World"—Common phrase, immortalized by James Bisset, "A Poetic Survey Round Birmingham," excerpted in *The New Oxford Book of Eighteenth-Century Verse*, ed. Roger Lonsdale (Oxford and New York: Oxford Univ. Press, 1984), p. 837.

Notes

35. influential lawyers—See, e.g., Governors' Order Book, Vol. 2, in the archives of the King Edward VI School, Birmingham; obituary notices from the *Birmingham Post* collected by G. H. Osborne, pp. 38, 91 (BRL Local Studies).

36. with its theater—John E. Cunningham, *Theatre Royal: The History of the Theatre Royal Birmingham* (Oxford: George Ronald, 1950), pp. 10ff.

36. destroyed . . . during the Priestley riots—Skipp, *Centre of England*, p. 217.

37. "Petition for an Absolute Retreat"—*The Poems of Anne Countess of Winchilsea*, ed. Myra Reynolds (1903; rpt. New York: AMS Press, 1974), pp. 68-77.

38. William Shenstone . . . a "putrid fever"—E. Munro Purkis, *William Shenstone: Poet and Landscape Gardener* (Wolverhampton: Whitehead, 1931), p. 116.

38. Randle Darwall . . . corresponded . . . signing up subscribers—Unpublished manuscript letter by Randle Darwall, January 28, 1764 (Salt); Randle says he and John both correspond with Miss Whateley.

38. the finishing touches—She revised her work considerably; see pp. 46-48 below.

Chapter 3

40. "the Hon. Lady . . ." widow of the fourth baronet—1764, p. 3; VH *Staffordshire*, Vol. 20, 25.

40. granddaughter in Shenstone's garden—Shenstone, *Letters*, p. 456, lists Miss Wrottesley among visitors in 1762.

40. Wrottesley . . . carried a great deal of weight—See VH *Staffordshire*, especially Vols. 5 and 20.

Notes

40. John Welchman—DNB, "Welchman, Edward"; John Burman, *Warwickshire People and Places* (Birmingham: Cornish Brothers, 1936), p. 73.

40. "To the Rev. Mr. Welchman at Tanworth"—1764, pp. 90-94.

41. Dr. John Wall—DNB; Franklin A. Barnett, *Worcester Porcelain and Lund's Bristol* (London: Faber and Faber, 1966), pp. 1-2, 12, 21; VH *Worcestershire*, Vol. 2, 276-77.

41. Shenstone . . . valued—Shenstone, *Letters*, pp. 223, 337.

42. Shenstone . . . wrote to his friend Mrs. Bennet—See note to p. 16.

42. A lively letter—See note to p. 38.

43. A versifier himself—A long blank verse poem, "Health and Content, written in sickness," was published in the *London Magazine* in September, November, and December 1739, signed R. Darwall; others, many on music and signed R.D., appeared in later years. His lively letter of 1764 concludes with a curiously formless poem about health. Also in manuscript is a long and charming verse letter to his wife lamenting her absence, expressing his love, and claiming that the baby "Jack" sympathizes with his woes (dated Haughton, January 15, 1732/33; from the papers of Mrs. Penelope Darwall).

43. "Elegy on the Uses of Poetry"—1764, pp. 109-13.

44. Shenstone would have agreed—For a detailed comparison of their poetics, and their poems, see my " 'Like—but oh, how different!': William Shenstone and Mary Whateley," in *Gender at Work: Four Women Writers of the Eighteenth Century*, ed. Ann Messenger (Detroit: Wayne State Univ. Press, 1990), pp. 15-33.

44. "To Mr. O———y"—1764, pp. 62-63.

45. it was linked with the letter—His letter contains a parenthesis referring the reader to Miss Whateley's poems in the previous month's issue.

Notes

45. the *Annual Register* for 1761—Despite the date, a later publication than the January and February 1762 *London Magazine*.

45. "a pretty Large Collection"—Shenstone, *Letters*, p. 420.

46. two September letters—Ibid., pp. 418-20.

46. letter thanking Mrs. Bennet—See note to p. 16.

46. in two versions . . . in three—"To my Garden" in GM June 1759, p. 282, and 1764; "An Address to my Pen" in GM October 1759, p. 483, and 1764; "Liberty" in GM Supplement 1761, p. 636, in the *London Magazine*, January 1762, p. 46, and 1764. I omit here consideration of "Liberty" in the *Royal Female Magazine* (May 1760, p. 232), which except for one two-word phrase (contributed by a creative printer?) cannot be considered a "version" different from the GM text; other variants between these two texts, otherwise explainable, are insignificant. For versions of the Anacreontic, a special case, see pp. 71-72 and note.

46. "more correct than I almost ever saw"—*Letters*, p. 419.

47. "simplicity rather than surprize"—*The Works in Verse and Prose of William Shenstone, Esq.*, 6th ed. (London: J. Dodsley, 1791), Vol. 2, 181.

48. country people really were more virtuous—Ibid., p. 134.

49. "Florence wine"—Purkis, *William Shenstone: Poet and Landscape Gardener*, p. 16, quoting Richard Graves.

49. Women are inferior . . . "genuine esteem" . . . fancy and imagination—*Works*, Vol. 2, 194, 206, 212.

49. "tenderness" and "sensibility"—Robert Dodsley, preface to Shenstone's *Works*, Vol. 1, 8, 11.

49. "On the left side . . ."—*London Chronicle*, February 16, 1763.

Notes

50. Thomas Percy . . . ascribed it to Miss Whateley—*Shenstone's Miscellany*, ed. Gordon, p. 1.

50. Shenstone valued modesty—*Works*, Vol. 2, 48, e.g.

50. "A man possessed of intellectual talents"—Ibid., p. 4.

50. considered the possibility and fretted—*Letters*, p. 429.

50. *Annual Register*—1761, p. 247.

50. "Fame to lose . . . kind Opinion"—1764, p. 4.

51. he had urged Lady Luxborough—*Letters*, p. 307.

51. planned to ask . . . Dartmouth—Ibid., pp. 419, 420.

51. his own publisher and friend—Dodsley could also have been personally acquainted with Miss Whateley; he often visited Shenstone at the Leasowes, as she sometimes did. (James E. Tierney, ed., *The Correspondence of Robert Dodsley, 1733-1764* [Cambridge and New York: Cambridge Univ. Press, 1988], p. 19.)

51. John Langhorne—DNB; George Atkinson, *The Worthies of Westmorland* (London: Robinson, 1850), pp. 85-118; J. T. Langhorne, ed., intro. ("Memoirs") to John Langhorne, *Poetical Works*, 2 vols. (London: Mawman, 1804), Vol. 1, 5-25; anon. intro. to *The Poetical Works of John Langhorne* (London: Cooke, [1789?]).

51. considered himself "liberal"—*Monthly Review*, June 1764, p. 445.

51. comfortably conservative . . . social conscience—See, e.g., *Works*, ed. Cooke: "The Amiable King" (p. 62); "The Country Justice" (pp. 83-101); "Proemium" (p. 48); et passim.

51. One early memoirist—Intro., Cooke's ed., p. 5.

52. a lively essay—*The Effusions of Friendship and Fancy* (2nd ed., 1766; rpt. New York: Garland, 1970), Vol. 1, 93-100.

Notes

52. "literary acquirements" . . . Italian—J. T. Langhorne, "Memoirs," pp. 10-11.

52-53. her later poem . . . an ancient debate—"An Epistle to a Friend," 1794:1, pp. 19-25. For the relationship between friendship and married love, see Bonnie S. Anderson and Judith P. Zinsser, *A History of Their Own* (Harmondsworth: Penguin, 1990), Vol. 1, 440-41, tracing the beginnings of the debate to the fifteenth century. See also Orest Ranum, "The Refuges of Intimacy," in *A History of Private Life: III, Passions of the Renaissance*, ed. Roger Chartier, tr. Arthur Goldhammer (Cambridge, Mass., and London: Belknap Press, 1989), pp. 252-57; Sylvia Harcstark Myers, *The Bluestocking Circle: Women, Friendship and the Life of the Mind in Eighteenth-Century England* (Oxford: Clarendon Press, 1990), pp. 85, 234.

53. Hannah More . . . one of his early biographers—Atkinson, *Worthies of Westmorland*, p. 97.

53. "Precepts of Conjugal Happiness"—Cooke's ed., pp. 73-76.

53. admire each other's poetry—In an essay advocating simplicity in the diction of poetry, Langhorne quotes "an ingenious lady" (Mary Whateley) for both example and precept (*Effusions*, Vol. 2, 97): "Enough, the Muse her Wreath of Ivy twines, / Mixt with each smiling Field-flow'r's fragrant Bloom" (from "Elegy Written in a Garden," 1764, p. 59).

53. "Elegy on the Search of Happiness"—1764, pp. 78-80.

55. other women poets who shared the tradition—For example, Katherine Philips, in "Happiness," Lady Mary Chudleigh, in "On the Vanities of this Life," and Elizabeth Carter, in "On Fortune," emphasize virtue; Anne Finch, Countess of Winchilsea, in "All Is Vanity," and Mary Masters, in "The Vanity of Human Life," emphasize futurity; Anne Killigrew, in "The Discontent," seeks only oblivion—she is unique in the tradition.

Notes

55. stoicism may be useful . . . fraudulent—Eliza Haywood makes a similar point in *The Female Spectator*, Book, 24; see my *His and Hers* (Lexington: University Press of Kentucky, 1986), pp. 145-47.

55. "TO A LADY"—Cooke's ed., p. 134.

56. *Visions of Fancy*—Cooke's ed., pp. 140-47.

56. Langhorne . . . wrote at the age of twenty-seven—DNB.

56. "a despairing lover"—J. T. Langhorne, "Memoirs," p. 12.

57. "To the Rev. Mr. J. Langhorne"—1764, pp. 114-17.

58. "To Miss W———"—1764, pp. 11-12.

Chapter 4

61. Shenstone . . . Elegy I—*Works*, Vol. 1, 29-31.

61. Dr. Johnson caustically remarked . . . read and imitate—*Lives of the English Poets* ("Pope"), intro. Arthur Waugh (London, New York, and Toronto: Oxford Univ. Press, 1952), Vol. 2, 309; *The Rambler*, intro. S. C. Roberts (London: Dent, 1953), p. 81 (No. 36).

61. *Monthly Review*—June 1764, pp. 445-50.

63. "tow'ring *Fancy* . . ."—1764, pp. 74-76.

63. "Satire on Men . . ."—1764, p. 104.

64. "tuneful Maid"—1764, p. 11.

64. notoriously partial when reviewing—Margaret Strickland, *A Memoir of the Life . . . of Edmund Cartwright* (1843; rpt. New York: Kelly, 1971), p. 31.

64. *Critical Review*—August 1764, pp. 114-18.

Notes

66. "Elegy written in a Garden"—1764, pp. 56-59.

66. mottoes and inscriptions—"A Description of the Leasowes," in Shenstone, *Works*, Vol. 2, 298-99, 319-20.

67. "Occasioned by reading some Sceptical Essays"—1764, pp. 53-55.

68. Silly girls are a frequent target—See, e.g., Anne Killigrew, "The Fourth Epigram. On Galla"; "Ephelia," "To a Proud Beauty"; Aphra Behn, "The Coquet," from *The Lover's Watch*; Anne Finch, Countess of Winchilsea, "Ardelia's Answer to Ephelia."

68. "Ode"—1764, pp. 26-28.

69. "The Power of Destiny"—1764, pp. 13-16.

71. "*Russel*'s Land, or *Gideon*'s Purse"—Russell, probably the Duke of Bedford, who had substantial and lucrative landholdings in London and elsewhere; Gideon, millionaire London financier active in national affairs.

71. three Anacreontics—*Royal Female Magazine*, May 1760, pp. 232-33; 1764, pp. 21-22, 84-85. I cannot with certainty identify Shenstone's editorial hand in the changes made from one version to another; for the most part, these changes differ in kind from those discussed in Chapter 3.

71. Anacreon's first ode—Miss Whateley's title is "The First Ode of Anacreon, imitated"; this is No. 23 in most modern editions, No. 1 in Abraham Cowley's 1683 translation.

72. "Liberty" . . . further interpretation—1764, pp. 17-20. For further argument about its allegorical meaning, see my "Women Poets and the Pastoral Trap: The Case of Mary Whateley," in *Eighteenth-Century Women and the Arts*, ed. Frederick M. Keener and Susan E. Lorsch (New York, Westport, and London: Greenwood Press, 1988), pp. 93-105.

Notes

Chapter 5

75. "Written in Spring 1764"—1794:2, pp. 72-73. When quoting from 1794, I silently correct obvious typographical errors.

77. about one hundred pounds—I thank Betty Rizzo for help in working out this sum, which is based on the number and cost of subscriptions.

77. letters to John—See note to p. 38.

77. Two of her poems—*Birmingham Register*, Vol. 1 (Birmingham: Sketchley, 1765), 30, 32; I thank Isobel Grundy for this reference.

78. "Song"—1794:2, pp. 14-16.

79. a cure for love—Steven F. Walker, *A Cure for Love: A Generic Study of the Pastoral Idyll* (New York and London: Garland, 1987), Chapter 2 et passim.

80. fragment of a diary—Diary.

80. The diarist's mother—Mary Whateley Darwall (1771-1857), the daughter of the poet's brother George and wife of her oldest stepson, John.

80. married love . . . friendship—in "An Epistle to a Friend," 1794:1, pp. 19-25; and see pp. 142-43 below. Compare Katherine Philips, who reverses the idea, calling friendship "Love's Elixir" (*Poems. By the Incomparable Mrs. K.P.* [London: Marriot, 1664], p. 160).

81. eight books for sale—Advertised together in the *London Chronicle* for April 29-May 1, 1766.

81. appointment as rector of Blagdon—Announced in GM August 1766, p. 392.

81. Mrs. Hewan—Probably the wife of Lieut. Thomas Hewan of the 4th Dragoons. I thank Miss E. Talbot Rice of the National Army Museum, London, for this information.

Notes

81. "Ode, Addressed to Mrs. Hewan"—1794:2, pp. 34-40.

83. "Elegy, Addressed to Mrs. Hewan"—1794:2, pp. 65-68.

Chapter 6

89. Clarence Tracy—*A Portrait of Richard Graves*; see especially p. 78.

90. Family legend has it—D. W. Darwall, "A Walsall Poetess," *Walsall Observer*, June 1923; in WLHC. I thank Alan Darwall-Smith for identifying the newspaper in which this article appeared.

90. all sixty-two of them—Today there are fifty-nine; for the eighteenth century, see GM September 1799, p. 763.

90. John Langhorne's jogging—Atkinson, *Worthies of Westmorland*, pp. 114-15.

90. a modern commentator—N. Temperley, *The Music of the English Parish Church* (Cambridge: Cambridge Univ. Press, 1979), p. 223.

90. "a great Variety of Dancing"—*Aris*, November 10, 1766.

91. local amateurs . . . Home's *Douglas*—Stebbing Shaw, *History and Antiquities of Staffordshire* (London: Nichols, 1798-1801), Vol. 2, 75.

91. young William Siddons—Roger Manvell, *Sarah Siddons: Portrait of an Actress* (London: Heineman, 1970), pp. 16-18.

91. A dazzling success . . . a fervent Scot—Richard W. Bevis, *English Drama: Restoration and Eighteenth Century, 1660-1789* (London and New York: Longman, 1988), p. 205.

91. Shenstone . . . partial to Scots—[Richard Graves], *Recollection of Some Particulars in the Life of the late William Shenstone* (London: Dodsley, 1788), p. 165.

Notes

92. heavy snows—*Aris*, January 12 and 19, 1767.

92. Langhorne's long-delayed marriage—DNB.

92. flour was scarce—*Aris*, January 12, 1767.

92. Beoley had to ration—Barnard, "Some Beoley Parish Accounts," p. 39.

92. to count . . . the Catholics—There were over one hundred, listed by name and occupation (George Every, "The Catholic Community in Walsall 1720-1824," in *Recusant History*, Vol. 19, No. 3 [May 1989], 316-17).

92. a short poem to his tuneful darling—I thank John Whiston of Walsall for supplying this manuscript poem from his own copy of 1764 and for permission to reproduce it here.

93. John Wesley had discovered her—*The Journal of John Wesley*, ed. Nehemiah Curnock (London: Kelly, [1910]), Vol. 5, 252.

93. intervals between "domestic duties"—1794:1, [i]; a few of the poems bear definite dates; a few can be dated from internal evidence. In restoring them to probable intervals, I hope to show in general what Mrs. Darwall's life was like, since they were integrated with her daily routine. The exact dates do not always matter.

94. "On the Author's Husband . . ."—1794:2, pp. 55-57.

95. "To Mr. F. now Earl of W . . ."—*Poems*, ed. Reynolds, pp. 20-23.

95. Robert Felton, was suffering—*Aris*, May 1, 1769, reports his death "after a long and painful Illness."

95. housekeeper-cum-secretary, Mrs. Preston—Elizabeth Pratt, a.k.a. Mary Preston, of Little Sutton, Middlesex, bore Lord Mountrath's only child (*The Complete Peerage*, ed. H. A. Doubleday and Lord Howard De Walden [London: St. Catherine Press, 1936], Vol. 9, 361 note); she inherited various properties (bond from Charles Henry Coote Earl of Mountrath to Elizabeth Pratt . . . August 4, 1775; Bradford [Mountrath]

Notes

Papers D1287/22/5-6, SRO). Many letters in these papers from or mentioning her confirm her influence; see also Chapter 9.

96. probably built of red brick—In 1795 it had been "recently" faced with rough-cast: GM April 1795, p. 281.

96. "four bays of Building"—Glebe terriers (B/V/6, Walsall, LJRO); the house therefore was sixty to eighty feet across the front.

96. young David Davenport—Pearce, *History and Directory of Walsall*, p. 103.

96. 130 to 300 pounds . . . "is rather more"—John Darwall, Visitation Return, April 10, 1772 (B/V/5/1772, Walsall, LJRO).

98. occasional tussle with his churchwardens—St. Matthew's Churchwardens' Account Books for 1771, e.g. (WLHC).

98. as a "surrogate"—*Aris*, November 27, 1769, announces the appointment.

98. vigilante association—*Aris*, March 30, 1772; Oct. 20, 1788; etc.

98. Henry Whateley . . . plans for a canal—*Aris*, August 27, 1770.

98. Martha Baylies was now established . . . recently widowed—Sketchley's *Walsall Directory* for 1770 (WLHC) lists Martha Baylies, mercer and draper. Several Robert Baylieses had died in relevant parishes in recent years; I cannot determine which one had been her husband.

99. "Lines Addressed to a Young Lady"—1794:2, p. 61.

99. presented as a verse letter—I thank Isobel Grundy for this reference.

100. published for the first of many times . . . metrical "New Version" . . . other words—I thank Ian Ledsham, of the Music Library, University of Birmingham, for these details.

Notes

100. Psalmody had already begun declining—W. H. Frere, intro. to *Hymns Ancient and Modern, Historical Edition* (London: Clowes, 1909), pp. xci-xcviii. See also Horton Davies, *Worship and Theology in England from Watts to Wesley to Maurice, 1690-1850* (Princeton: Princeton Univ. Press, 1961), pp. 33-34, 64-65, 234-36.

100. found the pace tedious—GM February 1800, pp. 124-25, "Historical Sketch of the Organs in Walsall Church."

100. "Dr. Watts's flights of fancy"—Quoted in Frere, *Hymns Ancient and Modern*, p. xcii.

100. "the hymnody, like the cuckoo . . ."—Ibid., p. xciii.

100. Darwall's manuscript book of sacred music—British Library Add. Ms. 50891 A, B.

101. Walsall's charity school—Pearce, *History and Directory of Walsall*, p. 20.

101. in Mrs. Darwall's hymn—1794:2, pp. 116-18.

101. the other two charity hymns . . . Hallelujah—I thank Robin Darwall-Smith for his detailed description of the manuscript and his informed comment on the music.

101. a morning and an evening hymn—"Morning Hymn, Sung by the Congregation of Walsall," "Evening Hymn, Sung by the Congregation of Walsall," 1794:2, pp. 119-22.

101. advertised for sale—*Aris*, September 23, 1771.

101ff. a new organ . . . Psalm 150—GM February 1800, pp. 124-25.

103. as . . . John Wesley had done—Richard Arnold, " 'Those Damn Sacred Hymns': Some Problems in the Ontology of 'Text,' " in *Man and Nature: Proceedings of the Canadian Society for Eighteenth-Century Studies*, Vol. 9, ed. Hans Gunther Schwarz, David McNeil, and Roland Bonnel (Edmonton, Alberta: For the Society, 1990), 67 n. 11.

Notes

103. Mr. Stanton's travelling company—*Aris*, January 3-March 28, 1774.

104. an epilogue about ghosts and witches—Stephen Chatterton, "An Occasional Epilogue, Written for and Spoken by Mr. Holcroft, at Walsall Theatre, after the Tragedy of Mackbeth," *Poems*, pp. 96-97.

104. "Invocation"—1794:1, pp. 5-13.

106. *The Female Advocate*—See note to p. 16.

106. "not intended *vainly* . . ."—John Darwall, *Visitation Sermon Preached in the Parish Church of Walsall May 18th 1775* (Wolverhampton: Printed for the Author, [1775]), p. 1.

106. "strenuously oppose . . . *Satan*"—Ibid., p. 5.

107. "when the *spiritual Labourer* . . . rob God himself"—Ibid., pp. 19-21.

107. "*grate* the *Ears* . . ."—ibid., p. ii.

107. bells . . . recast . . . new spire—VH *Staffordshire*, Vol. 17, 233; GM April 1795, p. 281.

107. "the first essay . . ."—John Darwall, preface to the first "Political Lamentation" poem in *Political Lamentations . . . To which is annex'd a Political Sermon* (Printed by the Author, sold by W. Nicoll, London, [1777]), p. 1. The two poems and the sermon all are paginated separately.

107. "UNGRATEFUL BLOWS . . . fost'ring Hand"—Ibid., p. 2.

107. "braver Foes"—Ibid., p. 7; the diction here is remarkably similar to that of the report on Lexington and Concord in GM June 1775, p. 293.

107. "But let us turn . . ."—*Political Lamentations*, pp. 8-9.

108. her brother Henry . . . married—*Aris*, April 24, 1775.

Notes

108. coal mines—D. P. J. Fink, *Queen Mary's Grammar School 1554-1954* (Walsall: Queen Mary's Club, 1954), p. 243.

Chapter 7

110. "Invitation to the same, In Winter"—1794:1, pp. 29-33. The complete poem has thirteen stanzas.

111. poem that she wrote last autumn—"To a Friend, on her recovery from sickness," 1794:1, pp. 26-28.

112. snow, which . . . is still falling heavily—GM January 1776, p. 44; March 1776, p. 117; *Aris*, January 15, 1776; for this and other weather for 1776, see Gilbert White, *The Natural History of Selborne*, new edition (London: Whittaker, Treacher, 1833), pp. 319-24, 395, 401.

112. rioted until trade became impossible . . . additional constables—Lewis and Woods, *Book of Walsall*, p. 49.

113. part of the time with his grandparents—Diary.

113. preference given to her own blood—Among other distortions, the diary of Dr. John Darwall claims that such preference was given, in that Mary Fox's sons were apprenticed to trades and Mary Whateley's to professions (military, medical, legal). But the sons of the two marriages were treated equally in terms of the money spent for their education. In fact, Mary Whateley's sons might have cost the family less. Charles Henry lived at home and studied law with his uncle; money need not have changed hands. Frederick was apprenticed to a surgeon and Leicester to a stained-glass artist; when these two took up military careers, it was in the militia, which paid them a bounty for serving. Even at the rank of ensign and lieutenant, they did not have to purchase commissions. See J. R. Western, *The English Militia in the Eighteenth Century* (London: Routledge and Kegan Paul; Toronto: Univ. of Toronto Press, 1965), Part 3, especially pp. 309, 314, 320.

Notes

114. sonatas for pianoforte—Date conjectural; the sonatas are mentioned in the *Musical Times*, October 1909, p. 650. I thank John Wilson for this reference. The sonata manuscripts have not been located.

114. Mrs. Parkes's bookshop—Advertised in *Aris*, December 19, 1774, e.g.

114. "Poetess" a "reproachful name" . . . Pilkington— *Letters Written by the Late Right Hon. Lady Luxborough to William Shenstone, Esq.* (London: J. Dodsley, 1775), pp. 21, 49.

115. winter fair—For list of major sources of information about Walsall, see note to p. 26.

115. restoring the old rates—Glebe terriers for Walsall, 1762 to 1791 (B/V/6, LJRO).

115. *8 March* . . . the excitement—*Aris*, March 4, 1776.

116. They must assume the latter—"A woman who concealed the birth of a child which died was considered [in law] to have murdered it, unless she could prove otherwise." The law was changed in 1803. (Alice Browne, *The Eighteenth-Century Feminist Mind* [Brighton: Harvester, 1987], p. 17.)

116. Mrs. Langhorne's death—DNB.

118. "Sonnet, on Removing a Bay-Tree"—1794:2, pp. 104-05.

119. As they walk along the boundary—Rosamund Bayne-Powell, *English Country Life in the Eighteenth Century* (London: John Murray, 1935), pp. 20-21 (quoting *Hones Year Book*).

119. Whit-Tuesday Fair—Here I conflate various descriptions of fairs, including Parson Woodforde's references and *Aris*'s details about zebras and lions shown in Walsall.

120. a Bill has been introduced—GM June 1776, pp. 252-53.

121. "Eleonora"—GM June 1776, pp. 255-57.

Notes

121. "an affectionate Husband"—GM June 1776, p. 280.

121. sounded like a song—See "Song, Adapted to a favorite Gavot of Avison's," 1794:1, pp. 48-49, and p. 191 below.

122. "Lines addressed to a Gentleman"—1794:2, pp. 91-95.

124. A total eclipse—GM June 1776, p. 269; August 1776, p. 344.

125. "Declaration" . . . burned to death—GM August 1776, pp. 361-62, 383.

125. Thomas Jackson nearly drowned—Billy Meikle manuscript booklet 64, WLHC; date approximate; attribution of rescue invented.

125. Mr. Rutter . . . fireworks—*Aris*, September 16, 1776.

126. "The Wood-Nymph"—1794:2, pp. 81-85.

126. crowning of . . . Signora Corelli—GM September 1776, p. 432; October 1776, p. 482 (I conflate these two reports). Her correct professional name was Corilla Olimpica, her personal name Maria Maddalena Morelli (1727-1800). Her career in the Accademia dell'Arcadia began in 1750. In 1776, she scored a spectacular triumph, improvising verse on a wide range of both assigned and unexpected topics, before a large and distinguished audience. See E. Portal, *L'Arcadia* (Remo Sandron, 1922), pp. 61-70. I thank Maria Pia Chisu for identifying this poet and supplying the reference.

127. loves the theater . . . Shakespeare—Diary.

127. "Hymn to Plutus"—First published in Langhorne's *The Effusions of Friendship and Fancy* (London: Becket and Hondt, 1763), pp. 120-22; the Delia passage is lacking in the second edition (1766); it was restored in Cooke's edition of the poems (1789?) and subsequent editions. I thank Charles Greene of the Princeton University Library for information about the earlier editions.

128. Mrs. Darwall's answer—1794:1, pp. 41-44.

Notes

129. We are also to ask God—GM November 1776, p. 505.

130. the Green Dragon . . . ladies may be admitted—John Money, *Experience and Identity: Birmingham and the West Midlands 1760-1800* (Montreal: McGill-Queen's Univ. Press, 1977), pp. 111-12.

130. his father . . . had been taken ill—Conjectural; he died early in the next year.

130. Fast Day with the sermon—"A Political Sermon," the third part of *Political Lamentations*.

130. punished for our own sins—John Darwall was not alone in holding this odd opinion. See, e.g., *Letters of Anna Seward* (Edinburgh: Constable, 1811), Vol. 4, 278-79: Miss Seward deplores "the cant of despondency, which imputes the bad consequences of state impolicy to our individual sins. The same weak lamentation was plentifully uttered in the eve of the disastrous American war—as if we had not been unsuccessful on account of our attempted tyranny over that country, but on account of our gaming, lasciviousness, and Sabbath-breaking. . . ." Miss Seward's language suggests that she had read John Darwall's sermon.

Chapter 8

132. Randle's death—Details of inheritances from his will, dated 1772 (B/C/11, LJRO).

132. a glover . . . a month . . . Westminster Abbey—Diary.

133. the dissipation that hastened his end—DNB.

133. young Randle . . . an ironmonger—Apprentice records, PRO Kew, IRI 62.

133. William . . . a haberdashery, . . . Randle . . . a druggist and grocer—Letter from Mrs. Darwall to Mrs. Preston, April 14, 1790 (Bradford [Mountrath] Papers, D1287/9/11, SRO).

Notes

133. a course of reading—Diary.

133. for sale at two shillings—*Aris*, April 7, 1777.

133. *Monthly Review*—May 1777, p. 390.

133. the death of his curate . . . Rutter—Pearce, *History and Directory of Walsall*, p. 103.

134. overcrowded burial ground—St. Matthew's Churchwardens' Account Books for 1779 (WLHC).

134. the Corporation's debts . . . Taylor died—Homeshaw, *Corporation of the Borough and Foreign of Walsall*, pp. 105-07.

134. The usual conflicts—Ibid., pp. 99, 116, et passim.

134. old parishioner . . . Holt's peal—*Aris*, June 4 and 11, 1781.

134. a strong program—*Aris*, January 20 and 27, 1777; February 10, 1777.

134. Nunns . . . had joined—He first appears in *Aris* advertisements for the Stantons in 1775.

134. Nunns married Miss Elizabeth—Date of marriage (late 1777 or 1778) is conjectural but probable: Highfill dates the marriage "by the summer of 1779 at the latest," when they were acting together at Birmingham ("Nunns, Mrs. John," in Philip Highfill, Jr., Kalman A. Burnim, and Edward A. Langham, *A Biographical Dictionary of Actors, Actresses, Musicians, Dancers, Managers, and Other Stage Personnel in London, 1660-1800*, Vol. 11 [Carbondale and Edwardsville: Southern Illinois Univ. Press, 1987], 82); *Aris* mentions "Miss Stanton" in early 1777.

134. "Epilogue Written for a Favourite Actress"—1794:2, pp. 76-78. I conjecture that Mrs. Nunns is the actress indicated: as Miss Stanton she had long been a fixture on the Walsall circuit, and Mrs. Darwall's association with her continued for many years after this. That would mean the epilogues were delivered in 1778 or 1779.

Notes

134. "Epilogue Spoken by the Husband"—1794:2, pp. 79-80.

135. her own marriage lasted—Highfill, *Biographical Dictionary*, loc. cit.

136. Hockley Abbey—Charles Pye, *A Description of Modern Birmingham* (Birmingham: Talbot, [1823]), pp. 101-02; Robert K. Dent, *Old and New Birmingham* (1878-80; rpt. Wakefield: E. P. Publishing, Ltd., 1972), p. 209.

136. "Close by yon Lake's pellucid stream"—Quoted in a newspaper article on the Abbey, from John Macmillan, "Newspaper Cuttings relating to Old Birmingham" [1864-1905], p. 69 (BRL Local Studies).

138. Four of her poems—1794:1, pp. 50-59.

138. "Elegy on the Ruins of Kenilworth Castle"—1794:2, pp. 1-7.

138. the extinct title had been revived—*Encyclopaedia Britannica*, 11th ed., "Clarendon, George William Frederick Villiers."

139. "To Mr. D——"—1794:2, pp. 123-24.

140. hungry colliers . . . fixed the prices—Homeshaw, *Corporation of the Borough and Foreign of Walsall*, pp. 95-96.

140. thanked with a poem—*Aris*, December 16, 1782.

141. apprenticing of Leicester . . . Eginton—Apprentice records, PRO Kew, IRI 64.

141. Eginton . . . "polygraphs" . . . Windsor Castle—DNB; VH *Warwickshire*, Vol. 2, 245.

141. John had convinced a board—Ordination recorded in subscription book (B/A/4/38, LJRO).

141. St. Bartholomew's . . . charity sermon—*Aris*, September 15, 1783.

Notes

142. "Female Friendship" . . . *British Magazine*—*British Magazine and Review, or Universal Miscellany*, Vol. 1 (September 1782), 220; I thank Roger Lonsdale for this reference.

142. a friend of long standing—"Monimia" appears as a sympathetic listener to "Delia's" lament in "'Delia, A Pastoral" (1764, pp. 64-67); later, Mary Darwall consoled "Monimia" for her father's death (1794:2, pp. 31-33).

142. "Why does vain man accuse"—I quote "An Epistle to a Friend," 1794:1, pp. 19-25; the differences between this and the earlier text are insignificant.

143. is not new—See pp. 52-53 above and note.

143. "Ode on the Peace"—1794:2, pp. 24-28.

144. preliminary peace treaty . . . generally expected—T. H. McGuffie, *The Siege of Gibraltar 1779-1783* (London: Batsford, 1965), pp. 180-81.

144. "William and Susan"—1794:2, pp. 96-99.

146. health began to decline . . . Young John came over . . . assume some of his father's tasks—Letter from Mrs. Darwall to Mrs. Preston (see note to p. 133).

146. "*outward* Forms" . . . "*indecent Whisperings*"—John Darwall, *Discourse on Spiritual Improvement from Affliction* (Walsall: Milward, 1789), pp. 10, 14.

147. typical contemporaries—My comparisons come primarily from sermons by William Paley and Hugh Blair; I have also looked at sermons by Benjamin Hoadley and Joseph Butler.

147. "avoid . . . *burning zeal*"—*Visitation Sermon*, p. 33.

147. Richard Graves's spokesman—*The Spiritual Quixote* (1773), ed. Clarence Tracy (London: Oxford Univ. Press, 1967), p. 453.

Notes

147. "from whom the author has experienced . . ."—I thank Barry Nicholas, Principal of Brasenose College, Oxford, for sending me a copy of the dedication.

148. Charles Henry . . . Frederick . . . Randle . . . William . . . The two girls—Letter from Mrs. Darwall to Mrs. Preston (see note to p. 133). P. J. and R. V. Wallis, in *Eighteenth-Century Medics* (Newcastle-upon-Tyne: PHIBB, 1988), identify Frederick's master as Richard Green of Lichfield and give the date of his apprenticeship as September 30, 1789—perhaps an error, as Mrs. Darwall's letter would make it 1788.

148. Young John's affairs . . . assistant to the headmaster . . . the library—Philip B. Chatwin, ed., *Records of King Edward's School Birmingham*, Vol. 5 (Oxford: Oxford Univ. Press, 1963), 66; "An Epitome of the History of King Edward the 6th School Birmingham" (manuscript book, school archives), p. 20.

148. Henry Francis Cary—DNB; R. W. King, *The Translator of Dante: The Life, Work, and Friendships of Henry Francis Cary (1772-1844)* (London: Martin Secker, 1925), pp. 19-22, 25-33.

150. "STANZAS Addressed to the Author"—1794:2, p. 69.

150. "Thanks to the gen'rous Bard"—"To Mr. Cary, in reply," 1794:2, pp. 70-71.

150. Thomson's "Winter"—Line 876 (1746 edition): "And fring'd with Roses *Tenglio* rolls his Stream." The Tenglio is a river in Finnish Lapland, which actually has roses on its banks.

151. "strains ecstatic," "beauteous HELEN's . . . lyre"—"Lines, occasioned by seeing a beautiful print of the River Clyde," 1794:1, pp. 14-18.

151. Helen Maria Williams's poems . . . liberal—*Poems by Helen Maria Williams*, 2 vols. (London: Rivington and Marshall, 1786); "An American Tale," Vol. 1, 3-13; "An Epistle to Dr. Moore," Vol. 2, 3-20; see also "An Ode on the Peace," Vol. 1, 35-57.

Notes

151. supporter of the French Revolution—Janet Todd, "Williams, Helen Maria," in *A Dictionary of British and American Women Writers 1660-1800*, ed. Janet Todd (Totowa: Rowman and Allenheld, 1985).

151. the quality of women's writing—"To Mrs. Montagu," Vol. 2, 47-51.

151. "Edwin and Eltruda"—Vol. 1, 59-94.

151. "To Sensibility"—Vol. 1, 19-28.

152. W. Hamilton Reed—GM August 1788, p. 733.

153. Graves . . . *Recollection*—Pp. 157-58.

153. not suffer rivals gladly—The sonneteer Charlotte Smith, e.g. See Anne Henry Ehrenpreis, intro. to Charlotte Smith, *Emmeline* (London: Oxford Univ. Press, 1971), p. viii note.

153. wrote them a verse letter—"To H. and E. Darwall, October the 31st 1788—Vicarage Garden," manuscript (not in Mrs. Darwall's hand) from the papers of Mrs. Penelope Darwall. I thank Mrs. Darwall for having a copy of this manuscript and other papers sent to me. The manuscript may be one verse letter or two: the title refers specifically only to the verses on the first two sheets, which are quite serious; the second two sheets are comic in tone and in a different verse form, but untitled. It is not possible to determine the date of the comic verses or their exact connection with the serious ones.

154. Walsall celebrated—*Aris*, March 16, 1789.

154. Lord Mountrath . . . sent a letter—Noted in Mrs. Darwall's letter to Mrs. Preston (see note to p. 133).

155. at midday on December 18—Letter from Thomas Hodgkins to James Bradfield, December 21, 1789 (Bradford [Mountrath] Papers, D1287/9/5 [A/192], SRO).

Notes

Chapter 9

159. sequestered her husband's salary—Sequestration document dated at Lichfield, December 19, 1789 (B/A/8, Walsall, LJRO).

159. borrowed ten guineas—Unless otherwise noted all information in the first part of this chapter (pp. 159-69) is from letters in the Bradford (Mountrath) Papers, D1287/9/5 (A/192), D1287/9/11 (A/192), and D1287/22/5 (K/7) (SRO). I am grateful for the permission of that office to cite these letters.

160. Mrs. Darwall's finances—She might have had other resources; her brother Henry's will indicates that he loaned or gave her money from time to time. But I have not traced any further sources of regular income for the early years of her widowhood.

161. the Corporation . . . mayor for a year—Glew, *History of the Borough and Foreign of Walsall*, pp. 7, 124.

161. the petition . . . platitudinous testimonials—Undated, eighty signatures (Bradford [Mountrath] Papers, D1287/22/5, SRO).

162. something of a recluse—*Annual Register* for 1802, pp. 500-01.

163. his only child—See note to p. 95.

168. lifted the sequestration—Document dated June 14, 1790 (B/A/8, Walsall, LJRO).

169. "Elegy"—1794:2, pp. 108-15.

171. a fine country house—Date unknown, but the *Universal British Directory* for 1790 does not list Henry Whateley as living in Walsall (extracts in WLHC); presumably he had moved by this time. His name appears in the active Law List for the last time in 1789. The 1801 local census lists him at Birchills (WLHC). VH *Staffordshire*, Vol. 17, 159, mentions a "Birchills Hall . . . [which] existed by the late eighteenth century," possibly Henry's.

Notes

171. George . . . center of Birmingham—Pye's *Birmingham Directories* for 1785, 1788, 1798 (BRL Local Studies).

171. Henry . . . his will—PRO B11/1370 PFFP 1896.

171. curacy of St. John's . . . the old minister . . . elected young John Darwall—Deritend parish registers. See also L. F. Crowder, "Ecclesiastical History," in *A Handbook for Birmingham and the Neighbourhood*, ed. George A. Auden (Birmingham: Cornish Brothers, 1913), pp. 85-86.

171. Deritend . . . run-down old suburb—Terry Slater, *A History of Warwickshire* (London and Chichester: Phillimore, 1981), p. 108.

172. eighty pounds a year—W. Hutton, *An History of Birmingham*, 2nd ed. (Birmingham: Pearson and Rollason, 1783), p. 112.

172. the agreement he signed—"Copy of the terms to be proposed to the Rev. Mr. Darwall upon his being presented to Deritend Chapel," manuscript, 1791, Ref. No. 393872 (BRL Archives).

172. matriculate, at the age of twenty-nine—*Alumni Oxonienses* mixes this John and his father together, but other evidence confirms his late matriculation; see p. 209 and note.

172. her new urban environment—Deritend is described by Jones in *Manors of Aston Parish*, p. 35, and "Birmingham and Deritend: An Introduction to their Historical Geography" (typescript, 1968), pp. 13-14 (BRL Local Studies).

172. regular music festivals—J. Sutcliffe Smith, *The Story of Music in Birmingham* (Birmingham: Cornish Brothers, 1945), pp. 16-26.

173. (John served on the committee . . .)—Dent, *Old and New Birmingham*, p. 178.

173. regular acting company . . . *The Monk*—Cunningham, *Theatre Royal*, pp. 15-16, 23-25, 126-29.

Notes

173. John Fawcett, Jr.—Highfill, "Fawcett, John, 1768-1837," *Biographical Dictionary*, Vol. 5 (1978), 197.

173. Mrs. Nunns, who had spent some time—Ibid., Vol. 11, 82.

173. "Address"—"Address, spoken by Mrs. Nunns, on her first appearance at the Theatre, Edinburgh," 1794:1, pp. 78-80.

174. benefit some time earlier—"Address, spoken by Miss Mellon, on her Benefit Night, at the Theatre, Walsall," 1794:1, pp. 75-77.

174. when she joined Stanton's company—Highfill, *Biographical Dictionary*, "Mellon, Harriot."

174. "Epilogue, spoken by Miss Mellon"—1794:2, pp. 100-03.

175. Frederick . . . Leicester—C. H. Wylly, *Historical Records of the 1st King's Own Stafford Militia* (Lichfield: Johnson's Head, 1902), p. 10.

175. promoted to lieutenant—In 1793; noted in the 1795 Militia List. I thank Miss E. Talbot Rice of the National Army Museum, London, for this and other military data (below).

175. for reasons of health . . . a china factory—Letter from Mrs. Darwall to Mrs. Preston (see note to p. 133); I conjecture Dr. Wall's works in Worcester because Leicester is said to be "about thirty miles" from Walsall, and because of the old Wall connection.

175. a tour of ceremonial duty—Wylly, *Historical Records*, p. 13, but see note to p. 202.

175. Frederick had transferred—Army List.

175. Priestley riots—Gill, *History of Birmingham*, Vol. 1, 144-45; Jones, "Bordesley and Deritend," p. 15, and map in his *Manors of Aston Parish*.

176. Birmingham's economy—Gill, *History of Birmingham*, Vol. 1, p. 146; Dent, *Old and New Birmingham*, p. 179.

Notes

176. They took a petition—Lee, *Short History of Walsall*, p. 40.

177. next door to Mary's brother—Pye's *Birmingham Directories* for 1785, 1787, 1788 (BRL Local Studies).

177. anonymous letters—In the archives of King Edward VI School, Birmingham; I thank Mr. C. A. Boardman, archivist, for copies of these letters and an explanation of the wrong kind of boarders.

177. governors issued a resolution—Chatwin, ed., *Records of King Edward's School*, Vol. 5, 98.

177 f. Darwall's resignation . . . one hundred pounds—Ibid., pp. 99-100.

178. living in Wales in July 1794—1794:2, p. 172 (a dated poem).

178. she quotes with approval a line—1810, p. 151.

178. one could live there for a fraction—One of the main reasons why the Ladies of Llangollen chose Wales.

178. seventy-five pounds a year—Ann B. Shteir, "Botanical Dialogues: Maria Jacson and Women's Popular Science Writing in England," in *Eighteenth-Century Studies*, Vol. 23, No. 3 (Spring 1990), 310.

178 f. Newtown was . . . small—E. V. Jones, *History of Newtown (1221-1970)*, 3rd ed. rev. (Newtown: Severn Press, 1970), p. 15; *The Life of Robert Owen, Written by Himself*, Vol. 1 (London: Wilson, 1857), 1-2.

179. the thrifty Fords—*Local Notes and Queries*, Vol. Q, p. 29 (BRL Local Studies). No date for the move is given, but in 1793 Mr. Ford was seventy and probably retired.

179. to be with their son—John Bourn Ford, Newtown's doctor, witnessed Harriet Darwall's wedding. The Newtown parish register indicates that he was the son of Richard Ford and that both father and son were living in Newtown when they died; I thank Mr. P. W. Davies, of the National Library of Wales, for this information.

Notes

Chapter 10

180 f. Booker . . . book of poems . . . first clerical position—DNB.

181. preached a charity sermon—*Aris*, September 18, 1780.

181. Rev. Mr. Parry . . . well-off—I thank Mr. P. W. Davies of the National Library of Wales for this financial information.

181. neglected to arrange for advertising—I have found no advertisements in the usual literary magazines or in the (admittedly incomplete) Burney collection of newspapers (microfilm).

182. the *Critical Review*—July 1795, pp. 344-45.

182. The *Monthly Review*—September 1795, pp. 95-96; the poem quoted is "On Hearing a Blackbird Sing Early in March" (1794:1, pp. 60-61).

182. "Circumstances of no consequence"—1794:1, p. [i].

183. "The following pages . . ."—1794:1, p. [i].

183. "The Triumph of Liberal Sentiment"—1794:1, pp. 1-4.

184. "Sonnet to Time"—1794:2, pp. 125-26.

185. "Written on walking . . ."—1794:2, pp. 168-72.

185. Arthur Blayney—*Dictionary of Welsh Biography; Montgomeryshire Collections*, Vol. 30 (1896), 110-16, quotation from p. 114.

185. "Delia to Philander"—1794:1, pp. 34-38.

186. "Philander" . . . elsewhere—"Invitation to the same, In Winter," 1794:1, pp. 24-33.

186. "Impromptu"—1794:1, pp. 81-82.

186. "Lines . . ."—1794:2, pp. 22-23.

Notes

186. "Ode . . ."—1794:1, pp. 62-65; I have been unable to identify this young nobleman.

186. to Mrs. C—— and Mr. F—— —1794:2, 106-07; 1794:1, pp. 45-47; Mrs. C—— remains unidentified.

187. "Down the Bourn"—1794:2, pp. 44-46.

187. "A Scotch Pastoral"—1794:2, pp. 86-90.

187. "The Self-Exiled Minstrel"—1794:2, pp. 47-52.

187. she does so unequivocally—A very few of her poems could be read as having a male or female speaker, e.g., "A Pastoral Song" (1764, pp. 42-44).

187. "The Death of Mary"—1794:2, pp. 41-43.

187. "pathetic ballad" . . . John Lowe—R. H. Cromek, *Remains of Nithsdale and Galloway Song* (London: Cadell and Davies, 1810), pp. 342ff. ("pathetic ballad," p. 342); DNB.

187. "cold is my clay . . ."—John Lowe, "Mary's Dream," in *The Edinburgh Book of Scottish Verse*, ed. W. MacNeile Dixon (London: Meiklejohn and Holden, 1910), No. 195.

188. "Song of the Sisters of Ivar"—1794:1, pp. 68-74.

188. Thomson and Mallet's masque—Her wording is slightly closer to David Mallet's revision (1751), but she refers specifically only to Thomson. Whichever edition she was reading, she detached and used the same passage; my argument is essentially unaffected, except that the Mallet version has more plot action.

189. "pictur'd *Raven*" . . . "Wrought by the sisters . . ."—[James Thomson and David Mallet], *Alfred, A Masque* (London: Millar, 1740), pp. 37-38.

190. "Advice to a Young Lady"—1794:2, pp. 29-30.

Notes

190. much earlier "Song"—1794:2, pp. 14-16; and see pp. 78-79 above.

191. "Song, adapted . . ."—1794:1, pp. 48-49.

191. "Valentine's Day"—1794:1, pp. 83-118.

192. Her allusion elsewhere—In "The Self-Exiled Minstrel," 1794:2, p. 49.

192. Shenstone . . . "Erse fragments"—John Butt, *The Mid-Eighteenth Century*, Oxford History of English Literature, Vol. 8 (Oxford: Clarendon Press, 1979), 105.

193. "The Moanings of Ella . . ."—1794:2, pp. 159-67.

193. "the maiden's meadow"—John Edward Lloyd, *A History of Wales* (London: Longmans, Green, 1912), Vol. 2, 748 note.

193. drowning of . . . Sabrina—Maxwell Fraser, *West of Offa's Dyke: North Wales* (London: Hale, 1959), p. 73.

193. "Sonnets, &c."—1794:2, pp. 127-58.

193. "two young friends"—1794:1, p. [ii].

194. "native plains" . . . "parted friends"—1794:2, p. 154.

194. "Tears of Affection"—1794:2, pp. 132-34.

194. When she first sees—"Sonnet, On the first sight of the Severn," 1794:2, pp. 157-58.

194. "a Gentleman going . . ."—"To a Gentleman going to join the army on the continent," 1794:2, pp. 152-53.

194. "give the hour serene"—1794:2, p. 142.

194. "dark DESPONDENCY" . . . "musing . . . maid"— 1794:2, pp. 128, 137.

Notes

194. "languish . . ." . . . "guileless heart" . . . "faithful HENRY"—1794:2, pp. 145, 156.

Chapter 11

196. Newtown until 1803—List of Preston Hospital widows, dated November 18, 1803, includes Mary Darwall of "New Town in Wales" (Bradford [Mountrath] Papers, D1287/13/1, SRO). These same papers include receipts for the pension, dated, signed, and specifying amounts paid. Lord Mountrath (d. 1802) arranged for the pension in his will.

197. Probably a Roman Catholic—Catholics were common in and around his birthplace; he had no public career; both Harriet and Elizabeth became Catholic converts (see p. 208 and note).

197. second son of a . . . cider merchant—Will of Yerrow Arrowsmith, dated September 30, 1779 (PRO B11/1078).

197. private schools . . . medicine—Shrewsbury census, 1851.

197. Elizabeth's poem about leaving—"Stanzas, written in London, on the recollection of leaving Hope Mansell," 1810, pp. 96-99.

197. Another poem in Elizabeth's book—"Addressed to E.D. by her Mother," 1810, pp. 150-54.

197. live with . . . a daughter—Oliven Hufton, "Women Without Men: Widows and Spinsters in Britain and France in the Eighteenth Century," *Journal of Family History*, Vol. 9 (1984), 362.

198. Rutter died, suddenly—Willmore, *History of Walsall*, p. 138.

198. September 1796 . . . complicated arrangements—Manuscript letter from John Darwall to the Bishop of Lichfield and Coventry, August [1796] (B/A/10/1784, LJRO).

198. "the democratic spirit" . . . "armed associations"—Letter from John Darwall to Lord Mountrath, May 23, 1798 (Bradford [Mountrath]

Notes

Papers, D1287/13/11, SRO); see also Glew, *History of the Borough and Foreign of Walsall*, pp. 12-13.

199. an appropriate sermon—Published in Pearce, *History and Directory of Walsall*, pp. 212-15.

199. negotiated, with some difficulty—John Darwall, "Correct Statement, respecting the subscriptions, entered into in 1803 to augment the income of the Minister of St. John's Chapel, Deritend," 1824 (BRL Archives, Ref. No. 62463).

199. return to his teaching job—Governors' Order Book, Vol. 2, January 20, 1804 (manuscript; archives of King Edward VI School).

199. a new headmaster—Rev. John Cooke (Chatwin, ed., *Records of King Edward's School*, Vol. 5, 102 note).

199. moved his family, twice—Holden's *Birmingham Directory* for 1805; Wrightson and Thomson's *Directory* for 1812 (BRL Local Studies).

199. settled into his own house—1801 local census (WLHC).

199. His garden stretched down—Mason's "Plan of the Town of Walsall," 1824 (WLHC).

199. Maria Riddell included "Liberty"—I thank Isobel Grundy for this information.

199. four . . . in Elizabeth's book—Only one of these is clearly attributed: "Addressed to E.D. by her Mother, who was first known to the poetical world as *Miss Whateley*" (1810, pp. 150-54). It is followed by "Addressed to the Author of a Sonnet, entitled 'The Sketch' " (pp. 155-56), which is not in Elizabeth's style. A third follows that: "The Victory of the Nile, by the same" (pp. 157-59), so it looks as if "by the same" was accidentally omitted from "Addressed to the Author. . . ." I argue for the authorship of the fourth in my text.

200. "Impromptu"—1794:1, pp. 81-82.

Notes

200. "To an Old Acquaintance"—1810, p. 75.

200. "The Sketch"—"Addressed to the Author of a Sonnet, Entitled 'The Sketch,' " 1810, pp. 155-56; for the authorship of this poem, see note above.

201. "LINES . . ."—*Monthly Magazine,* June 1801, p. 423; for the tour journal, unsigned but obviously written by an "Eliza," see the *Monthly* for August 1800 (pp. 11-16) and September 1800 (pp. 119-23). The same magazine includes another poem by "M.D." in May 1807 (p. 360): "Impromptu, On being presented by a friend with an Eolian harp made by Robert Bloomfield." Despite the blank verse, a form that Mary Darwall seldom used, its style and tone resemble hers. But it is dated from Broughton, and I have not found the name Darwall in the most likely of the many Broughtons; yet there are many Arrowsmiths in the various Lancashire Broughtons.

202. Leicester Darwall . . . died—*Staffordshire Advertiser,* March 20, 1802.

202. The Staffordshire militia . . . (. . . two miles . . .)—Wylly, *Historical Records,* p. 13. (Wylly dates the disembodiment 1801, an error, since it followed the Peace of Amiens [March 1802].)

203. saw the world . . . disease took a higher toll—Donald Creighton-Williamson, *The York and Lancaster Regiment (65th and 84th Regiments of Foot)* (London: Cooper, 1968), pp. 33-39.

203. Frederick . . . died . . . in Calcutta . . . "talents and humanity"—*Staffordshire Advertiser,* August 23, 1806.

203. "transport" . . . "after a long silence"—"Addressed to an Absent Brother, on hearing from him after a long silence. Written on the Banks of the Clywedog," 1810, pp. 78-81. On brother-sister love, see Leonore Davidoff and Catherine Hall, *Family Fortunes: Men and Women of the English Middle Class, 1780-1850* (Chicago: Univ. of Chicago Press, 1987), p. 351.

203. dated November 1804—"Stanzas, written during a state of painful suspence," 1810, pp. 82-85.

Notes

203. agony of loss—"Written in 1805, and Addressed to a Friend" (1810, pp. 86-87) is the most powerful of these; news of Frederick's death in 1805 probably did not arrive until early 1806, but Elizabeth could have adjusted the date on her poem to commemorate the actual year of her loss.

204. "Author & Critic"—1810, pp. v-viii.

204. (a phrase Shenstone had used . . .)—*Letters*, pp. 419, 420.

204. ". . . Homage to Cupid"—1764, p. 6.

204. except for one early poem—See pp. 17-18 above.

205. pair of women . . . memorialized at length—GM February 1801, p. 126; see also William Pitt, *A Topographical History of Staffordshire* (Newcastle-under-Lyme: Smith, 1817), pp. 276-78.

207. Honor's property—Will dated May 18, 1799 (PRO B11/1349).

207. William Whateley . . . appointed secretary . . . succeeded his father—"An Epitome of the History of King Edward the 6th School Birmingham," p. 31.

207. "young" John's oldest son—Ibid., p. 5.

207. Charles Henry became a churchwarden—Glew, *History of the Borough and Foreign of Walsall*, p. 128.

207. John Clements Whateley—Pearce, *History and Directory of Walsall*, p. 130.

208. his father appears there—Poor rate book, Brewood (D880/4/1/10, SRO).

208. cider growers had been uprooting—VH *Herefordshire*, Vol. 1, 413-14, 426-27; John Duncombe, *General View of the Agriculture of the County of Hereford* (London: Phillips, 1805), pp. 87, 154; see also grain prices in the *Annual Register* for 1812ff.

Notes

208. distinguished career as a surgeon—John Yerrow Arrowsmith was one of the original Fellows of the Royal College of Surgeons (1843). I thank Mr. M. M. Derrick, of the Library of the Royal College, for this information.

208. Harriet . . . in reduced circumstances—She might have been widowed. After 1815, Samuel Arrowsmith disappears; the burial of a son puts the family in Shrewsbury in 1824. But Samuel was not buried in Brewood or Shrewsbury. I conjecture that the family moved to another town where he died, and that Mary Darwall's return to Walsall (1817) marks the time of the move or of his death.

208. daughters had become Roman Catholics—So noted on family tree from the Darwall-Smith archives.

209. some evidence that his wife resented—A reasonable explanation for the distortions of her son's diary.

209. two Oxford degrees . . . chancellor's letters—*Alumni Oxonienses*. The letters are in the university archives. I thank Miss M. Macdonald, Oxford archivist, for reconstructing John Darwall's academic career from the few records that survive.

209. "Children intended . . . the Jews"—Manuscript letter of John Darwall to the Board of Governors, December 31, 1804 (archives of King Edward VI School Birmingham).

210. tried . . . to gain control—Letters to the governors and bailiff dated March 19, 1814; August 9, 1814 (school archives).

210. anything but classics—Carl Boardman, *Foundation and City* (typescript book, school archives), Chapter 8, pp. 52-53.

210. a stern address—"Address to the parents of poor children in the hamlets of Deritend and Bordesley" (1815) (BRL Archives, Ref. No. 60763).

210. demanded a formal request—Noted in the Deritend parish register.

Notes

210. When George IV was crowned—John Darwall, *A Sermon, Preached in St. John's Chapel, in Deritend, on the 19th of July, 1821* (Birmingham: Hodgetts, 1821).

210. his doctor son ... rabid Tory—John Conolly, "A Biographical Memoir of the late Dr. John Darwall, of Birmingham," *Provincial Medical and Surgical Association Transactions*, Vol. 2 (1834), 489-546; see especially pp. 533-36. Conolly's memoir is an odd mixture of eulogy and balanced analysis. Despite his various limitations, Dr. Darwall, who was a pioneer in industrial medicine, was highly respected. He died in 1833 at the age of thirty-seven from an infection contracted while performing an autopsy.

210. bitter pamphlet war—John Darwall, "A Correct Statement"; R. Webb, "Reply to Rev. John Darwall's attempt to answer a statement respecting a subscription entered into in the year 1803 ..." (1824) (BRL Archives, Ref. No. 260822).

210. his declining health—John's health was poor from 1821 to 1824, noted in the Deritend parish register February 1827. He died in 1828.

211. an annuity ... in his will—Will dated 1835; probated May 6, 1843 (copy of probate, WLHC).

211. Churchwarden and mayor ... a solid citizen—Glew, *History of the Borough and Foreign of Walsall*, pp. 124, 128; Pearce, *History and Directory of Walsall*, pp. 98, 176; Fink, *Queen Mary's Grammar School*, appendix.

211. equally solid and much loved Charles Frederick—See Fink, Glew (previous note); W. H. Robinson, *Local History and Reminiscences ... in the Walsall Observer, from 21 Dec. 1918 to April 19, 1919* (in WLHC), includes a lavish tribute.

211. Walsall had changed—See list of Walsall sources, note to p. 26.

211. Elizabeth Nunns had run—Pearce, *History and Directory of Walsall*, p. 132.

Notes

212. restored to the light—Not only by my own work but also in *Eighteenth-Century Women Poets*, ed. Roger Lonsdale (Oxford and New York: Oxford Univ. Press, 1989), and in *British Women Poets 1660-1800: An Anthology*, ed. Joyce Fullard (Troy, N.Y.: Whitston, 1990). This latter unfortunately includes numerous errors in the biographical sketch of Mary Darwall (pp. 553-54).

212. her obituary—*Staffordshire Advertiser*, December 10, 1825.

Index

Aikin, Anna Laetitia (Mrs. Barbauld), 105, 153.
Airy, Harriott; *see* Darwall, Mary Whateley.
Arrowsmith, Samuel (son-in-law), 195, 197, 208.
Avison, Charles, 121, 191.

Bennet, Mrs., 42, 46, 51, 66.
Beoley, described, 10-11.
Bordesley Hall, 35-36, 172, 176.
Birmingham, description and history, 35-36, 172-73, 175-76; *see also* Bordesley Hall, Hockley Abbey.
Bisset, James, "Poetic Survey Round Birmingham," 136-38.
Blayney, Arthur, 185, 193.
Booker, Rev. Luke, 180-81; "The Triumph of Liberal Sentiment," 183.
Brooke, Frances Moore, 105; *Rosina*, 192.
Burke, Edmund, *Reflections on the Revolution in France*, 176.
Burns, Robert, 91, 150-51, 152, 174, 187.

Carter, Elizabeth, 58, 64, 105.
Cary, Henry Francis, 148-50, 153; "An Irregular Ode to General Elliot," 149; "Stanzas Addressed to the Author," 150; *Sonnets and Odes*, 149.
Chatterton, Stephen, 28-29, 33, 78, 104; "The Walsall Beauties," 28-29.
Churchill, Charles, 78.
Coleridge, Samuel Taylor, 203.
Copywell, Jemmy; *see* Woty, William.
Corelli, Signora (Corilla Olimpica), 126-27.
Cracroft, Ann, later Langhorne, 52-53, 56, 58, 92.

Dacier, Mme., 183.
Dartmouth, Lord and Lady, 51.
Darwall, Charles Henry (son), 95, 98, 113, 125, 148, 153, 154, 168, 169, 171, 195, 199, 207, 209, 210-11, 212.
Darwall, Elizabeth (daughter), 114, 116, 117, 118, 148, 153, 168, 190-91, 200-202, 207, 208, 211; as poet, 193-94, 196, 197, 200, 203-204.
Darwall, Frederick (son), 103, 113, 148, 175, 198, 203, 211.
Darwall, Harriet, later Arrowsmith (daughter), 103, 113, 131, 148, 153, 168, 178, 195, 196-97, 198, 199, 207, 208, 210; as poet, 193-94.
Darwall, Honor (sister-in-law), 31, 77, 132, 133, 204-207.
Darwall, Honor (stepdaughter), 77, 103.
Darwall, Rev. John (husband), 22, 30-58 passim, 67, 75-163 passim, 180, 186, 192, 194, 198; "Darwall's 148th," 100; *Discourse on Spiritual Improvement from Affliction*, 146-48; *Political Lamentations*, 107-108 (poem), 130-31 (sermon), 133 (both); *Visitation Sermon*, 106-107, 120.
Darwall, John (stepson), 32, 34, 113, 115, 127, 132, 133, 141, 146,

269

Index

148-49, 160-61, 165, 167-68, 171-73, 175, 177-78, 196, 198-99, 205-207, 209-210.

Darwall, Leicester Yonge (son), 92, 113, 141, 153, 175, 202-203.

Darwall, Mary (stepdaughter), 32, 34, 103.

Darwall, Mary Fox, 30, 31-32, 33-34, 77, 80, 207.

Darwall, Mary Whateley: birth, 9, 11, 13; girlhood, 13-16; her reading, 15; appearance, 16, 29; begins to write, 16-17; as "Harriott Airy," 19-22, 29, 30, 49, 50, 53; poems about, 29, 81, 93, 150, 152-53; meets John Darwall, 30; first book reviewed, 61-65; as woman poet, 69-74; marriage, 83-84; children born, 92, 95, 103, 114; widowed, 155; move to Wales, 178-79; second book reviewed, 182; daughter's marriage, 195; return to Walsall, 208-209; death, 212.

Poems (mentioned) "Address, spoken by Mrs. Nunns," 173-74; "Advice to a Young Lady," 190-91; "Down the Bourn," 187; "Epilogue Spoken by the Husband," 134, 135; "Hymn to Solitude," 65, 99; "Impromptu," 186, 200; "An Invitation in Winter," 80-81; "Lines for a sampler," 186; "Ode to Summer," 64, 65, 77; "Ode . . . to a Young Nobleman," 186; "A Pastoral Song," 65; "The Pleasures of Contemplation," 63, 99, 106; "A Scotch Pastoral," 187; "The Self-Exiled Minstrel," 187.

Poems (discussed and/or quoted in part): "Address, spoken by Miss Mellon," 174; "An Address to my Pen," 46-47; "Addressed to E.D.," 201-202; "Addressed to the Author of a Sonnet, Entitled 'The Sketch,'" 200; "Author and Critic," 204; "The Death of Mary," 187-88; "Delia to Philander," 185-86; "Elegy," 169-71, 184; "Elegy, Addressed to Mrs. Hewan," 83; "Elegy on a much lamented Friend, Who died in Autumn, 1759," 17-18, 63, 77; "Elegy on Leaving———," 24-26, 65; "Elegy on the Ruins of Kenilworth Castle," 138-39; "Elegy on the Search of Happiness," 53-55, 67; "Elegy written in a Garden," 66-67; "Epilogue, spoken by Miss Mellon," 174-75; "Epilogue Written for a Favourite Actress," 134-35; "An Epistle to a Friend," 142-43; "The First Ode of Anacreon, imitated": first version, 71; second version, 72, 74, 76; hymns, 100-101; "Invitation to the same, In Winter," 110-11; "Invocation," 104-105, 183; "Lines occasioned by . . . the River Clyde," 152; "The Moanings of Ella," 192-93, 202; "Occasioned by reading some Sceptical Essays," 67-68; "Ode," 68-69; "Ode, Addressed to Mrs. Hewan," 81-83; "Ode on the Peace," 143-44; "Ode to Friendship," 33; "Ode to May," 62-63, 65, 76, 99; "Rural Happiness," 35-38, 63, 65; "Song, adapted to a favorite Gavot of Avison's," 191; "Song

Index

of the Sisters of Ivar," 188-90; "To H. and E. Darwall," 153-54; "To Mr. Cary," 150; "To Mr. Copywell," 19-20; "To Mr. D―― on his fifteenth wedding day," 132, 139-40; "To my Garden," 19, 46-47; "To the Rev. Mr. J. Langhorne," 57-58; "To the Rev. Mr. Welchman," 40-41; "Valentine's Day," 186, 191-92; "The Vanity of external Accomplishments," 63, 68; "The Victory of the Nile," 200; "William and Susan," 144-45; "The Wood-Nymph," 126.
Poems (quoted in full―* text): "An Anacreontic," *72, 73; "Elegy on the Uses of Poetry," 43-44, *214-16; epitaph on Shenstone, *49-50, 145; "Hymn to Plutus," 127, *128-29; "Liberty," 24, 25, 26, 30, 37, 42, 46-48, 64, 72-74, 99, 199, *213-14; "Lines addressed to a Gentleman," *122-24; "Lines Addressed to a Young Lady," *99; "Lines occasioned by reading . . . the Journal . . .," *201; "Ode to Truth," *21-22; "On the Author's Husband Desiring her to Write Some Verses," 94, 94-95; "The Power of Destiny," 69-71, 74, 77, *217-18; "Song," 78, *79, 190; "Sonnet, on Removing a Bay-Tree," *118; "Sonnet to Time," *184; "To Mr. O――y" [Mr. S――, Mr. L――], *44-45, 48, 49, 50, 64, 99; untitled, 154, *218-19; "Written in Spring 1764," *75-76; "Written on walking in the Woods of Gregynog . . .," 185, 193, *220-21.

Darwall, Mary Whateley (1777-1857) (niece/daughter-in-law), 177, 209.
Darwall, Randle (father-in-law), 31, 38, 42-44, 67, 75, 130, 132, 178, 180.
Darwall, Randle (stepson), 33-34, 113, 119, 125, 132, 133, 148, 172, 207, 209.
Darwall, Whateley (son), 92, 95, 203.
Darwall, William (stepson), 38, 113, 119, 121, 133, 148, 207.
Davenport, Rev. David, 96, 98-99, 133, 181, 207.
Dodsley, Robert, 45, 49, 50, 51, 74, 75, 76, 99.
Dryden, John, 44, 149, 173.
Duncombe, John, *Feminead*, 152.
Durbach, Anna Louisa, 78.

Eginton, Francis, 141.
Elliot, General Sir George Augustus, 143-44, 149.

Fawcett, John, Jr., 173.
Finch, Anne, *see* Winchilsea, Lady.
Ford, Richard, 136-38, 179, 186, 195, 196.
Friendship, 22, 33, 52-53, 142-43, 154; among women, 13-14, 104, 142-43.

Garrick, David, 124.
Gay, John, 192; *The Beggar's Opera*, 191.
Gentleman's Magazine, 14-15, 18-20, 22, 24, 36, 42, 53, 76, 77-78, 81, 106, 120-21, 124, 125, 126, 145, 149, 152-53, 205.

271

Index

Graves, Richard, 46, 89, 153; *The Spiritual Quixote*, 147.
Gray, Thomas, 15, 93; "The Bard," 178, 202; "Elegy," 150.
Greville, Frances, 105; "Prayer for Indifference," 151.
Griffith, Elizabeth, 105.

Handel, George Frederick, 17, 31, 63.
Hellier, Sir Samuel, 31.
Hewan, Mrs., 81-83, 91.
Hewitt, Jane, 205-207.
Hockley Abbey, 136-38, 179.

Johnson, Samuel, 15, 18, 36, 61, 109; *Rasselas*, 26, 30, 48, 73; *The Vanity of Human Wishes*, 36, 53-55, 67.
Jones, Mary, 64.

Kauffman, Angelica, 141.
Killigrew, Anne, 44.

Langhorne, John, 15, 36, 39, 44, 51-59, 60, 61-64, 67, 75, 76, 77, 81, 90, 92, 116, 133, 153, 180; "The Country Justice," 117; "Hymn to Plutus," 127-28; *Letters on the Eloquence of the Pulpit*, 78; *Poetical Works*, 81; "Precepts of Conjugal Happiness," 53; "To Miss W———," 58; "To a Lady," 55-56; *Visions of Fancy*, 56-57.
Lennox, Charlotte, 105.
Loggin, Edward, 75, 83-84.
Loggin, Elizabeth, 14-15, 16, 26, 30, 42, 50, 53, 77, 78, 114, 132.
Loggin, Rev. William, 11, 13, 15, 16, 18, 44.
Lowe, John, "Mary's Dream," 187-88.

Luxborough, Henrietta, Lady, 15-16, 25, 51, 114.
Lyttleton, George, Lord, 42.

Macaulay, Catherine, 64.
Mallett, David, *Alfred*, 188-89.
Mellon, Harriet, 174-75.
Milton, John, 15, 17, 63, 69.
Milward, Frederick, 148, 164, 181, 193.
Montague, Elizabeth, 105, 106, 183.
More, Hannah, 53, 105.
Mountrath, Earl of (Charles Henry Coote), 95, 140, 147, 154, 160-68, 196, 198.
Music, 28, 31, 32-33, 99-103, 114, 121, 154, 172-73, 186.

Nelson, Horatio, Viscount, 198, 200.
Nunns, Mrs. John (Elizabeth Stanton), 134-35, 173-74, 211.

Ossian (James Macpherson), 78, 91, 187, 192-93.

Parry, Rev. Edward, 181, 195.
Pepys, Samuel, 159.
Percy, Thomas, 46, 50; *Reliques of Ancient English Poetry*, 78, 91.
Philips, John, *Cyder*, 197.
Pilkington, Laetitia, 114.
Politics (especially rel. to American revolution), 107-108, 112, 129, 130-31, 143-44, 151, 175-76.
Pope, Alexander, 15, 18, 36, 63, 149; *Epistle to Dr. Arbuthnot*, 70; *Essay on Man*, 39, 67-68; *To a Lady*, 69.
Preston, Mary, 95, 162-63, 165-69, 198.

Index

Price, Richard, *Discourse on the Love of Our Country*, 176.
Priestley, Joseph, 176.

Reed, W. Hamilton, 152-53.
Rodney, Admiral Sir George, 143-44.
Rutter, Rev. John Simpson, 125, 133-34, 141, 146, 159-68, 181, 198.

Scott, Mary, *The Female Advocate*, 44, 106.
Seward, Anna, 1, 149, 153, 183, 185.
Shakespeare, William, 15, 18, 61, 104-105, 127, 143, 173, 183, 198.
Shenstone, William, 15-16, 18, 25, 36, 38, 39, 40, 41, 42, 44-51, 52, 63, 65-67, 68, 73, 76, 88, 89, 91, 106, 114, 145, 153, 180, 192, 204; Elegy I, 61; *Essays on Men and Manners*, 48-49.
Siddons, Sarah (Kemble), 91, 173.
Siddons, William, 91-92.
Smith, Charlotte, 185.
Stone, Lawrence, 13.

Talbot, Catherine, 106.
Taylor, John, 35.
Theater, 28, 91, 103-104, 134, 173-74; Home's *Douglas*, 91-92.

Thomson, James, 17, 63, 143; *Alfred*, 188-89; *Winter*, 150.
Tracy, Clarence, 89.

Wall, Dr. John, 14-15, 41-42, 50, 75, 114, 124, 175, 180, 181.
Walsall, description and history, 26-28, 112-30 passim, 134, 140-41, 154, 211-12.

Welchman, Rev. John, 40-41, 67, 76.
Wesley, John, 93, 103, 130.
Whateley, family, 9-10, 11.
  Ann (sister), 9, 98, 169, 181.
  George (brother), 10, 13, 35, 136, 171, 172, 177, 181, 207.
  Henry (brother), 9, 10, 14, 15, 24, 29, 35, 38, 70, 95, 98, 108, 121, 148, 169, 170-71, 181, 182, 196, 204, 207.
  John (brother), 9-10, 181, 204.
  Martha (Baylies) (sister), 9, 98-99, 120, 169, 181.
  Mary, *see* Darwall, Mary Whateley.
  Mary (mother), 9, 13, 15, 38, 40, 132.
  William (father), 9, 10, 11-13, 15, 38.
  William (brother), 9-10.
Wilkes, John, 51, 198.
Williams, Helen Maria, 91, 150-52.
Winchilsea, Lady (Anne Finch), "Petition for an Absolute Retreat," 36-38; "To Mr. F.," 94-95.
Wollstonecraft, Mary, *Vindication of the Rights of Men*, 176.
Women, as writers, 61-62, 74, 83, 151.
Woodhouse, James, 42.
Wordsworth, William, 203.
Woty, William (Jemmy Copywell), 19-23, 24, 39, 49, 53, 78; "The Female Advocate," 22; "Ode to Friendship," 20; "To Miss Harriet Airy," 20.
Wrottesley, Lady, 40.

Young, Edward, 78.

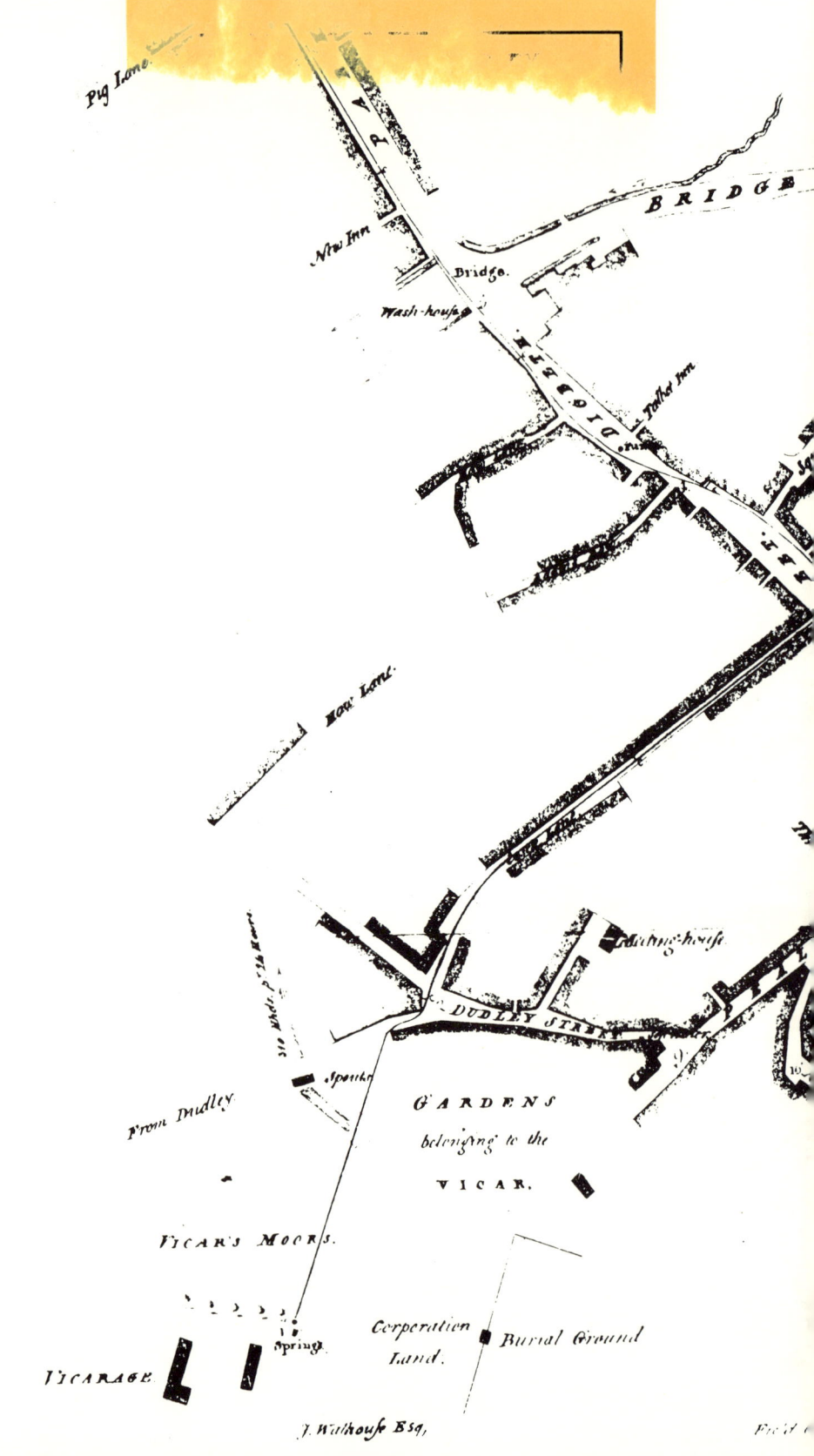